A YEAR WITH
Selwyn Hughes

SPECIALLY SELECTED THOUGHTS,
WRITINGS AND TEACHINGS

CWR

INTRODUCTION

One of the favourite items in many people's music collections is a 'best of' album or CD. Whether it's Beethoven or the Beatles or Britney, a compilation of their greatest hits is nearly always a bestseller. Sometimes we forget just how much we loved an individual track, but after only a few bars we are singing along to the familiar words rich in emotion and often personal meaning. Indeed some people these days even pay others to download a selection of their much loved artists onto an iPod. Selwyn Hughes was the founder of CWR and author of the daily Bible-reading notes, *Every Day with Jesus*. Selwyn was also a gifted pastor, counsellor, preacher and author. His work is still read and loved by Christians throughout the world from America, Africa and Australia to New Zealand and Zimbabwe. At CWR we have taken the time to revisit many of the books Selwyn wrote over forty years of ministry and compile our own selection of some of his greatest work. We have chosen a wide variety of passages from twenty-three of his books, including his autobiography, *My Story*, and his magnum opus, *Christ Empowered Living*.

The Bible is a timeless piece of literature as it is inspired by a timeless, eternal God. Because Selwyn wrote about its timeless truths, his writings still have the power to encourage, inspire, comfort, challenge and teach us today. The diverse subjects covered include prayer, evangelism, revival, Psalm 23, marriage, the Holy Spirit and keys to enjoy the presence of God, as well as many others. Selwyn's simple expositional style combines anecdotes, humour, illustration and a deep understanding of Scripture, in a way that helps us apply God's Word to everyday life and relationships. Through it all, Selwyn's love of Scripture and of his Saviour shines out from his writings as light and heat – light for our minds and passion for our hearts. This compilation truly represents some of the 'best of Selwyn'!

Each selection has been adapted, with the inclusion of a relevant heading and Bible reference, into 365 individual passages. This makes the book ideal as a resource for daily scriptural reading and meditation throughout the course of a year. To those of you who have read Selwyn's work before I believe you will enjoy reading some of his familiar and much loved themes. To those of you who are new to Selwyn's writings, I hope you will find much to inspire as you join over one million Christians throughout the world who benefit from the writings of Selwyn Hughes.

Mick Brooks
May 2011

The grace of God

'... God's abundant provision of grace ...' Romans 5:17

Whatever else you may lack in the coming years, I can assure you in the name of Him who sits upon the throne that there is one thing you will not lack, and that is the gift of grace. No year has yet dawned that has not brought difficulties and problems. Yet you can be sure that whatever happens in your life, grace will be there to sustain you and support you. You may run out of many things but you will never run out of grace.

One observation I have made is that Christians can be divided into two categories: those who appear to be thriving and those who are merely surviving. You must have noticed this yourself – some believers seem to travel faster along the path of Christian discipleship than others. We grow old at the same rate but we do not all seem to grow in the spiritual life at the same rate. Some people, even though they have been on the Christian pathway for fifty years or more, appear to have progressed at a snail's pace, while others have covered the same distance in five. Why is this? There are many possible answers but I am sure that one of the chief ones is this: they have appropriated for themselves what is described as 'God's abundant provision of grace' (Rom. 5:17). They have opened themselves to it and thus they stride along the Christian pathway at speed becoming 'pacesetters' – people who set the pace for others.

REFLECTION: Tell the Lord now you want to receive His gift and get back in the race again, moving forward with the most ardent believers you know.

What is grace?

'Now I commit you to God and to the word of his grace,
which can build you up ...' Acts 20:32

U sually grace is defined as 'God's unmerited favour'. 'Grace', says one writer, 'is shorthand for God's redeeming love.' Grace as undeserved favour is a concept that is still used in the business world. Companies sometimes say concerning a claim: 'We do not accept liability for this claim, but we will make an ex gratia [out of grace] payment.' They acknowledge no liability, but out of goodwill they make a token payment. And agreements sometimes contain a grace period in which one party freely gives another party time to rectify a fault.

One person made this memorable comment: 'Grace always has a stoop in it. Love reaches out on the same level, but grace reaches down to pick us up.' The best definition of grace I have come across, though, is this: 'Grace is the strength God gives us which enables us to live or do as Jesus would do were He in our situation.'

However, we should not think of grace merely as unmerited favour or the loving kindness of God. It is important to recognise also that it is the inner strength He lends to men and women like ourselves, who need a power other than their own to cope with the various issues and problems that life brings. Nothing can happen in your life today for which divine strength will not be given. Through God's grace we can face anything that comes providing, of course, we avail ourselves of it.

REFLECTION: The problem is never God's unwillingness to give His grace, it is always our unwillingness to receive it.

Joy – now

'But the fruit of the Spirit is love, joy, peace ...'
Galatians 5:22

We cannot absorb Christ's joy without it affecting our own joy. 'I have told you this, that my joy may be within you and your joy complete', says Moffatt's translation of John 15:11. Our Lord's joy completes our joy. The idea that Christians will one day discover that joy in heaven instead of having a joy that supports us while we are still on earth is false. Some Christians may be heading for glory but there's nothing of being on the glory road about them right now!

Let's look at some more Moffatt translations of Scripture about joy. '... let us enjoy the peace we have with God ...' (Rom. 5:1). Some have peace with God but don't enjoy it. 'we enjoy our redemption ...' (Eph. 1:7). To be redeemed and not enjoy it is a contradiction in terms. 'we ... enjoy our access to the Father in one Spirit' (Eph. 2:18). 'we enjoy our confidence of free access' (Eph. 3:12). These scriptures show us that joy is overflowing because of peace, redemption and access to the Father. Your situation may be dark and dismal but if you meditate on the fact that God is your heavenly Father, Jesus is your Saviour, the angels are your companions, heaven is your home and you have free access to the throne of God I guarantee that joy will spring up in you. It must. Joy to a Christian is a necessity – not a luxury.

Joy is for now – not just for eternity

REFLECTION: Read John 15:5–17 and use what these verses say about the conditions for being able to experience complete joy.

Get close to God in prayer

'Then Jesus told his disciples a parable to show them that they should always pray and not give up.' Luke 18:1

D o you pray? There is no way we can build a close relationship with God if we scrap the disciplined practice of prayer. Dr John Stott says, 'The thing I know will give me the deepest joy, namely to be alone and unhurried in the presence of God, aware of His presence, my heart open to worship Him, is often the thing I least want to do.' I can identify with that. And so, I am sure, can you. Most Christians know that to develop their spiritual life they must spend time with God in prayer, yet there is something within them that resists that responsibility.

That is why we must make a daily *appointment* with God – a specific time when we meet with Him – for such an important thing as prayer cannot be left to the vagaries of feeling. If you come to think in terms of having a daily appointment with God, then you are more likely to keep it even when you don't feel like it.

A regular prayer habit will soon build itself into your life, and will come to have the regularity and naturalness of other daily responsibilities. You should not, of course, limit your praying to that early morning prayer time. You can pray anywhere and at any time. But let those prayers be extras. Growth in the Christian life demands discipline, and so whatever you do, be firm with yourself about a fixed period of daily prayer.

REFLECTION: Determine now with God when you will make that daily appointment – early morning is a good time when you are fresh and rested and ready for a new day.

Listen for God's voice

'Speak, Lord, for your servant is listening.' 1 Samuel 3:9

I am astonished at the number of books that are written on the subject of prayer that make no mention of cultivating the art of active listening. Prayer is not just talking to God: it involves listening as well. Prayer has been defined as 'conversation with God'. All polite conversation is a two-way thing. It is the same with prayer. We talk to God and He talks to us. After you have talked to God, before you rise from your knees, spend a minute or two letting God talk to you.

How do we learn to recognise the voice of God when He speaks to us? The alert and courageous soul making its first venture upon the spiritual life is like a wireless operator on his trial trip in the Pacific. At the mercy of a myriad electrical whispers the novice at the receiver does not know what to think. In the same way the Christian who waits and listens for the voice of God must learn to disentangle His voice from the other voices that clamour for his attention – the ghostly whisperings of the subconscious, the noise of traffic in the street, the sounds of children at play. To learn to keep one's ear true in so subtle a labyrinth of sound is indeed a venture. It doesn't come easy but the more we practise it the more we will be able to detect the voice of God when He speaks to us.

REFLECTION: With practice it is possible for us to distinguish God's voice speaking to us.

The sound of God's voice

'The voice of the LORD is powerful; the voice of the LORD is majestic.' Psalm 29:4

B ut what does God's voice *sound* like? An old lady in Wales told me many years ago that God is Welsh. I asked her why she thought that. She replied, 'Well, He always speaks to me in that language!' Naturally God's voice will filter through our personalities and will come to us in the language or the idiom with which we are most familiar. But it is still God's voice for all that. God's voice is like the voice of conscience, only richer and more positive. Conscience merely approves or disapproves, but God's voice does much more. It informs, instructs, encourages and guides. It *never* argues but is quietly insistent and authoritative.

Not every day will the voice of God be equally clear. The closeness of our walk with God will determine that and, of course, the divine awareness of our need. Jesus referred to Himself in one passage in the New Testament as a good shepherd and said that His sheep follow Him because they *know* His voice (John 10:4). They do. You may be saying at this moment, 'I have been praying for years but I have never once heard the voice of God.' Ah, but did you pray *believing* that God would speak to you? It is possible to pray, and pray often, without such a sense of expectation. Expect God to talk to you. Incline your ear unto Him and in time you will not be disappointed.

REFLECTION: God will speak to us in ways that are familiar to our own personality, language and culture.

Unconditional love

'For I am convinced that neither death nor life ...
nor anything else in all creation, will be able to separate
us from the love of God that is in Christ Jesus our Lord.'
Romans 8:38–39

'One of the disadvantages of growing up in a Christian home,' said the late Dr W.E. Sangster, 'is that one always hears talk about the love of God and one becomes used to the phrase, we take it as part of the order of things ... though all the time we are living in it and are utterly dependent upon it, we take it for granted and seldom with gratitude. There is no wonder in it and no realisation in it either. God is remote and love is but a word.'

Although we cannot 'explain' the love of God perhaps it might help us if we thought for a moment how different it is from human love and also how much higher. Human love, for example, is conditional; divine love is unconditional. There are no strings to God's love. He does not love us if we will do this or that. He loves us for ourselves alone. It is love without condition and it is love without end. In the face of this amazing love does not the poverty of our own love sweep over us? So much human love is love for something even when it masquerades as the love of God. None of this is like the divine love. The unconditional love of God means that because we are not loved for anything no failure on our part can rob us of that love. We cannot even sin God's love away. We can never escape this inexorable and aggressive Lover. Blessed be His holy name.

REFLECTION: Are you truly aware of how much God loves you – that you are so very precious to Him? Revel in that today.

Thinking as God thinks

'... but be transformed by the renewing of your mind.'
Romans 12:2

B iblical meditation is designed by God to bring about major changes in our personality, especially our thoughts, feelings and decisions. Having 'rescued us from the dominion of darkness and brought us into the kingdom of the Son he loves, in whom we have redemption, the forgiveness of sins' (Col. 1:13–14), God wants to change us to be more and more like Jesus, and meditating on the Bible is a key part of this process.

Since the fall of Adam and Eve in the Garden of Eden the human personality has been thrown out of line. So it badly needs readjustment and realignment. Original sin took place when Satan, instead of attempting to put pressure on Eve's will to take the forbidden fruit, simply dropped an insinuating doubt into her mind. He knew only too well that God had built the personality in such a way that what a human believes affects the way they act. Our thoughts affect our emotions and our emotions affect our decisions. Instead of rejecting the doubt Satan dropped into her mind, Eve allowed it to mingle with her thoughts and the doubt quickly led to her disbelieving God – and eventually to disobeying God. So from that day to this our natural mind has been directly contrary to God's principles. This means that every thought needs to be brought into line with God's thoughts. We do this through continual and persistent biblical meditation, getting to know His thoughts, principles and purposes.

REFLECTION: How do my thoughts need to be brought in line with His thoughts?

Feasting on His Word

'How sweet are your words to my taste, sweeter than honey to my mouth!' Psalm 119:103

What exactly is biblical meditation? It is the process of holding a phrase or verse of Scripture in mind, pondering it, continually contemplating it, dwelling on it and viewing it from every angle we can think of until it begins to deeply affect us. Andrew Murray defined meditation as 'holding the Word of God in the mind until it has affected every area of one's life and character'. Meditation has also been described by someone else as 'gazing long at a prism of many facets, turning it from angle to angle in a bright spotlight'.

Bill Gothard likens meditation to a person slowly turning a many-faceted diamond in the light to feast upon its beauty from every possible angle. Campbell McAlpine described it as 'the devotional practice of pondering the words of a verse, or verses of Scripture, with a receptive heart, allowing the Holy Spirit to take the written Word and apply it as a living word to the inner being'.

The word 'meditate' or 'meditation' can be found in many parts of the Bible. Psalm 1:2 tells of the person whose 'delight is in the law of the LORD, and on his law he meditates day and night.' The Hebrew word for 'meditates' here is *hagah*, which means to murmur (in pleasure), to ponder. Scripture meditation is the digestive system of the soul. The person who reads, studies and memorises the Bible without meditating on it is like one who chews their food but refuses to swallow it.

REFLECTION: Contemplation of His Word is the springboard for living His life.

This God is *your* God

'Will your courage endure or your hands be strong in the day I deal with you?' Ezekiel 22:14

God is powerful not only in creation and preservation, but He is powerful in *judgment* also. When He acts no one can resist Him. The flood of Noah's day is one example of God's intervention, when the entire human race – with the exception of eight people – was wiped out (Gen. 6:1–9:18). A shower of fire and brimstone from heaven destroyed Sodom and Gomorrah and all the cities of the surrounding plain (Gen. 19:1–29). And Pharaoh and his army were impotent when God swept them into the Red Sea (Exod. 14:1–31).

Now what does the contemplation of God's great power do for us? First, it causes us to *tremble* before Him. The trouble with many modern men and women is that they do not *tremble* before God. Another thing the contemplation of God's great power does for us is to cause us to *adore* Him. Who can consider the might of this awesome God without wanting to worship Him? The rebellious heart will resist this, of course, but the heart cleansed by the blood of Christ will bow in homage and say, 'Who is like you – majestic in holiness, awesome in glory, working wonders?' (Exod. 15:11). Well may we, as believers, *trust* such a God. No prayer is too hard for Him to answer, no need too great for Him to supply, no predicament too difficult for Him to solve. Grasp this great and gripping truth: this God is *your* God.

REFLECTION: Tremble before God till that trembling turns to adoration and ever-increasing trust.

The mind of Christ

'Let this mind be in you which was also in Christ Jesus ...'
Philippians 2:5, NKJV

Paul never ceased to wonder at the fact that Christ was living in him, empowering him and motivating him towards a life that he had never imagined possible. Previously he had constantly struggled in his thinking, feeling and willing; now there was steady success. He was strong in the strength of his resident Lord. Consider this: in the thirteen letters Paul wrote, one phrase is repeated over and over again – 'in Christ'.

Adolf Deissmann, the German scholar, has counted the number of times Paul uses this and similar expressions and found they total 164. How important it seemed to Paul that he was in Christ and that Christ was in him. It seemed to be the pivotal point around which he constructed all his writings. The victorious life, the empowered life, is the life lived in Christ. When He is at the centre of our being – thinking, willing and feeling in our responsive hearts – then we begin to experience the kind of life God intended for us in the beginning.

How do we allow Christ to be at the centre of our thinking, our willing and our feelings? We begin with the mind. The mind plays a great part in human functioning. Some would say a primal part. '... as he thinks in his heart,' says Scripture, 'so is he' (Prov. 23:7, NKJV). With the imagination – so powerful a segment of the mind – even the will is strongly shaped and influenced.

REFLECTION: The way we think needs to be transformed by the renewing of our mind so we stop following worldly lies and believe God's truth in Christ.

Looking after the temple

'Therefore honour God with your body.'
1 Corinthians 6:20

I n 1 Corinthians the apostle Paul also says: 'Do you not know that your body is a temple of the Holy Spirit, who is in you, whom you have received from God? You are not your own; you were bought at a price' (6:19–20).

Could the matter be put more clearly? The Christian's body belongs to God. It is His property, and we are expected to pay as much concern to its welfare and upkeep as we would to the building in which we worship God every Sunday.

Think of it! Our bodies are the dwelling places of the Holy Spirit's presence. We are the custodians of the Lord's property. So take a good long honest look at your body right now. Are you caring for it in such a way that it truly glorifies and honours God? Is it a fit place for the Lord of glory to dwell?

God expects us to care for our bodies in the same way that we care for our spirits, and we shall have to give an account to Him for both. It is my conviction that thousands of Christians have died before their time because they have failed to keep their bodies in proper repair. You and I have a responsibility to keep our bodies in the best shape we can, barring accidents and genetic failure, of course, and to stay as long as possible on this earth, sharing the love of Jesus with our friends and families.

REFLECTION: Think prayerfully of some of the things you consider the main ingredients of good physical care.

A real disciple?

'This is to my Father's glory, that you bear much fruit,
showing yourselves to be my disciples.' John 15:8

My friend, are you a disciple of Christ? Is your Christian life shaky and lacking real dedication and commitment to Jesus Christ? Are you ready to take your place with that breed and brand of disciple that Jesus is asking for in this generation? Are you willing to redefine discipleship so that it means something so radical that the Church can stand in the midst of a pagan society and show the world that twenty-first-century discipleship is similar to first-century discipleship? That's what the world is crying out for.

Perhaps the greatest need of the Church at this moment is for disciples. I am asking you whether you want to commit yourself now to Jesus Christ, to be His disciple. Maybe you have been a half-hearted Christian, lacking in dedication and commitment, but God can turn you into a flaming brand of fire in His kingdom. If you have come to feel that the test of discipleship is something you can't pass, then that is good, because as you realise that it is impossible to do in your own strength, you are in the place to make the greatest breakthrough of your life. What you are asking God to give you now is a new brand of discipleship, not just to be a Christian, wonderful as that is, but a true disciple of Jesus.

REFLECTION: Lord Jesus, I give my life into Your hands. I want to be a disciple, totally committed to You. Now fill me with Your Spirit from the crown of my head to the soles of my feet so that every part of me shall be Yours, indwelt by You, dominated by You. Amen.

'My' not 'our'

'Who may ascend the hill of the LORD? Who may stand in his holy place? He who has clean hands and a pure heart ...'
Psalm 24:3–4

One of the great evidences of the Welsh Revival in 1904 when God's breath blew over the Principality in a powerful way was the fact that people's lives were cleaned up in the most amazing manner. Old debts were paid, bad language gave way to the praises of God and people would cross the valleys to each other's homes in order to clear up any bad feeling that had been between them.

It was like this in the Hebrides Revival in 1959 too. A group of people were praying in church and some stood up and read from Psalm 24. One of the congregation followed the reading with a prayer that went something like this: 'O God, forgive us if our hands are not clean and our hearts are not pure.' A young man immediately stood up and startled the congregation by crying out: 'It is so much humbug to talk about our hands and hearts not being clean. We need to drop the "our" and replace it with "my".' Then he proceeded to pray, 'Oh God, my hands are not clean, my heart is not pure ... forgive me ...', and falling to the ground in repentance provoked others to follow in the same vein.

People made their praying very personal and cried out to God in such a way that the Holy Spirit fell on the island ushering in one of the great movements of the Spirit in the twentieth century.

REFLECTION: Do you long for such Holy Spirit revival?

'He' not 'it'

'And do not grieve the Holy Spirit of God ...'
Ephesians 4:30

The Holy Spirit is not merely an influence; He is a *Person*. This is why, when we talk about Him, we must refer to Him as 'He' and not 'it'. Some Christians believe He is an impersonal influence yet use personal pronouns such as 'He' and 'His' when referring to Him. One man said, 'I use a personal pronoun when talking about the Holy Spirit in the same way that people use the term "Jack Frost" when speaking about icy conditions.' What nonsense. He is a Person in the same way that you and I are persons. He has individuality, intelligence, hearing, knowledge, wisdom, sympathy, and so on. He can see, speak, rejoice, love, whisper, and when we spurn Him by turning to other resources, or resist Him when He seeks to work within us, He is grieved in the same way that a close friend would be hurt.

The Bible says He is God, with the very same attributes as God. In Job 26:13 He is seen as having the power to create. In Psalm 139:7 He is shown to have omnipresence – being everywhere present. In Hebrews 3:7 He is spoken of as issuing commands – something only God can do. And in 2 Corinthians 3:17 He is referred to as 'Lord'. My dear friend, if you are a Christian there is an unseen deity in your life – the Holy Spirit. He doesn't want to hide from you, and He doesn't want you to hide from Him.

REFLECTION: The Holy Spirit is not the personification of an influence, the sense of fellowship Christians experience or an 'atmosphere'. He is a Person.

The Divine Gardener

'I am the true vine and my Father is the gardener.'
John 15:1

Many times during the years in which I have been a minister and a counsellor, I have had occasion to sit and talk with those who have been undergoing the painful process of 'spiritual pruning'. During such periods innumerable questions rise unbidden in the mind: What is God doing to me? Why does it hurt so much? When will it all end? Spiritual pruning is an experience from which many shrink – myself included – but one that is essential if we are to become the people God wants us to be. Christian fruitfulness and productivity do not just happen: they are the result of careful planning and pruning.

Our Lord put the truth in these gripping and arresting words: 'I am the true Vine, and my Father is the Gardener. He lops off every branch that doesn't produce. And he prunes those branches that bear fruit for even larger crops' (John 15:1–2, TLB). Someone has said: 'He who knows the *why* of things can always cope with the *what*.' It is my prayer that as you learn the 'why' of God's intentions, you will be able to give yourself more confidently to the purposes of the Divine Gardener. Always remember, no matter how often the secateurs snip or how painful the pruning, your life is in good hands: it is your *Father* who is the Gardener. Let us be quite clear about one thing – there is no way to spiritual fruitfulness except through careful and relentless pruning.

REFLECTION: It is our heavenly Father who goes about the task of pruning our lives in order to make them more fruitful and productive.

Pruning

'... he trims clean so that it will be even more fruitful.'
John 15:2

C onversion may be described as being grafted to Jesus Christ, the Vine, whereby His divine life begins to flow in us and through us. We are made partakers of the divine nature. The pruning process – cutting away the things that hinder or prevent our growth – provides for a continuous conversion in which we are converted from the irrelevant to the relevant, from being just busy to being fruitful. The useless non-fruit-bearing growth – the suckers that take life but give no fruit – must be cut away. In Japan, land is so scarce compared with the population, that everything must be cultivated to the maximum. In a hotel room in Tokyo some years ago, I saw an apple that was twice the size of an ordinary one. I said to myself, 'This isn't an apple, it's a whole tree!'

How do the Japanese achieve such amazing results? Mainly in two ways— fertilisation and pruning. And especially pruning. Every useless branch and every bit of unproductive growth is cut away so that everything is prepared for maximum fruitfulness. This is how it must be with us. If we are not able to give up, then we will not be able to give out. It is vital that we see this process of pruning in positive terms, for a negative attitude can greatly hinder the purposes of the Divine Gardener.

REFLECTION: The shears, or knife, which cut away at the non-fruit-bearing growth are held in the hands, not of an angel, nor an archangel, but in the hands of our loving heavenly Father.

Realignment of the will

'I wrote for them the many things of my law, but they regarded them as something alien.' Hosea 8:12

O ne reason God encourages us to meditate on His Word is: realignment of our wills. The will responds to feelings and feelings respond to thoughts. We generally choose what makes us feel good – in line with our basic assumptions and thinking. From the moment each of us enters this world our will responds to the basic egocentricity within us. We want what we want when we want it. Conversion to Christ means that the will has to be trained to respond to God's directions and purposes, but it cannot be trained unless those directions and purposes are stored in our memory through meditation.

Many Christians regard the Christian life as simply a battle of the will. They get up every morning gritting their teeth and with the attitude that they must strive as hard as they can to please God and do everything He wants them to do that day. No wonder that they fall back into bed at night utterly exhausted and frustrated! Instead of trying to conquer a rebellious will by forcing it to obey God's commands, flood your mind with God's Word by systematic meditation. The more you think God's thoughts the more your emotions delight in Him and you will want to obey Him more and more. When the mind is taught to think God's thoughts in meditation it is not long before the rest of the personality follows the same pattern – and feels and acts in response to right thinking.

REFLECTION: Realignment of my will means becoming God-centred not self-centred. Are there any of His ways from which I shy away?

Putting our roots down

'Your statutes are my delight; they are my counsellors.'
Psalm 119:24

A nother way we gain from biblical meditation is we become able to discern between right and wrong: 'I have hidden your word in my heart that I might not sin against you' (Psa. 119:11). God appeared to Solomon and told him he could have anything he wanted. Solomon's response was to ask for 'an understanding heart … that I may discern between good and bad' (1 Kings 3:9, AV). This request pleased God so much that He not only gave Solomon wisdom and understanding but riches and honour as well.

The ability to discern between right and wrong is an important part of our spiritual development and comes about mainly through exposure to the Word of God. When we read and meditate in the Scriptures, God uses the Word hidden in our hearts to show us when our thoughts, actions and attitudes are displeasing to Him. Failure to meditate in the Scriptures is one of the major reasons why so many Christians live barren and unfruitful lives. Psalm 1 explains that the secret of a spiritually fruitful life is to send one's roots down into the Word of God by meditation. As we do this we draw upon the life of God in His Word that, in turn, produces the spiritual fruitfulness the Bible everywhere encourages us to reveal. The picture is of a tree planted by the river, bringing forth fruit in its season and whose leaves never wither. Can you say that this is a picture of your Christian life?

REFLECTION: When I put down roots in His Word God waters them.

JANUARY 20

Prayer revision

'... not my will, but yours be done.' Luke 22:42

An elderly Welsh preacher of my acquaintance used to define prayer as 'revision'. Because, as he put it, 'a revised version of your life is put out every time you pray – really pray'. When we open up our heart to God, then more and more of our life is brought under His control and is pruned.

A Christian psychologist once undertook some research into the matter of what causes Christians to lapse into prayerlessness. He found that the chief reason was that they were harbouring things in their hearts they did not want to give up. They knew that if they prayed, God would have an opportunity to challenge them about these matters. When you want to hold on to guilt, self-pity, resentment and such like, then it is better not to pray.

If prayer is revision, then prayer involves pruning. 'He ... cleans every branch which does bear fruit, to make it bear richer fruit' (John 15:2, Moffatt). Cleans it of what? He cleans it of suckers that sap the life of the branch, suckers that bear no fruit, that only keep the branch from bearing fruit. It is because of this that when Christians say to me they are too busy to pray I respond, 'Then you are busier than God intends you to be.'

REFLECTION: When we open up our heart to God in prayer then we are bringing more of our life under His control and consequently our will is brought into alignment with the will of God.

Ruminating

'It is the man who shares My life and whose life I share who proves fruitful.' John 15:5, J.B. Phillips

As we explore the meaning of biblical meditation we come to another word to describe it: ruminate. Many animals – sheep, goats, camels, cows and giraffes – are known as ruminant animals because they have stomachs with several compartments, the first of which is called the rumen. The way a ruminant animal digests its food is quite fascinating. First it bolts its meal down, then later regurgitates the food out of its first stomach, the rumen, back into its mouth. This regurgitation process means the food is thoroughly digested, causing it to be absorbed into the bloodstream and become part of the animal's life. Rumination and meditation are parallel words.

When a Christian takes a thought from the Scriptures and begins to meditate on it they actually pass that thought from their mind into their spirit, backwards and forwards, over and over again, until it is absorbed into the spiritual bloodstream and translated into spiritual faith and energy. Just as a ruminant animal gets its nourishment and energy from the grass through regurgitation so does a Christian extract from the Scriptures the life of Christ through meditation. Meditation on the Word of God transfers the life of Christ into the believer's personality. So remember: it is not enough simply to read the Bible, study the Bible or memorise the Bible. To extract the life of God that He has deposited in it – that His life may flow in us – we must meditate upon it.

REFLECTION: I must chew on God's Word to be fully fed.

Saved *and* sustained

'Grace and peace be yours in abundance.' 1 Peter 1:2

Many Christians go through life relying on their own resources. Though they know in theory that God's strength is available to help them face anything that comes, in practice they do not draw upon it. Something that has surprised me greatly over the years is the number of Christians who go about as if God's dealings with them ended when they surrendered to Him. They talk about being saved by grace, but they seem to know nothing about being sustained by grace. God does not just call us to be saints – His grace is available to make us saints. Those who accept this truth are conscious there is a power that far exceeds their own resources and that they do not have to stumble along the path of Christian discipleship unaided.

Do you know someone who is younger than you in terms of discipleship yet demonstrates Christian qualities that you seem to struggle to put into effect – qualities such as an ability to forgive injuries, freedom from jealousy, lack of censoriousness, or joy when others do better at the things they themselves would like to do and praise them for it? And perhaps some of these people just a year or two ago were wallowing in sin! You can be sure of this: they are believers who live in constant awareness that God's grace is available to meet their every spiritual need. God has more to give than saving grace.

REFLECTION: There are multitudes of Christians who live as if their commitment to Jesus Christ were a completion rather than a commencement.

Spiritual laws

'... there is now no condemnation for those ... in Christ Jesus, because through Christ Jesus the law of the Spirit of life set me free from the law of sin and death.' Romans 8:1–2

I am convinced that the Creator built into the human personality spiritual laws that are as sure, certain and reliable as those in the natural realm. The apostle Paul introduces us to one of these spiritual laws in his epistle to the Romans. I have often illustrated this thought of his by holding a book on the palm of my hand and saying, 'There is a law – a law of gravity – trying to pull this book to the floor. Why doesn't it fall?' The answer is of course that a stronger law – the law of suspension operating through my hand is in those circumstances stronger than the law of gravity.

The law of the Spirit of life, the controlling power of the Holy Spirit – who is life-giving – is stronger in the believer than the controlling power of sin which ultimately produces death. How many occasions have we had to be grateful for the controlling power of the Holy Spirit working in us to counter the downward effects of the law of sin? Where would I have been, where would *you* have been but for the blessed Holy Spirit? At our first foolish fingering with sin, as soon as sin seduced our hearts and inflamed our desires, if He had not been there to sustain and support us, where would we have been? How grateful ought every Christian to be for the Holy Spirit who is at work within us pleading against the sinful desires with which every one of us is acquainted.

REFLECTION: The Holy Spirit not only pleads against every argument of sin, He breaks its power and hold over us, if we let Him.

Homeward bound

'We ... would prefer to be away from the body and at home with the Lord.' 2 Corinthians 5:8

One thought above all others should dominate our thinking as we make our way through this alien world is that we are going home. Many years ago, on the East Coast of the United States, two ships passed each other – one a large sailing ship, the other a small steamer. The small steamer was just a run-down vessel that visited the ports on the East Coast, dropping off supplies such as tea, coffee, mechanical equipment and so on. The great sailing ship with its white sails billowing in the wind was a tremendous sight and the men on the small steamer caught the scent of spices and perfumes as it passed by. As was the custom in those days the captain of the little steamer picked up his megaphone and hailed the great sailing ship in this way: 'I am the captain of the *Mary Anne* and I have been out of Miami 12 days carrying little bits and pieces to the different ports. And I am on my way to New England. Who are you?' In response, a strong voice boomed out from the megaphone on the other ship: 'I am the *Begun of Bengal*, 123 days out of Canton, having delivered perfumes and spices to many ports of the world, and now, homeward bound.'

As Christians we can make a similar claim. We are happily engaged in dropping off the perfume of heaven on our way through this world, but our greatest joy is this: we are homeward bound.

REFLECTION: Homeward bound where our eternal lover awaits us.

Meditating on the Bible

'Be still, and know that I am God.' Psalm 46:10

Biblical meditation is, without doubt, one of the greatest ways we can ever discover of realising God's presence in our lives but, regrettably, it is one that is little understood and little used. David Ray, an American minister and author, says: 'I used to look with suspicion on people who talked about Bible meditation as being out of touch with reality. Then someone showed me how to take a verse such as Psalm 46:10, 'Be still, and know that I am God', and allow it to soak into my thoughts. Within days, I became more aware of God's presence in my life than ever before.' May I suggest that you begin right now to practise the art of Bible meditation by letting this same verse lie on your mind throughout the day.

If necessary, put down this book, think about the verse, probe it, contemplate it and draw from it all that God has put into it, view it from every angle, ponder on it, letting it affect the deepest parts of your being. Bible meditation must not be confused with other types of meditation, particularly those that come out of the East. They focus on emptying the mind; Bible meditation focuses on filling it – filling it with the truths and insights of Scripture. As I said before, you can read the Bible, memorise the Bible, study the Bible, but unless you know how to meditate on it, you will not get the best out of it.

REFLECTION: Through meditation, a Christian extracts from Scripture the life and energy that God has put into it.

A giant tourniquet

'For I am convinced that neither death nor life ... neither
height nor depth, nor anything else in all creation, will be
able to separate us from the love of God that is in Christ
Jesus our Lord.' Romans 8:38–39

More than almost any other New Testament writer (perhaps with the exception of the apostle John), Paul seemed to revel in the fact that his life was circumscribed by the love of God. He saw it as encircling his life like a giant tourniquet holding him spiritually safe and secure in the midst of all life's problems. And the apostle seemed to have to face an endless array of problems But read what he says in Romans 8:35–37 prior to our verse above: 'Who shall separate us from the love of Christ? Shall trouble or hardship or persecution or famine or nakedness or danger or sword? As it is written: "For your sake we face death all day long; we are considered as sheep to be slaughtered." No, in all these things we are more than conquerors through him who loved us.'

Paul was convinced that everything that happened to him had first to pass the protective walls of God's love that encircled him and unless it furthered God's purposes in his life it would not be permitted to happen. When writing to the Philippians he said, 'Now I want you to know, brothers, that what has happened to me has really served to advance the gospel ...' (Phil. 1:12–14). Clearly the love of Christ was not only the secret of his spiritual drive, *it was also the secret of his spiritual defence.*

REFLECTION: So encompassing is the love of God that nothing can ever get through it unless God foresees that He can work it for good in a Christian's life.

The homing instinct

'I spread out my hands to you; my soul thirsts for you like a parched land.' Psalm 143:6

Not only are we physical beings but we are spiritual beings also. And, as such, we have within us the capacity of longing. When the Divine Architect planned our make-up, He decided to place within the heart of every one of us a longing for Himself. The great majority of men and women do not understand this; they just know there is something in them which earth cannot satisfy.

One naturalist writes, 'All students of natural history know of the wonderful instinct of direction displayed by birds and beasts and fish. It is called "the homing instinct". Cats and dogs find their way home across miles and miles of unknown country. Pigeons fly direct to their homes after being taken hundreds of miles from their lofts. Swallows and other birds take a confident journey between destinations which are thousands of miles apart. Salmon return to spawn in the rivers of their birth.'

Deep in the heart of every human being, too, is a homing instinct – a longing for God. It is obvious that the psalmist was in touch with the longings God had built into him. He expresses this by saying that he 'thirsts', but the words 'thirst' and 'longing' are interchangeable, as a careful examination of Scripture will show. What the psalmist was feeling was akin to the homing instinct in many animals. However, such a feeling is much more than an instinct – it is a personal yearning of the soul after God.

REFLECTION: These longings God has built into us cannot be cured by anything except 'home' – home in Him.

A psalm of comfort

'The Lord is my shepherd ...' Psalm 23:1

Psalm 23 is a passage that particularly speaks to people who, like David, are experiencing a major upheaval in life. Do you feel let down by someone who has been extremely close to you? Is a longstanding friendship about to break up? Then this psalm is for you. Begin memorising it and repeating it out loud to yourself. Roll every word around on the tip of your spiritual tongue and suck every precious drop of refreshment from it. Let it lie upon your mind until you feel its peace and serenity invading and penetrating every cell of your being. I promise you that if you will make the effort to absorb the truths that lie buried in this matchless psalm, you will never again be overwhelmed by life's difficulties and problems.

David begins by putting his problems in their proper context – he focuses his gaze directly upon God: 'The Lord is my shepherd.' Have you learned yet how to get your spiritual focus right when caught up in a crisis? If you don't immediately bring God into the problem, then you have no proper frame of reference in which to deal with your difficulties.

Knowing the psalm is one thing – hearsay – but knowing the Shepherd is quite another – heartsay. If you do not know Him in this personal way, then I urge you – surrender your life to Him this very moment.

REFLECTION: Perhaps one of the saddest situations is to hear so many recite Psalm 23 without having a personal relationship with the One of whom it so tenderly speaks.

He is my Shepherd

'The LORD is my shepherd ...' Psalm 23:1

Why did David choose to think of God as his Shepherd? The picture of God we carry deep in our hearts is the one we relate to whenever we find ourselves surrounded by trouble or difficulties. But perhaps what is more important is this – we will interpret every event of our lives in accordance with the inner picture that we have of Him.

I have referred before to the fact that, when I have asked people during counselling to describe to me their primary view of God, I have been surprised that so often they see Him, not as a loving Shepherd but as an austere and stern Judge. God is a Judge, of course – as David discovered when he committed adultery with Bathsheba – but that is not His primary relationship to His children. Someone has pointed out that the two most beautiful illustrations of God's relationship to His people given in Scripture are those of a Father and a Shepherd. It is interesting also that the two best-known passages in the whole of God's Word – the Lord's Prayer and Psalm 23 – use these analogies.

What kind of picture of God, I wonder, do you carry deep down in your heart? David, in the midst of his trials, consoled himself with the thought that God was not his Judge, but his Shepherd. This was his primary view of God, and thus the image of the divine Shepherd's tender love and care filled his heart as he meditated upon Him.

REFLECTION: Make no mistake about it – the image of God that you carry deep in your heart is the one that you will relate to in a moment of crisis.

I shall not want

'... I shall not be in want.' Psalm 23:1

Here is David in the midst of intense privation, hunted and hounded by hostile enemy forces, deserted by many of his former supporters – yet quietly affirming, 'I shall not want'. In the past I have known many Christians who have had great difficulty in understanding this phrase. They have said, 'How can I recite this verse when I want so many things?'

The meaning of what David is saying here becomes clear when we dig a little deeper into the original Hebrew words. One translation says: 'I shall lack nothing.' Another puts it like this: 'I shall not lack any good thing.' 'The main thought', says one commentator, 'is that of not lacking – not being deficient – in proper care, management or husbandry.'

So what David is really saying is this: no matter what hardships or privations come my way, I am confident of this one thing – that I shall not lack the expert care and tender supervision of my Master and my Shepherd. There were many things that David lacked – he lacked the comforts of life, family affection, physical security, and so on. What he did not lack, however, was the assurance that God was with him in his difficulties, David, in making this statement, is boasting in the fact that no matter what hardship he might endure, he would never want – never lack – the expert care and management of his tender, loving Shepherd.

REFLECTION: Our security is not in material possessions, achievements or people but in the One who counts the hairs on our head.

A different perspective

'Cast all your anxiety on him because he cares for you.'
1 Peter 5:7

There are many who believe that once we become Christians, we ought to be exempt from the ordinary ills that afflict humanity. Those who adopt this attitude go down like ninepins when trouble strikes. The same thing happening to two different people may have an entirely different effect. It all depends on our inner attitudes.

During a counselling session, a man said, 'I have found a verse in the Bible that describes my life perfectly.' He picked up a Bible that was lying on the desk and opened it at Job 5:7. 'Here, read that – aloud,' he said to the counsellor. The counsellor read: 'Man is born to trouble as surely as sparks fly upward.' 'I was born to trouble,' complained the counsellee. 'I live in trouble and I'll probably die in trouble. There's always a new burst of sparks, and they are burning me something awful.' The counsellor, with a flash of divine insight, said, 'There's another verse which accurately describes your life also: it's 1 Peter 5:7.' Then, handing him the Bible, he said: 'Now you read it – aloud.'

The man read these thrilling words: 'Cast all your anxiety on him because he cares for you.' He was silent for a time, and then, with a tear trickling down his cheek, said, 'Thank you for putting the perspective back into my life. I needed a word from God.'

REFLECTION: The difference between a Christian and a non-Christian is not in what happens to us, but what we are able to do with what happens.

The great triune God

'Thomas said to him, "My Lord and my God!"' John 20:28

D r W.E. Sangster told the story of how one Trinity Sunday he followed three children out of church. One of the children remarked to the others, 'I can't understand all this "Three in One, and One in Three" business.' 'I can't either,' said one of the other children, 'but I think of it like this: my mother is Mummy to me, she is Mabel to Daddy, and Mrs Douglas to lots of other people.' Is that the answer then? Is it just a question of names? Are we right in finding the doctrine of the Trinity in Matthew 28:19 where we are told to baptise in the name (not 'names') of the Father, Son and Holy Spirit?

No, that is just part of it. One of the better explanations of the Trinity is this. God, we know, is one God. But there stepped into the world one day Someone who also claimed to be God. He came from Nazareth and His name was Jesus. He forgave sins, disclosed that He had existence before Abraham, and accepted worship as His right. Worship, remember, is for God alone. After Jesus was resurrected and had returned to heaven He sent back the Holy Spirit, who is also seen as God (2 Cor. 13:14). He – the Holy Spirit – came *into* the disciples and brought with Him the resources of the Godhead, breaking the sin in their nature, moulding them to holiness, pleading in prayer, and exalting the Saviour. Thus we see that God is One, but also Three in One.

REFLECTION: God above us, God among us, God within us. The Father in majesty, the Son in suffering, the Spirit in striving. The triune God. This is the central mystery of our most holy faith.

Proprietors or stewards?

'But seek first his kingdom ... and all these things will be given to you as well.' Matthew 6:33

The question of material possessions is a sharp one. Some Christians prefer not to face it as it raises all kinds of emotions in their hearts. But, I assure you, if we don't face it, here and now, then we leave God with no alternative but to deal firmly with us. God will not have our heart fixed on things: He wants our gaze fully focused on Himself.

There is nothing wrong with being the possessor of great riches, providing these are held in trust for God and that we see our role not as proprietors but as stewards of the Lord's treasury. I have seen many Christians become preoccupied with riches and I have watched as God overturned their nest. A man I once knew, a Christian with a brilliant business mind, launched an enterprise that, within a few years, made him a fortune. When I talked to him about his spiritual life, I was reminded of the words of Edna St. Vincent Millay: 'I cannot say what loves have come and gone. I only know that summer sang in me a little while, and in me sings no more.' The icy winter of materialism had set in, chilling his spiritual life. But then God overturned his nest. He was stripped of everything he owned. At first he was stunned and crushed. Out of the bewilderment and pain, however, came a new vision of God. He rose up to build a new and better business – one in which God was the principal shareholder.

REFLECTION: God is not against us having possessions; He is against possessions having us.

A vital issue

'Jesus ... watched the crowd putting their money into the temple treasury.' Mark 12:41

A Christian's relationship to material possessions is a vital issue. We read that 'Jesus sat down opposite the place where the offerings were put and watched ...' It is a solemn moment when we review our relationship to our money and material possessions with Him sitting beside us, watching the effect of money on us. The real question for us to ask, then, is this: Who owns my possessions, God or I? Whether we acknowledge it or not, we do not in reality own anything. We are only in possession of our possessions for a brief period.

In the Bible God teaches us how to acknowledge His ownership – by giving Him one-tenth. But, remember, when we give one-tenth we are not really giving, we are only paying an obligation. When we give out of the remaining nine-tenths, only then are we giving. A Christian businessman put it wisely when he said, 'God has prospered me. Now I want to know how much of God's money I can keep for my own needs.' Unless we develop the right attitude towards our money and our material possessions then God may have to overturn our nest in order for us to learn the lesson that our gaze must be focused on God – not gold.

When we learn to put all our possessions at God's disposal, we do more than settle a money issue – we settle a life attitude. We then become men and women under orders, people with a sense of mission, a sense of direction and goal.

REFLECTION: Our attitude towards money reveals our attitude towards God.

What Jesus taught most

'You cannot serve both God and Money.' Matthew 6:24

When you let go of your possessions and let God have them then life takes on a sense of stewardship. You are handling something on behalf of Another. That does something to the whole of life – puts sacredness into the secular and lifts the sordid into the sacred. Surrender of your possessions to God makes them sanctified and sanctifying. Your Christianity functions in and through the material. Many years ago I heard an old Welsh preacher begin a sermon with these words, 'Tonight I want to speak to you on the subject: "What Jesus talked about most".'

Immediately my mind jumped ahead of him and I tried to work out for myself just what it was that Jesus talked about most. I thought to myself, could it be 'prayer' or 'faith' or 'heaven'? No, I concluded, it was none of these. It must be this – 'salvation'. Imagine my surprise when the preacher said, 'The subject Jesus talked about most was a man's relationship to his possessions.'

Consider the facts for yourself. Half of Jesus' parables focus on the issue of money. In Matthew's Gospel alone Jesus talks about money close on 100 times. In fact, extending the argument further than the Gospels, although in the New Testament there are about 500 references to prayer, there are over 1,000 references to a person's relationship to his possessions. God will not have our gaze focused on things but only on Himself. The central issue is what is most important – our possessions or God?

REFLECTION: Our attitude to possessions can cripple or boost our spiritual life.

The only answer

'Will you not revive us again, that your people may rejoice in you?' Psalm 85:6

Six out of the seven churches in the book of Revelation had quenched the Spirit so that they had to be severely reprimanded by the Lord Jesus Christ. Look around at the state of the contemporary Christian Church here in Great Britain. Yes, there are some good things happening, but the fact is Christianity in the mainstream churches is declining. According to Peter Brierley, a reliable research expert, we are losing about 1,000 young people a week. The level of spiritual energy in the contemporary Christian Church seems no match for the fast developing agnosticism of this postmodern generation. And while Christianity appears to be declining, non-Christian religions are growing and developing at an astonishing rate. In today's Britain there are more Muslims than Methodists, and the way Buddhism is growing who knows but one day there may be more Buddhists than Baptists. And this is what was once called a Christian country.

While we must be thankful for the good things that are happening such as Spring Harvest, Alpha and the large summer conferences that draw thousands of Christians, we have to confess that, generally speaking, after several decades of charismatic renewal we are making about as much impact on the nation as a peashooter on the rock of Gibraltar. Something much bigger and more powerful is needed if the spiritual situation is to be redeemed. It is going to take something much more than our methods and techniques to turn things around spiritually. As I see it, revival is the only answer.

REFLECTION: Revival is the only answer.

Pilgrims passing through

'He has also set eternity in the hearts of men ...'
Ecclesiastes 3:11

Ecclesiastes 3:11 suggests that when God designed us He put within us longings for immortality – a yearning for eternity. Is it this – the fact that we came from God – that accounts for the mysterious homesickness felt by every human heart? We were made by God for God, and there is a restlessness in us that will never go away until we find our home in God. Over the years I have met some very godly people and one thing that has always impressed me about those who live close to the Lord is that they have about them the 'air of an exile'. This earth, they seem to say both by their actions and their demeanour, is not their place. They are just pilgrims passing through.

How busy Paul was for the kingdom of God, but he expressed his true longing in 2 Corinthians 5:8 to be 'at home with the Lord'. It seems that the more godly people are, the more they will view the things of this world as a hotel room. Though it may be tasteful and appealing, it is not all that important. They are not staying.

In 1 Peter 1:1–9 the apostle reminds his readers of the hope given to every believer of an inheritance that can never perish – *kept in heaven*. The more godly a person is the more aware he or she seems to be of heaven. My soul aches for something more satisfying than I have ever discovered on earth.

REFLECTION: I have had a taste of heaven down here on earth, but it is only a *taste*. The full banquet comes later.

Son or sun lamp?

'... all you who ... provide yourselves with flaming
torches, go, walk in the light of your fires ... You will lie
down in torment.' Isaiah 50:11

This world is not our final destination. It is just a stopover. However comfortable one may make it, it simply will not satisfy the soul. If you have ever read C.S. Lewis's *The Silver Chair*[1] you will be familiar with the section where the beautiful Queen of the Underworld tries to convince the children from the Overworld that her dismal kingdom is the only reality and their world is but an imagined dream. 'There is no sun,' she says. 'You have seen my lamps and imagined that there was a sun.' This tactic used by the Queen of the Underworld is practised by many today, especially those who are part of what is called 'the psychological society' walking in the light of their own torches.

This passion to explain matters is our way of bringing them under our control. I heard one psychologist say during a television programme: 'The yearnings that we feel inside us can all be explained in terms of our sexuality, and the yearning that Christians say is the yearning for heaven or the homeland they are looking for is nothing more than a desire to return to their mother's womb.' Do you hear the tactic of the Queen of the Underworld? 'You have seen my lamps and imagined that there was a sun.' Perhaps in the light of Romans 8:7 we should not blame unbelievers too much for their blindness. But there again, as the saying goes, 'There are none so blind as those who do not wish to see.'

REFLECTION: Some people seem to settle for a sunlamp instead of the Son.

Utopia

'Come, let us build ourselves a city, with a tower that reaches to the heavens ...' Genesis 11:4

One way in which people deal with the fact that there is within their hearts a feeling that something very important awaits us elsewhere is by interpreting it as the desire for Utopia. The word 'Utopia' is not much used nowadays, but when I was growing up it was frequently mentioned. Utopia is an imaginary place with a perfect social and political system, an ideally perfect place or state of things.

In the 1920s and 30s politicians fervently believed they could bring about such a state of perfection. 'With more advanced education,' they said, 'with increased knowledge, better understanding of social forces, we are coming to the point where we should be able to provide healthy, happy and useful lives for all. The day is not far off when no need will have to go unsatisfied and no child go unloved.' Then came World War II, after which we learned that in one of the best educated societies of the day millions of Jews had been gassed. There has not been much talk of Utopia since. But now and again I hear some befuddled politicians talk about their desire to see the world become a kind of heaven on earth, which could easily be achieved, they believe, 'if we learned to control the variables that affect happiness'. They do not realise that a pleasant and civilised environment is inadequate to deal with the sinful desires of the human heart. Time and time again the attempt to improve conditions has been made and has failed.

REFLECTION: When will we understand that deep change only comes from within and that God is the only one who can effect that change?

A world of fantasy

'They exchanged the truth of God for a lie ...' Romans 1:25

T hose who allow themselves to be persuaded that the world is our home, our *only* home, discover, like Alice in the fantasy of Wonderland, that they are growing smaller. And not only do they themselves grow smaller, the world grows smaller too. A world such as this, beautiful though it may be, is not good enough to properly be called home. A waiting place – yes. A dwelling place – yes. But not *home*.

To trivialise the built-in desire we have for heaven and eternity has the same effect on the soul as psychotropic drugs have upon the mind: they dull it and deaden it. Far better to listen to the urge deep within us. As soon as we think we have put these built-in longings to sleep they spring up again and cry out for satisfaction. None of the remedies the experts prescribe for dealing with this inner yearning do the trick. The modern nostrum for dealing with personal discomfort is to 'discover yourself ', 'accept yourself', 'get a good self-image'. But those who have discovered their self usually don't like the self they have discovered. How can you accept a sinful self? And those who have discovered themselves and say, 'This is what I have been looking for all my life' know full well that it really isn't what they have been looking for. They settle for something that deep down they know is not what they want to settle for. It's all so sad. So very sad.

REFLECTION: Sin desensitises the soul to such a degree that some do not even realise that deep within them is a yearning for eternity.

The authority of Jesus

'I am going there to prepare a place for you.' John 14:2

I s the longing for heaven which God has placed within our hearts enough evidence that there is a heaven? A young scientist once put it to me like this: those who have travelled across a desert know the deception of the mirage. A person sees water in front of him. He would bank his life on it being there, but as he reaches out to drink, it fades away. This shows how our human senses are subject to illusions. When we long for something our mind sometimes persuades us that it is available. So how do we know the longing for heaven isn't just a mirage, that it isn't a form of self-delusion? I pointed the young scientist to John 14:2 in which Jesus says, 'I am going there to prepare a place for you.' We have the best proof possible: Jesus has told us there is a heaven and that a place in it is reserved for the men and women who believe in Him. What better evidence do we need than the words of Jesus?

Of course, if a person doesn't believe in Jesus or accept His credibility then that is another matter. Jesus' word is good enough for me, however, and I am sure for most of you who are reading these lines. He has told us in the clearest of terms that He will meet those of us who are His one day in heaven. The One who said, 'I am the truth' has given us His word.

REFLECTION: What better evidence do we need than the words of Jesus?

Double vision

'I pray that out of his glorious riches he may strengthen you with power through his Spirit in your inner being ...'
Ephesians 3:16

The real 'you', I believe, is not the person others see, not even the person you see, but the person God sees. Only He knows the real you. One of the characteristics of a good counsellor is to have a clear vision of a person's potential so that they can encourage that person to move towards it. This is not so much human potential but our potential in Christ. In John 1 Jesus looks at Simon and declares: '"You are Simon ... You will be called Cephas" (which, when translated, is Peter).'

What was Jesus really saying here? He was saying that He saw within Peter the potential to be a rock, for that is what the name 'Peter' means. Simon was the kind of vacillating character who could walk on the water with Jesus and yet 'followed afar off' when he was on the land. But Jesus had the double vision and insight to see people not just as they are but as they can be. This is a characteristic of the Holy Spirit also. He sees us as we are, loves us as we are, but yet loves us too much to let us stay as we are. Lovingly and gently He prods us towards perfection. Just as Jesus looked on Simon the reed and saw Peter the rock, so the Holy Spirit looks on you and sees you maybe as ineffective, beaten, cowed and fearful, but He also sees you as confident, effective, sanctified and strong, moving ahead along the Christian pathway.

REFLECTION: The Holy Spirit not only sees your potential in Christ, but helps you achieve it.

Experiencing the Holy Spirit?

'... be filled with the Spirit.' Ephesians 5:18

What stops us getting close to the Holy Spirit? Mainly it is our unwillingness. When our will is intent on getting closer, we *will* find a way. The divine Counsellor is at work within us seeking to make us into the kind of person He sees that we can be. Emerson said: 'Could'st thou in vision see Thyself the man God meant, Thou never more could'st be The man thou art, content.'

How does the Holy Spirit go about the task of enabling us to see the man or woman God *meant*? No counsellor is effective unless he or she has the confidence *and* attention of the person being counselled. Sadly, many of us keep the Holy Spirit at a safe distance. Charles Swindoll said, 'As theologians and teachers of the Word we study the Holy Spirit from a safe doctrinal distance; we are loath to enter into any of the realms of His supernatural workings or even to tolerate the possibility of such. Explaining the Holy Spirit is one thing; experiencing Him another.' I believe with all my heart that the Holy Spirit yearns to transform us in the same way that Christ yearned to transform Simon Peter (2 Cor. 3:17–18). But the cost is great. It means taking time to develop our relationship with Him. Once we do that, however, He goes to work, inflaming, enlightening, prodding, enticing, and moving us on until the difference in us is so marked that we too need a new name.

REFLECTION: To you now, as to one long ago, the Spirit says, 'You are ... But you shall be ...'

Pruning through the Word

'... they received the message with great eagerness and examined the Scriptures every day ...' Acts 17:11

H ave you ever found yourself reading the Scriptures when suddenly a verse seems to leap out at you, fasten itself to your conscience and plead with you to put something right in your life that you know to be wrong? That was God at work, pruning your life through His Word. In order for the Divine Gardener to prune us through the Word, we must soak ourselves in that Word. What liberty it brings if we give God the opportunity He desires to prune away the suckers that take life, but give no fruit.

I believe that the *chief* method by which God desires to prune our lives is through His Word. The Bible is eminently suitable for this, because it is both searching and sensitive. People ask: Doesn't an emphasis on reading the Bible *daily* bring Christians into a state of bondage and legalism? Yes, it can, but with the right approach it need not necessarily be so. My own view is this – it is of immense spiritual benefit to spend some time daily in the Bible, but we must be careful not to think that if we miss out on reading a portion of the Scriptures each day, God might push us under a bus. Try to read the Word of God daily, but if for some reason, such as tiredness, sickness or a period of unusual pressure, you are not able to do so, don't be too hard on yourself, but return to a regular schedule as soon as you can.

REFLECTION: The goal in every Christian life ought to be that of spending some time every day reading the Bible.

Don't neglect the Bible

'All Scripture is God-breathed and is useful for teaching, rebuking, correcting and training in righteousness ...'
2 Timothy 3:16

N one who seek to be conformed to the image of Christ can afford to neglect the Bible. This doesn't mean, of course, that the only reason we ought to read the Bible is so that God can have an opportunity to knock us into shape. I doubt whether I would be motivated to open the Scriptures daily if I thought that every time I did so God would reprimand me. Of course, if my life was way out of line, then God would be justified in doing this, but *normally* God's way of ministering to us is to mix His blessings and speak through His Word right into the area of our current need. One day our greatest need might be for comfort; and so He says: 'My grace is sufficient for you' (2 Cor. 12:9). Or it might be counsel. Then He says: 'This is the way, walk ye in it' (Isa. 30:21, AV).When our greatest need is reproof, then, of course, He speaks with the same authority and love.

As our needs are so varied, we should spend time with the *Bible* and not with substitutes. 'Promise boxes' or booklets that contain selected verses dealing only with comfort, may be useful as sweetmeats, but they must never become the whole meal. If God is to develop our lives through Scripture, then we must take care to read as much of it as possible. As far as the Bible is concerned, God can develop most those who read it most.

REFLECTION: There is no substitute for the very words of God recorded in the Bible.

Cleansed by the Word

'You are already clean because of the word I have spoken to you.' John 15:3

After Jesus had been with His disciples for nearly three years, He said: 'You are already clean because of the word I have spoken to you.' What was this 'word' that made them clean? Why did He use 'word' instead of 'words'? The reason could be that His words gathered themselves into such a living body of truth and insight, that they were no longer words – they were 'the Word'.

Over the period of time Christ spent with His disciples, His 'word' had been at work in their lives, cleansing, purifying and pruning. When the disciples first joined Christ, they had some pretty strange ideas about God and about life. But gradually, being exposed to the Word, their ideas were cleansed and purified. Jesus cleansed their ideas about God. He got them to see that the Almighty was not an autocratic, irresponsible despot but a Father and a Friend. He not only cleansed their ideas about God, but He cleansed their ideas about the kingdom of God. The kingdom of God was, to the Jewish mind, a setting up of a power base from which God would rule with strength and force. Jesus showed them that the rule of God would not be by the force of might, but by the force of love. He also cleansed their ideas about greatness, religion and prayer. When they first came to Him, they obviously thought of prayer as getting something out of God, but they came to see that it was God getting something out of them.

REFLECTION: Through His Word, Jesus cleansed the disciples' total conception of life.

Gain the most from Scripture

'Open my eyes that I may see wonderful things in your law.' Psalm 119:18

What steps do we take to get the best out of our daily reading of the Scriptures? 1. *Relax.* You are receptive only when you are relaxed. Nothing can be inscribed on a tense conscious mind. 2. *Recall.* Ask questions as you read a passage: Who is writing? What is the purpose? How does it apply to me? How shall I put it into practice? 3. *Rehearse.* If you find a verse or a thought from the Word that speaks to your condition roll it over in your mind. 4. *Retain.* If a verse or a part of a verse speaks to you decide to retain it by committing it to memory. When Jesus was pressed by temptation in the wilderness, He answered in the words of Scripture. 5. *Rejoice.* In reading the Word remember that the purpose of the Bible is to take you by the hand and lead you to the Word, which is Christ. So, as you read, look for Him, and when you find Him – rejoice. 6. *Realign.* I heard of a black preacher who used to pray, 'Prop us up, Lord, on our leaning side.' The problems of life often cause us to get out of alignment with God's purpose for our existence, so as you read God's Word keep realigning your life with His life. 7. *Release.* When something grips you from the Word, pass it on to someone that very day. The repetition will help you retain it and might also lighten the path of the other person.

REFLECTION: Take a choice portion of God's Word as you would a sweet – put it on the tip of your spiritual tongue and suck every precious drop of flavour from it!

Not wishy washy

'From this time many of his disciples turned back and no longer followed him. "You do not want to leave too, do you?" Jesus asked the Twelve.' John 6:66–67

Here is the first test of discipleship: that we put Jesus Christ first and foremost before every other person in our lives. Committing our lives to Jesus Christ automatically affects, cuts into, every other relationship that we have. There must be a willingness to put Christ first and others second.

Now it is important to understand that there is a reason why Jesus raises the standard to these almost unbelievable heights. The Church is suffering today from what I call 'easy believe-ism', but, when Jesus came He rigorously challenged people. Time and time again, He would work a miracle and then, when people wanted to applaud Him, He would prick the bubble of applause with astonishing messages saying, in effect, 'Now I have got your attention through miracles, this is what it means to be my disciple.' You see, Jesus calls people to a radical commitment to Him, not a wishy-washy kind of Christianity where you take Him on today and then maybe forget all about Him tomorrow.

What Christ is looking for is a disciple who will stand for Him, raise the standard and say, 'I am on His side and He is first and foremost in my life!' Now, if we don't preach that in our evangelism, people are going to slip into the kingdom of God without this radical commitment to Christ and they are going to be arguing with Him all the way through their Christian lives.

REFLECTION: If people come into the Christian life through radical repentance, their will capitulates, their ego surrenders before the cross and they serve Jesus without argument.

What is your goal?

'So we make it our goal to please him ...'
2 Corinthians 5:9

If our minds have a clear understanding where true life is found, then our goal will be to know more of Christ. If our minds are muddled on this issue, then the goals we pursue will be foolish and idolatrous. Paul's goal in life was this – *to please Christ.* That goal was not uncertain, could not be undermined, and because Christ was at work empowering him, it was not unreachable. Ah, but you might say, 'Paul was a spiritual genius. He had experiences ordinary Christians do not have.' It is true that he had unusual visions and revelations, but when he wrote those words to the Corinthians, you may be sure they were for all Christians, throughout the whole of time.

So if you have not already done so, do it now: based on the biblical belief that only Christ can give you what your soul aches for, set your will in the direction of pleasing Him. Make a choice that determines every other choice. When your overall goal is to please the Lord in every situation, then whoever you are – a businessman or businesswoman, a teacher, a student, a homemaker, an office worker, a musician, a singer or a minister – all you need to do when facing a challenging or difficult situation is to say, 'What must I do to please the Lord in this?' When you attempt to please the Lord in every situation, you are pursuing a goal that carries with it the guarantee of divine empowerment.

REFLECTION: A goal is an objective we pursue because we believe that is where life is to be found. And any ultimate goal that we pursue, believing that is where life is found, is an idol.

Take heart

'In this world you will have trouble. But take heart!
I have overcome the world.' John 16:33

Many believe that God should spare His children from troubles and calamities. But how ridiculous the world would be if calamities struck the wicked alone and the righteous were always saved. Its laws would have to be in process of suspension whenever the righteous were involved. Gravity wouldn't pull you over a parapet even though you leaned out too far – provided, of course, you were righteous. If a person was good the law would be suspended; if he were bad it would smite him. Now that is not to say that sometimes God does not intervene to save His children in particular situations, for He certainly cannot be straight-jacketed in His universe. The laws are His habitual way of running the universe, but to say He cannot overrule them is to make Him less than His modes of action.

If it could be proved that the Christian is infallibly spared trials and problems and suffering, the result would be a degradation of Christianity. People would flock to our churches to become Christians as if taking out an insurance policy. It would also be the degradation of the Christian, for he and she would miss the discipline of living in a universe of impartial law. Our Lord overcame the trials and difficulties that came His way and because He lives in us, He is able to provide us with the inner strength to persevere and overcome every obstacle that confronts us. All we have to do is provide the willingness; He provides the power.

REFLECTION: Persevering becomes essential to living, the key that unlocks the door of hope.

The power of imagination

'... to him who is able to do immeasurably more than all we ask or imagine ...' Ephesians 3:20

S ome Christians speak disparagingly of the imagination. This is because they mistakenly classify it in their mind with fancy, fantasy or speculation. But imagination is one of the greatest gifts God has given us. The proper use of the imagination is not to conjure up false or foolhardy things – that is fantasy – but to take things that are capable of achievement, albeit with great effort, and to turn them into reality. Part of the power of prayer is to harness the imagination and use it to turn ideas into facts.

How then do we employ imagination in prayer? Let's say that during your prayer time you become conscious of a number of spiritual deficiencies in your life. You become aware perhaps that you are lacking in genuine love, or joy – or even peace. Imagination comes to your aid when you *see yourself* receiving those qualities, and picture them flowing into you straight from the throne of God. Harness the imagination to your quest and you will discover that what the will cannot do, the imagination *used by the Holy Spirit* will bring into your life what you desire.

Link imagination with affirmation and *say* it as well as see it. Don't say, 'Oh God, please, please, give me the love I need', but using your imagination: Lord, right now I am being filled with Your love. Lord, right now I am being filled with Your peace. Lord, right now I am being filled with Your joy.

REFLECTION: You don't have to keep on asking for God's love, because through the blessings of imagination and affirmation it can flow into you right now.

Imagination and prayer

'Therefore I tell you, whatever you ask for in prayer,
believe that you have received it, and it will be yours.'
Mark 11:24

U sing the imagination in prayer centres on God and His will in situations. The right use of the imagination deals only with truth. We have no right, of course, to use the imagination beyond its proper limits and to expect all our desires to come to pass. This is why before employing the imagination we must ask ourselves three questions: Is what I am asking for clearly the will of God? Am I sure beyond all doubt that God wants me to have this thing – and have it now? Is there any uncertainty in my mind about its truth?

There are those, of course, who find it difficult to *see* things in their imagination. They don't think in terms of pictures, and have difficulty in putting their imagination to work. Let them not despair. Practise a few moments every day developing an image of yourself in different situations. The proud you, becoming humble. The fearful you, holding your head up high. The resentful you, offering the hand of forgiveness. Just hold the picture there, if only for a few seconds. The discipline of the moments, if observed *daily*, will, I assure you, be infinitely rewarding. When imagination is used to picture the realised end of a situation and it is held clearly in the mind's eye, then all the doors of the personality fly open and the power of God floods in. So see it done. Link imagination with affirmation and new power will flow into your prayers.

REFLECTION: Even Jesus used His imagination when for example, for the joy that was set before Him He endured the cross (Heb. 12:2).

Life is Christ

'For the love of money is a root of all kinds of evil.'
1 Timothy 6:10

A Christian businessman who decided to donate some important medical equipment to a hospital in China, went to see the ship on which the equipment was being carried. At the dockside he met another Christian and as they talked, the businessman shared with him what the moment meant to him. 'I, too, have a gift on board that ship,' said the other Christian, 'my only daughter is on board, going to China as a missionary.' The businessman said, 'My brother, my sacrifice is nothing compared to what you have given.' Both, however, were stewards of the entrustments of God. Both could say, 'Such as I have, I give.'

In the parable of the sower Jesus mentions two things that choked the growing wheat and made it unfruitful: 'As for him who is sown "among thorns", that is the man who listens to the word, but the worry of the world and the delight of being rich choke the word; so it proves unfruitful' (Matt. 13:22, Moffatt). Here 'worry' and 'the delight of being rich' are classed as the two outstanding enemies of growth. Note that Jesus didn't say that riches were the enemy of the soul but the delight of being rich, that is, wealth as an end in itself.

Someone has said, 'You can serve God with mammon but you can't serve God and mammon.' 'Life is food,' says the chef. 'Life is emotion,' says the sensualist. 'Life is possessions,' says the materialist. But the Christian says, 'Life is Christ.'

REFLECTION: 'Whoever craves wealth for its own sake is like a man who drinks sea water; the more he drinks the more he thirsts, and he ceases not to drink until he perishes.' (Welsh Proverb)

Surgery of the soul

'Examine yourselves to see whether you are in the faith ...'
2 Corinthians 13:5

I t is clear from what God is telling us in 2 Chronicles 7:14 and other scriptures that He is looking to us to operate on ourselves. I call it 'self-exploratory surgery of the soul'. While you are fully conscious, fully aware, I invite you to allow the Holy Spirit to assist you, handing you the only instrument you need to do soul surgery – the germ-free scalpel of Scripture. Hebrews 4:12–13 tells us that: '... the word of God is living and active. Sharper than any double-edged sword, it penetrates even to dividing soul and spirit, joints and marrow; it judges the thoughts and attitudes of the heart. Nothing in all creation is hidden from God's sight. Everything is uncovered and laid bare before the eyes of him to whom we must give account.'

With this reliable instrument, the Word of God, in your hand take an honest look into your soul and consider how much pride still lies within you. Pride is the implacable enemy of God and He gives some stern warnings in Scripture concerning it. For some it will be your first ever look, for others not the first, but perhaps one long overdue. Self-exploratory surgery should always be conducted in the presence of God and with the Word of God, in the realisation that God is not against us for our sin but for us against our sin. Remember C.S. Lewis's words, that if you think you are not proud then most likely you are.

**REFLECTION: Theologians in the past have listed what they
call the seven most deadly sins. And the first to head that list?
Not lust, not cruelty, not even murder, but pride.**

'I am the one Jesus loves'

'... the one Jesus loved ...' John 20:2

All commentators believe that when John wrote the phrase – 'the one Jesus loved' – he was referring to himself. Brennan Manning said in one of his seminars: 'If John were to be asked, "What is your primary identity in life?" he would not reply, "I am a disciple, an apostle, an evangelist, an author of one of the four Gospels", but rather: "I am the one Jesus loves."' What would it mean for us if we saw ourselves first and foremost not in the roles we play in life – as ministers, car mechanics, nurses, schoolteachers, engineers, shop assistants, and so on – but as 'the one Jesus loves'?

An Irish priest saw an elderly peasant kneeling by the side of the road praying. The priest was impressed and quietly going up to the man he remarked: 'You must be very close to God.' The peasant looked up from his prayers, thought for a moment, and said: 'Yes, He's very fond of me.' That peasant was probably closer to God than most because he saw himself as the one who was loved. We must get it in our hearts that there is nothing we can do to make God love us more for if we don't we will end up working to be saved instead of working because we are saved. No amount of spiritual discipline, attendance of seminars, study of the Bible in Hebrew and Greek, can make God love us more than He does. He loves us as much as it is possible for an infinite God to love. That's where our true identity must be found – in being loved.

REFLECTION: We should cease trying to impress the Lord by our performance and rejoice in the fact that we are the objects of His affection.

A child of His grace

'You who are trying to be justified by law ... have fallen away from grace.' Galatians 5:4

S ome years ago I talked to a woman who was caught up in doing dutiful things because she believed her acceptance by God depended on this. I said to her: 'I know what I am going to say is not really possible, but suppose you could lie down on this floor and go to sleep for a whole year. When you awoke do you believe God would love you as much as He did when you fell asleep?' She thought for a moment and replied: 'I don't believe so.' 'Why?' I asked. 'Well,' she said, 'I would not have been reading my Bible, attended prayer meetings, given my tithes, not done anything to bring people to Christ ...' 'No, I don't think that would make any difference,' I said quietly and firmly. 'This is where you are greatly mistaken. God would love you when you awoke as much as He did when you fell asleep. Nothing in you can extinguish His love, and nothing in you can increase it.' That simple statement seemed to break through her barrier of legalism and she caught such a glimpse of God's unconditional love that in a matter of days she became a transformed person.

A car hire company used to have as its slogan 'We try harder'. The Christian life is not a matter of trying but trusting – trusting that the grace by which we're saved is powerful enough to sustain us also. Never forget that.

REFLECTION: We work for God because we *are* saved, we do not work for God to be saved.

Overcoming irritations

'He makes me lie down ...' Psalm 23:2

S heep, especially during the hot season, can be driven almost to distraction by flies and ticks. At such times it is quite impossible for the shepherd to make them lie down: they remain on their feet, stamp their legs, shake their heads and are ready to rush off in any direction to find relief. A diligent shepherd can do several things to help his sheep overcome these irritations. He can make sure, for example, that they are regularly dipped, so that their fleeces are cleared of ticks. And he can see to it that they are put out to graze in areas where there is plenty of shade.

We now ask ourselves: how does our Good Shepherd go about the task of helping His sheep overcome the irritations that beset them? The answer is this – divine grace! The apostle Paul, in 2 Corinthians 12:7 tells of experiencing a 'thorn in my flesh'. What it was nobody quite knows. Eye disease, epilepsy, an unrelenting Satanic attack – each has been suggested. But still nobody is certain. One writer, commenting on this, says: 'Paul had a thorn in the flesh but nobody knows what it was: if we had a thorn in the flesh everybody would know what it was.' Paul tells us he sought three times for its removal – yet it remained. At last, however, came the comforting word: 'My grace is sufficient for you.' God's grace enabled Paul to cope with his irritation and, believe me, that same grace will enable you to cope with yours.

REFLECTION: Don't panic! God's grace is here.

Rest

'He makes me lie down in green pastures ...' Psalm 23:2

Sheep will not lie down until they are (1) free from all fear; (2) free from friction with the other sheep; (3) free from torment by flies and parasites, and (4) free from the pangs of hunger. Obviously, it depends on the diligence of the shepherd as to whether or not his flock is free from these disturbing influences. The very first thing a shepherd does in order to calm and reassure his sheep is to make them aware of his presence. Isn't it just the same in the Christian life? I don't know about you, but whenever I am beset by troubles and trials the thing that quietens and reassures my spirit is the keen awareness that my Shepherd is nearby. There is nothing like Christ's presence to dispel the tension, the panic and the terror of the unknown.

Perhaps at this very moment you are facing a tragedy or a crisis that threatens to send shock waves of fear through your whole being. Take heart – your Shepherd is not far away. His presence in the situation makes a world of difference. When I was a young child, I was terrified of thunder. When a thunderstorm came in the middle of the night, however, I had little fear because I knew that automatically my mother would come into my room, get into bed with me, and stay there all night to make me feel safe. Her loving presence made all the difference between calmness and fear.

REFLECTION: Perfect loves drives out fear (1 John 4:18).

Still waters of refreshment

'... He leads me beside the still waters.'
Psalm 23:2, NKJV

H ow, in an age of turmoil and strife, can we discover those 'still waters' of which the Bible so eloquently speaks? The answer is found in the Quiet Time, when, preferably at the beginning of the day, we meet with God in prayer and the reading of the Scriptures. One shepherd described his feelings of exasperation when, taking his sheep to a clean, quiet stream to be watered, he found many of them stopping to drink from small, dirty, muddy pools beside the trail. 'The water in these pools was filthy and polluted,' said the shepherd, 'but the sheep were quite sure it was the best drink obtainable.'

How sad that so many Christians are like those stubborn sheep – they stop to drink at any stream except the pure waters of God's eternal and inerrant Word. From what source do you draw your spiritual strength? I asked a man who was living a defeated Christian life if he kept a daily Quiet Time and the naive reply came: 'Yes, I spend ten to fifteen minutes every day reading Shakespeare.' Another couple said that their idea of a Quiet Time was to quietly sit and read the newspaper for half an hour after breakfast. These sincere but defeated souls found release and victory when they set up a real Quiet Time, in which they took on board the quietening and quickening resources of God. Shakespeare and the daily newspaper may make interesting reading, but they are poor and pitiable substitutes for the Word of God.

REFLECTION: Going without water results in dehydration; going without God's Word results in spiritual deterioration.

If

'... if my people ...' 2 Chronicles 7:14

M y prayer is that this great text will do for you what it has done for me – set your heart on fire for revival. It begins with the preposition: 'if'. A preposition, it has been said, can alter a proposition. And nowhere is that more evident than in the opening word of this illustrious text. Just as great doors swing open on small hinges so this word unfolds for us the truth that whatever part God plays in a spiritual re-awakening, we have a part to play too.

In the main there are two opposing schools of thought in relation to revival. There are those who say revival is a sovereign act of God and cannot be predicted or procured through any human means. Others say the Church can enter into revival anytime it wants to – providing it is prepared to pay the price.

When I was a student of theology I learned this: 'There are two rails laid down in Scripture – one is God's sovereignty and the other is human responsibility. If you do away with human responsibility you have nothing to save; if you do away with God's sovereignty you have nothing to save with. The Bible will not make sense to you unless you are prepared to run on both of those rails.' The Almighty delights to team up with His people. We could not experience revival without Him and He won't bring it about without us. The word 'if' is clearly a word of condition.

REFLECTION: Divine sovereignty does not relieve us of our human responsibility.

My people

'... if my people ...' 2 Chronicles 7:14

To whom is God speaking when He says 'if'? If '*my* people'. The message of revival is not for everyone; it is aimed specifically at the people of God. The responsibility for facing up to the challenge of revival is not on those outside the Church, but those *inside* the Church. That is you and me – if you are a believing Christian. One of the things I have observed among those with an interest in revival is a tendency with some to focus more on the desperate spiritual state of the nation than the low spiritual state of the Church.

Our strongest criticism and our deepest concern must be reserved for ourselves. God is concerned with the state of our nation, but He has an equal if not greater concern for His people. You and me. To start by lamenting the deplorable spiritual state of our nation is to begin at the wrong end. The initial focus should be on *ourselves*, what kind of people we are and what kind of people we should be. We are quick to point out the sins of non-Christians, but not so quick to look at our own sins. Revival starts then with the people of God. But is God talking to all men and women who call themselves Christians when He says 'my people'? No. For there are many who call themselves 'Christians' and may even go to church but have never had a *personal* encounter with Jesus Christ.

REFLECTION: Revival starts with the people of God.

My *people*

'... if my people ...' 2 Chronicles 7:14

G od chooses to begin with His own Church when He offers revival and that puts upon us an enormous responsibility. Not one person, but *all* His people. His true people. It is a tremendous responsibility to belong to the people of God. Every one of us carries a responsibility for the honour of God's name.

Let me deal with a difficulty that may be in some people's minds concerning the application of this Old Testament scripture to New Testament times. I have heard it said: 'You can't take a verse like this which was meant for the nation of Israel and apply it to the Church of the present day.' My answer to that objection is that while it is true that it is sometimes inappropriate to apply some Old Testament texts to New Testament situations, that does not apply in this case. Take, for example, the concept of 'the people of God'. That's a concept that is found everywhere in Scripture. God had a redeemed people in the Old Testament whom He called Israel and He has a redeemed people in the New Testament called the Church. And take the other concepts found in the text such as humility, prayer, intercession and repentance – these are all truths that are enunciated most clearly in the New Testament and apply to every generation of God's people.

I believe 2 Chronicles 7:14 has as much application to the Church of the New Testament as it did to God's people in the Old Testament.

REFLECTION: Every one of us carries a responsibility for the honour of God's name.

Confidence in our Father

'He cuts off every branch in me that bears no fruit ...'
John 15:2

Before we can entrust ourselves to the pruning shears of the Divine Gardener, we must have absolute confidence in His abilities and character. If God gave us a book containing the most intimate details of His heart, it would never have enabled us to know Him as He really is. He has to show His character where your character and mine are wrought out, namely in the stream of human history. So Jesus makes 'known' the character of God in the only possible way His character can be made known, namely through another character – His own.

Jesus, knowing the fears and uncertainties that linger in the human heart, went to great lengths to assure us that God's care for us runs down to the tiniest and most insignificant details. On one occasion, He took up the most extravagant metaphor He could find: 'the very hairs of your head are all numbered' (Matt. 10:30).

Jesus' own untroubled spirit arose, I believe, from the fact that He had complete confidence that His Father's purposes were loving, wise and good. We see this in the last testing hours of His life. After His agony in the Garden of Gethsemane, when He was arrested, He declared, 'Shall I not drink the cup the Father has given me?' (John 18:11) Can you see what He is saying? The cup which He had been given to drink was full of bitterness, but He found solace in the fact that *the cup was in His Father's hands.* And so, my friend, must you.

REFLECTION: Because Jesus had complete confidence that His Father's purposes were loving, wise and good, so can we.

Word alive

'The man without the Spirit does not accept the things
that come from the Spirit of God ... and he cannot
understand them, because they are spiritually discerned.'
1 Corinthians 2:14

The Christian life is one of progress – in spiritual maturity, of getting to know God better and better, of being more aware, more sensitive to His presence and His ways. One of the most effective ways is through biblical meditation. Notice I say *biblical* meditation, for there are many forms of meditation that claim to lead people to God but which, in fact, lead them away from Him. The only way a person can know God is through a personal encounter with Jesus Christ. The glorious message of the Bible is summed up in the fact that when there was nothing we could do to climb up to God, the Almighty God became the Son of Man in order that the sons of men might become the sons of God. The Bible is the only way through which Christians can increase their understanding and awareness of God.

Biblical meditation, along with an understanding of the power of God, will keep us from erring. Some Christians make the mistake of wholly concentrating on the Scriptures – past revelation – and ignore the power of the Holy Spirit who gives revelation from the Word: what God wants to say to us *now*. Others have experienced the power of the Spirit in their life and experience but do not know the Scriptures in any real sense. They too err, for we cannot correctly discern God at work in our lives and churches unless we continually check spiritual experiences with the revelation contained in the Scriptures.

REFLECTION: The abiding presence of the Holy Spirit enables us to understand Scripture as God meant it.

Taking up the cross

'Then Jesus said to his disciples, "If anyone would come after me, he must deny himself and take up his cross and follow me."' Matthew 16:24

Let's consider a second test of discipleship which we find in this text: What does it mean to take up a cross? It is amazing how many people misunderstand what Jesus is saying here. Let me tell you first of all what it does not mean. The cross does not mean the unavoidable irritations of life, the people we find difficult to cope with, nor does it, as some people think, mean the unavoidable sufferings of life. The cross is something you can avoid; it is something you choose to pick up. The cross that Jesus is talking about is that point at which our self-interest and our self-concern intersect with His will and with His demands.

Visualise now, if you will, with your mind's eye, a perpendicular line, running perfectly straight before you. Then imagine a horizontal line cutting right across the middle of it. At the point where the horizontal line intersects with the vertical line a cross appears, and that is what Jesus is talking about when He says, 'Take up your cross.' What Jesus is asking is, 'Are you willing to put your self-concern and your self-interest to one side and to make my cause and my claims a priority?' The test of discipleship is not only that you will put Christ first and foremost before every person in your life but also, secondly, that you will put Him first and foremost before every pleasure in your life. Are you willing to take up that cross?

REFLECTION: The commands and claims of Jesus Christ will sometimes intersect with your own demands and desires. Are you willing at that stage to say, 'He comes first'?

Everything except ...

'... any of you who does not give up everything he has cannot be my disciple.' Luke 14:33

T his verse is Christ's third test of discipleship. Jesus is talking here about possessions, and is clearly saying, 'If you are not prepared to pass this test, then call yourself a Christian but don't call yourself My disciple.' I love that word 'disciple' because it was the word Jesus used. It means putting Christ first and foremost before every other person, every other pleasure and every other possession. He that does not forsake all that he has cannot be a disciple of Jesus. Maybe He can have everything, or, as one person said to me some years ago, 'He can have everything except my money.' There was a young man like this in the New Testament, referred to as 'the rich young ruler'. He was mightily interested in Jesus Christ but, when Jesus probed that area of his possessions, he turned away and went down into oblivion (Matt. 19:16–30).

What Jesus is saying is that, if you really want to follow Him and be His disciple, then you must be ready and willing to give Him all that He is asking – and He is asking for all. As someone said, 'If you do not crown Him Lord of all you do not crown Him Lord at all.' C.T. Studd, the great missionary, said, 'If Jesus Christ be God and died for me, then no sacrifice can be too great for me to make for Him.' And our money is usually the last thing to be laid upon the altar.

REFLECTION: Do you call your possessions your own? Does the Lord have access to your bank account? Are you ready to give Him your all?

Amazing love!

'The Lord did not ... choose you because you were ...
numerous ... it was because the LORD loved you ...'
Deuteronomy 7:7–8

W hen the Bible says God is love, it is saying more than that God loves, or that God is loving, or even that God is lovely; it is saying that love is the energy behind everything He does – love is not merely one of His attributes but is His whole nature. God is not only the Author of loving acts; He is love in the very core of His Being. Sometimes you hear people talking rather sentimentally about the love of God as if it is some kind of amiable weakness, a sort of good-natured indulgence patterned after fallen human emotions. Our thoughts of God's love, however, must be built on God's revelation about Himself in the Scriptures, not by projecting our own ideas about love onto Him.

Let's focus, therefore, on what the Bible has to say about the God who is love. First, God's love is *uninfluenced*. By that I mean nothing in us can give rise to it and nothing in us can extinguish it. The love which we humans have for one another is drawn out of us by something in the object of our love. But God's love is not like that; His love is free, spontaneous and uncaused. He loves because He would love. He *is* love. To 'explain' it would require that He loves us for something outside of Himself, and, as we have seen, He loves us for ourselves alone. And that love has its beginning, not in us, but in Himself. He is love's source as well as its river.

REFLECTION: Reflect on God's love for you – that it will never be diminished and never be taken away. Why can we love others as God loves them?

Knowing God

'... they will all know me, from the least of them to the greatest.' Hebrews 8:11

We should understand four pivotal things about God: God is a personal being who relates. God is a rational being who thinks. God is an emotional being who feels. God is a volitional being who chooses. That same design can be seen reflected in His human creation, for we are made in the divine image. However, though a theological education can present you with understanding, only a personal encounter with God through His Son Jesus Christ can initiate you into a spiritual world where you pass from knowing about Him to knowing Him for who He is. Although it is possible to know something about God through the study of His attributes, it is not possible to know God intimately until one experiences what the Bible calls 'a new birth'.

Every Christian longs to live a new and divinely empowered life, a life that rises above circumstances and is not beaten or defeated by problems. This is precisely the kind of life that is offered to us in the New Testament. It tells us that through the 'new birth' we can have the life of Christ as our life. Those who commit their lives to the Saviour can say with the apostle Paul, 'For me to live is Christ.' This means more than receiving Christ's help, as a flower receives the energy from the sun. It means receiving Christ Himself. He is not saving us from without but actually living within us – thinking, feeling, willing in the life of His obedient servants.

REFLECTION: Knowing about God is different to knowing Him personally for ourselves.

Frozen at the mouth?

'Then Jesus declared, "I am the bread of life. He who comes to me will never go hungry, and he who believes in me will never be thirsty."' John 6:35

My old pastor (the man who led me to Christ and mentored me in the days following my conversion) used to say, 'You have been saved to serve. Seek now to win someone else to Christ.' The New Testament fairly bulges with accounts of people who, having been introduced to Jesus, race to tell others about Him. Take Andrew, for example, one of Jesus' first disciples. No sooner did he find Christ than he hastened to tell his brother Peter about Him which resulted in Simon Peter becoming one of the most prominent and productive of the twelve disciples. And of the many other personalities in the New Testament who, having met the Saviour, were gripped with a desire to tell others about Him. The instinct of every newborn soul is to share what they have received with others. It's a tragedy that so many suppress that instinct and remain like the Arctic rivers – frozen at the mouth.

Evangelism has been described as 'one beggar telling another where to find bread'. Not to tell a hungry and starving world where they can find bread to satisfy their souls is criminal. Soul winning is a biblical imperative. One of the problems of today's Church (generally speaking) is the fact that, albeit unnoticed, the urgency of soul winning taught so clearly in the New Testament is no longer being emphasised in the way it once was.

REFLECTION: Let us never forget that the two main illustrations of soul winning in the New Testament are that of a fisherman and a shepherd; so you see, souls must be saved by hook or by crook!

No other name

'... for there is no other name under heaven given to men by which we must be saved.' Acts 4:12

There are exceptions, of course, but it seems that attempts to convert other people are being seen by many of today's Christians as a gross infringement of people's individual liberties and a most distasteful form of arrogance. How can one faith religion claim a monopoly on truth? some ask. Are there not different ways to God? What right have we to interfere in other people's privacy or attempt to impose our views on them?

What accounts for this change amongst the youth of our day? I believe it is because a concept has swept the world that presents one of the greatest threats and challenges to the cause of Christ in any part of history. That concept is – *tolerance*. It's part of this postmodern age to be tolerant of other people's religion and not to say that Christianity is better than any other faith. But Christianity, as the late Archbishop William Temple said, 'is a profoundly intolerant religion'. There are not many ways to heaven; there is just one. There can be no tolerance in mathematics, in physics, in charting a path to the moon, and no tolerance when it comes to the way of salvation: '... for there is no other name under heaven given to men by which we must be saved' (Acts 4:12).

In the face of that text, believing that there is more than one way to heaven is as foolish as thinking that dialling any phone number will connect you to your home.

REFLECTION: Meditate again on Acts 4:12 – can we afford to be too tolerant?

Open yourself to the Spirit

'"… streams of living water will flow from within him."
By this he meant the Spirit …' John 7:38

S ometimes one hears the expression: 'I need all the help I can get.' Ever said that? Well, if Christians are to exercise their rights and privileges at the place of prayer, achieve great victories and reach new spiritual heights, then they are going to need all the help they can get. We have all the help we need in the Person of the Holy Spirit. Who is the Holy Spirit? He is the third Person of the Trinity and His executive function is to minister the resources of God and Christ to the weak and helpless believer. Paul says in Romans 8:26: 'In the same way, the Spirit helps us in our weakness. We do not know what we ought to pray for, but the Spirit himself intercedes for us with groans that words cannot express.'

The Holy Spirit helps us in many ways of course, but His chief aim and purpose is to enable us to pray, and pray effectively. John Wesley once said, 'God does nothing in this world redemptively – except through prayer.' Think of that for a moment. If it is true that God does nothing redemptively except through prayer then it means whenever God wants to do something important in a community, or even in a nation, He lays a prayerful burden deep in someone's heart and brings about change through the process of human/divine co-operation. God does nothing independently, but seeks to bring about change by working through His redeemed people in the place of prayer.

REFLECTION: The more you allow the Holy Spirit to flow into and through your life the greater will be your power in prayer.

Praying in the Spirit

'I will pray with my spirit, but I will also pray with my mind ...' 1 Corinthians 14:15

Andrew Murray, a great prayer warrior of the past, emphasised the need for utter dependency on the Holy Spirit when he wrote: 'In every prayer the triune God takes a part; the Father Who hears, the Son in Whose Name we pray, and the Holy Spirit Who prays for us and in us.' Some say we have the Spirit at our conversion and there is nothing more to seek. Others say we receive just one operation of the Spirit at conversion (regeneration) and we need to seek a further encounter with the Holy Spirit, which they describe as the baptism in the Spirit. At this moment I am not interested in arguing a doctrinal point, but want to encourage you to open your life to all that God has for you.

If you believe that you received all of the Holy Spirit at conversion then what steps are you taking to ensure that His Spirit is flowing in your life to the extent He should? And if you believe that the Spirit came to you subsequent to your conversion and you were baptised with the Holy Spirit and fire, then how up to date is that experience? Is He flowing in you now with as much force and energy as He once did? Whatever our experience in the past, let our eyes be uplifted, our hearts wide open for a greater supply of the Spirit to flow in us and through us than we have ever known before.

REFLECTION: How important it is that we should be in a right relationship to the Holy Spirit and understand His word?

Worship not just praise

'God is spirit, and his worshippers must worship in spirit and in truth.' John 4:24

I ought to make clear the difference between the words 'worship' and 'praise', as some see them as synonymous terms. Praise is appreciating God for what He does; worship is adoring Him for who He is. C.S. Lewis, with his characteristic lucidity, said in *Surprised by Joy*, that something can be revered not for what it can do for us but for what it is. It was then, he said, that he understood the difference between praise and worship. Worship is not just praising God but being in awe of Him, adoring Him – not for what He gives but for who He is.

Strictly speaking, in worship there is no prayer or intercession. It is gazing on God in love and adoring Him just for Himself. Christians who know this experience can think of no bliss in eternity which will exceed the bliss of gazing on Him. But it is not so much with corporate worship I am concerned here; rather it is with individual worship. I am thinking of it in the way that Jesus used the word when tempted by the devil in the wilderness: 'Again, the devil took him to a very high mountain and showed him all the kingdoms of the world ... "All this I will give you," he said, "if you will bow down and worship me." Jesus said to him, "Away from me, Satan! For it is written: 'Worship the Lord your God, and serve him only'"' (Matt. 4:8–10).

REFLECTION: 'We have good preaching here, good music and good services; everything always has to be upbeat. But we are so preoccupied with praising God that we have no time to worship Him.'

Designed for worship

'Yet a time ... has now come when the true worshippers will worship the Father in spirit and truth, for they are the kind of worshippers the Father seeks.' John 4:23

Deep within every heart is a desire to worship God. This is because in the beginning God designed us for worship. The primary purpose behind the creation of mankind was that we might freely and intelligently worship the Creator. Only when this truth is understood and practised will our souls function in the way they were designed. One of the failures of modern-day Christians is to put work before worship. We take our converts and immediately set about making workers out of them. God never meant it to be so. God meant that we should learn first how to worship Him and only after that become a worker. God is not primarily in the business of recruiting labourers for His harvest field. His chief aim is to restore fallen men and women to the condition where they can offer Him true worship. Our Lord made this point clear to the Samaritan woman at the well of Sychar (John 4:23).

Those whose main work is in the field of evangelism need not be frightened of this emphasis, for labour and service that do not flow out of a worshipping heart will appear only as wood, hay and stubble in the day when everyone's work is tried. No one can worship God for long without seeing and sensing the need to work for Him. A vision of God such as Isaiah experienced in the Temple leads ultimately to the obligation of service becoming too strong to resist. The true worshipper responds as Isaiah did: 'Here am I. Send me!' (Isa. 6:8).

REFLECTION: Our work for the Lord is of course important, but not as important as our worship of Him. Are we more taken up with working for the Lord than with the Lord Himself?

A right view of God

'For the Lord is good and his love endures for ever;
his faithfulness continues through all generations.'
Psalm 100:5

The concept we hold of God in our hearts is crucial to the way we will worship Him. For example, take the case of Dr Joseph Cooke, a brilliant anthropologist and one-time missionary to Thailand, who experienced a breakdown on the mission field and came to see that part of his problem arose because of a faulty view of God. In his book, *Free for the Taking*, he wrote: 'I invented an impossible God whose demands of me were so high and his opinion of me so low that there was no way to live except under his frown.' Can you understand how a man who held such a concept of God as that could have a breakdown? I most certainly can for I have found in my pastoral and counselling experience that underlying many emotional problems is often a faulty concept of God. I am convinced that many Christians when they worship do not worship the true God but a caricature of Him.

'How do you see God?' I asked one woman. She answered, 'Judgmental. Distant. Punitive.' It was no surprise to me when she told me that, although she tried to be a good Christian, she found great difficulty in developing a life of intimacy with the Lord. 'I pray to God,' she said, 'but I find it so difficult to worship Him.' Is it any wonder, when she carried in her heart such a false picture of the Almighty? I urge you to think about how you see God.

**REFLECTION: If you do not see God as He really is −
trustworthy, reliable and good − then those doubts and
misgivings will sabotage true worship.**

When you fall into sin

'... I write this to you so that you will not sin. But if anybody does sin, we have one who speaks to the Father in our defence – Jesus Christ, the Righteous One.' 1 John 2:1

How do you deal with yourself when you stumble and crash, when you are so engulfed in shame that you are ready to give up? Here is the advice I have given to thousands. First, don't try to minimise the sin. Many of our problems arise from the fact that we do not see sin in its proper light. Don't just call a sin a mistake or use other euphemisms. Adultery is adultery – not a misdemeanour. Glossing things over by using euphemisms is one of the ways in which we grease the path to waywardness. And don't be among those who say, 'Everyone sins, so I will too.' Paul answered that false reasoning when he said: 'Rather, clothe yourselves with the Lord Jesus Christ, and do not think about how to gratify the desires of the sinful nature' (Rom. 13:14).

Secondly, don't persuade yourself that the thing you did was justified by the circumstances. I once asked a woman who had got entangled in an affair how she had got into that situation. She said, 'My husband was away and I was lonely.' Other people are lonely and don't behave in that way. The loneliness was a factor but the real problem was the lack of firm moral resolve. Admit the sin and don't excuse yourself. Then go to God, tell Him how sorry you are and ask His forgiveness. Once you have done that, don't brood over the past – He will give you the grace you need.

REFLECTION: It is foolish to call a serious thing by a light name and try to sneak it past your moral guard. Sin is sin.

Just because

'The LORD did not set his affection on you and choose you because you were more numerous than other peoples ... But it was because the LORD loved you ...' Deuteronomy 7:7–8

One of the things that has intrigued me over the years is that when I have pressed fellow believers who have done a great work for God to give reasons for the love that has prompted them to give their lives in self-sacrificing service for the cause of Christ, they fall back on the pattern of their heavenly Father and simply say 'because'. I have a friend in India who gave up a large church in the USA and the offer of a high position in the denomination he served, to move into a village in the state of Kerala, South India, and minister to a small congregation of no more than 100. When I tried to get him to explain it to me; to come up with some logical reasons for his decision, he turned to me and with a smile, shrugged his shoulders and said, *'Because.'*

It is the same with others of God's servants too. Wherever you find people spending themselves in service for others, with no great fame, no earthly rewards; a minister working in a small church perhaps, a faithful woman standing at the side of the man she loves, a businessman or woman who gives up a lucrative career to work in unprepossessing circumstances, and you press them for reasons as to why – what do they say? They say ... The only reason I can give is a love flows in my heart begotten of the Holy Spirit. If you want a logical reason then I cannot give you one. It's just – *because.*

REFLECTION: As you allow God's love to flow in you so you will find yourself responding to Him and to others.

MARCH 19

And He replies 'Because'

'But it was because the LORD loved you ...' Deuteronomy 7:8

T he older I get in the Christian faith the more I realise that my faith does not rest on theological arguments. There was a time when it did. I knew all the arguments for the existence of God and all the other arguments as to why God allowed sin to intrude into His universe, why He allows suffering and so on but nowadays my faith rests not so much on them but on the experiential knowledge that I am loved by the world's greatest Lover. I know of nothing more wonderful in all of the experiences I have gone through in my life than sensing and feeling the divine love wrapping itself around my heart holding me safe and secure.

As the blazing sun is set in the heart of this universe and all things revolve around it and have their life from it, so the burning love of God is at the heart of all the life of the Spirit and without it life would be impossible. God can no more stop loving than He can stop living. Nothing can drive the eternal love away. It is love without condition and it is love without end. So, if next time you feel a little despairing towards yourself and you think you are not worth being loved and you say, perhaps rather petulantly, 'Lord, why do you keep on loving me?' don't be surprised if He answers you with 'the strangest, oldest, shortest and most intriguing response in the English language' – Because.

REFLECTION: You are loved by the world's greatest Lover.

Understanding failure

'... what has happened to me has really served to advance the gospel.' Philippians 1:12

Sometimes God uses *circumstances of deprivation and loss* to further His purposes in our lives. We begin by focusing on the issue of *failure.* Some of our failures are due to the fact that we didn't try hard enough, didn't study hard enough or didn't properly count the cost. Some failures, no doubt, are due to our physical condition – lack of energy, sickness and so on.

There are, indeed, many reasons for failure but there are some failures which are deliberately engineered in heaven. God often arranges for us to fail in a secondary thing that we might succeed in a primary thing. Many people are ruined by secondary successes. They become tangled up in them, and never get to the worthwhile things. I am sure that God prevented me from achieving the success in engineering that I had set my eyes upon when I was a youth. I left college with good results, and was chosen from many applicants for an apprenticeship in a first-class engineering firm. But after a few years, the targets I had set for myself were not being achieved. I knew I could do it, but somehow things eluded me. One day I woke up and concluded that God wanted me to be an evangelist, not an engineer. My conclusion was right. I might have been crippled by a secondary success. At first I found it difficult to countenance the apparent failure of my youthful ambitions, but now I am thankful for God's preventative grace.

REFLECTION: Failing at something does not make *you* a failure.

A good shaking

'... removing ... what can be shaken ... so that what cannot be shaken may remain.' Hebrews 12:27

I heard recently of a Christian woman, afflicted for many years with spinal trouble, who could not walk without crutches. One day as she was making her way downstairs, she slipped and fell to the bottom, her crutches remaining halfway up the stairs. She lay there for a long time, calling for help, but no one came. Eventually she said to herself, 'This is ridiculous. I can't stay here all day.' She pulled herself up and began to walk. And she has been walking ever since! The fall and the loss of those crutches was the best thing that could have happened to her.

There are many things in your life and mine upon which we tend to lean heavily – success, money, friends, family, position. They may not be wrong, but they become crutches which weaken our moral fibre. We depend upon them too much. Then something happens and they are taken away. At first we are stunned and crushed. Our crutches are gone – what's left? Why, our feet and our backbones, and the grace of God!

A medical doctor friend lost his practice, his possessions, everything. When a friend tried to console him, he said, 'Don't worry, the shaking has done me good. Christ has been on the margin of my life too long. Now He will be the centre.' He set out with his family to another country, and he is doing a marvellous and wonderful work for God. Do not weep over lost crutches. God is not punishing you, but pruning you.

REFLECTION: God sometimes removes the things we rely on so that we come to rely only on Him.

Shaken but not shattered

'We were under great pressure, far beyond our ability to endure, so that we despaired even of life.' 2 Corinthians 1:8

The more we acknowledge our deep longings and thirst and tune in to them the more clearly we will realise that no one can fully satisfy them apart from God.

When people ask me how they can tune in to their deep longings I tell them: take a sheet of paper and think of some of the major personal disappointments you have experienced in your life. Write them down. Focus on how many times you have longed for someone to come through for you but found that they didn't. How hurt were you at such times? If you were deeply hurt was it because you depended too much on others to give you what your soul longed for and only God can provide? Then consider how you would handle such difficult matters as disappointment, criticism and rejection if you were fully aware of how much you are loved by God, how valued you are by Him, and how convinced you are that He has a plan for your life. Is it not a fact that the reason why we get hurt so badly when people let us down is because our relationship with God is weak, and instead of drawing our security, self-worth and significance from Him we look to others for it?

Our relationship with God does not insulate us from the feelings of hurt or make us invulnerable to disappointment, but it does uphold us and enable us to go on loving in the same way that we ourselves are loved by God.

REFLECTION: Does it mean, then, that when we rely on God to meet the deep needs of our soul we will never experience hurt? No, but though we may be shaken we will not be shattered.

Listen to God

'My sheep listen to my voice; I know them, and they follow me.' John 10:27

I have talked to many Christians who have told me: 'The listening side of prayer baffles me. I sit still and listen, but all I hear are the sounds in the distance ... It just doesn't seem to work for me.' Listening to God is an art. It is not learned in a single session. It costs in terms of time but the rewards are worth far more than it costs. It took me well over six months to learn to quiet my soul and cultivate the art of listening to God's voice. I would sit sometimes for half-an-hour or so and hear nothing. But gradually I learned, how to 'disentangle the voice of God from the net of other voices'*.

As exercise strengthens the body and education enlarges the mind, so our sensitivity to God develops and grows as we learn to wait in silence before Him. What does God's voice sound like? Different people have different experiences. To some, God's voice comes in the form of a gentle impression. To others a verse of Scripture takes on a special power as God speaks directly to the heart. Sometimes one is conscious of one's own thoughts being accompanied by such a sense of the divine presence that one is convinced God is thinking through you. One thing, however, must be said in relation to the listening side of prayer. Those who would cultivate the power to know His voice must set time aside specifically for it and set it aside every day.

REFLECTION: Jesus wants to speak with us; do we want to listen to Him?

*Mrs E. Herman, *Creative Prayer* (R.A. Kessinger Publishing Co., 1998).

Renewing the mind

'Do not conform any longer to the pattern of this world,
but be transformed by the renewing of your mind.'
Romans 12:2

To function correctly our minds must be renewed. Today's text spells out that truth most clearly. Without the help of God provided through His Word our minds won't work in the way He intended. There is an interesting verse in the book of Proverbs that says, 'Folly [or foolishness] is bound up in the heart of a child, but the rod of discipline will drive it far from him' (Prov. 22:15). Because of the effect of Adam and Eve's sin on the human mind, everyone arrives in this world with the foolish idea that the route to happiness is to have their own way in everything. A little child takes up this self-centred position as soon as he or she is able to think or talk and this is why discipline is required. The whole purpose of discipline is to drive out foolishness and build in wisdom. Incidentally, when Proverbs talks about fools it is not referring to a person who does not have the intelligence to pass a simple examination appropriate to their age, but someone who thinks they know where life is found but doesn't. Left to ourselves, without the wisdom that comes from God through His Word, we are all foolish thinkers.

In our unconverted state we think erroneously about where life is found. That is what has kept people from Christ since the time their minds began to function – and that is what keeps them from Him still. But sadly, in our converted state, we also sometimes think erroneously about where life is found.

REFLECTION: Without the help of God provided through His Word our minds won't work in the way He intended.

A spiritual exercise

'... remember that ... you were separate from Christ ...
without hope and without God in the world.' Ephesians 2:12

Often before talking to gatherings about the subject of our deep longings – I invite those present to join me in a short spiritual exercise. I tell them to close their eyes and ask themselves this question: What deep down am I really longing for? I remind them that this is a spiritual exercise and therefore things such as a new car, a better house or an increase in salary are ruled out. I encourage them to tune in to their greatest spiritual desires and try to express what is coming to them in a word or a phrase.

These are the words people use most frequently to sum up their greatest longing: approval, affirmation, peace, relaxation, rest, value, power, acceptance, meaning. And this phrase never fails to be mentioned: *to be loved.*

I have noticed that the responses fall into three distinct categories: to be loved, to be valued, and for life to have meaning and purpose. Why should this be so? Because the soul cannot function effectively unless, to a reasonable degree, it experiences these three things. Listen carefully to what I am afraid is a long but very key sentence: it is only in a close, deep and ongoing relationship with God that we can experience the feeling of being loved and valued, and our lives find meaning to such a degree that we are enabled to function properly and effectively in the way God intended. Without God, as our text for today puts it, we are without hope.

REFLECTION: What deep down am I really longing for?

An altogether Christian

'I no longer call you servants ...' John 15:15

As John Wesley heard Luther's description of the change which God works in the heart through faith in Christ he said that he felt his 'heart strangely warmed'. He added: 'I felt I did trust in Christ, Christ alone, for salvation; and an assurance was given me that He had taken away my sins, even mine, and saved me from the law of sin and death.' John Wesley became what he called 'an altogether Christian', and said also that whereas before he had the religion of a servant, after his conversion he had that of a son.

It is true, of course, that we are called God's servants in Scripture, and that must not be denied, but when it comes to describing the relationship as opposed to the role the best word to use is 'son' or 'child'. A servant is appreciated on the basis of what he (or she) does; a child on the basis of who he is. The servant starts out determined to please the master; the child knows he already has his parents' pleasure. The servant is accepted because of his workmanship; the child because of a relationship.

When a servant fails, as Dr David Seamands points out, 'his or her whole position is at stake. In a normal home when a child fails or violates the laws of the home he or she may feel grieved that they have blundered or been ineffectual, and will submit themselves to discipline, but they know in their hearts they still belong and are deeply loved.'

REFLECTION: Always remember, your role may be that of a servant but your relationship is that of a child.

Being persecuted

'... Jesus ... suffered outside the city gate ... Let us, then, go to him outside the camp, bearing the disgrace he bore.'
Hebrews 13:12–13

O ur Lord was cast out, despised and rejected by men. So the author of the Hebrews says, 'Let's go to him there, outside the camp.' The epistle was written to men and women who were undergoing severe persecution for their faith and the author, writing under the inspiration of the Holy Spirit, seeks to encourage them to persevere. Don't give up meeting together, he says in one place; you can draw strength from one another as you fellowship together. The letter is filled with encouragement and advice on how to persevere.

We live in an age that is increasingly hostile to Christians – some countries more than others. There has always been a reproach in the gospel, always a shame at the heart of the cross. You cannot have the friendship of the world and the friendship of Christ. There is a choice to be made and if you are going to be a disciple of Christ then you have to make it. Many people give up the Christian faith because of that. One young man said to me, 'None of my friends would recognise me; they severed all friendship.' What do we do when that happens? We should exult in it! Listen again to the word from Hebrews: 'Let us go forth' (NKJV). Hear the eagerness in the phrase. We are not going to be dragged; we are going to do it willingly. Indeed we run! We are going to put our shoulders underneath His cross and bear whatever we can by His grace of His reproach.

REFLECTION: A hymn we used to sing puts it well: 'I'm not ashamed to own my Lord, Or to defend His cause, Maintain the honour of His Word, The glory of His cross.'

Restoration

'... he restores my soul ...' Psalm 23:3

It's interesting that the phrase 'cast down' is an old English shepherd's term for a sheep that has turned over on its back and can't get up again by itself. If this happens, and the shepherd does not arrive on the scene within a reasonably short time, the sheep panics and can easily die of fright. Are you feeling 'cast down' at this moment? Well, take heart, for the divine Shepherd will not let you down. 'A "cast" sheep is a very pathetic sight,' says Phillip Keller. 'Lying on its back, its feet in the air, it flays away, frantically struggling to stand up without success.'

The care and concern that the one-time shepherd, Phillip Keller, had for his sheep pales into insignificance, however, beside that of our Lord Jesus Christ. Many Christians hold the view that when they fall by the way or fail in their Christian experience, God becomes extremely angry with them. Not so. The revelation of Scripture is that Eternal God, the Almighty, the Lord of all creation has a shepherd's heart. He is infinitely more caring and compassionate towards the sheep of His fold than any human shepherd could ever be.

Reflect again on the tender and loving manner in which Jesus restored Peter after he had three times denied Him. The tenderness, the compassion and the patience He showed in restoring Simon Peter are just the same as He will show in restoring you.

REFLECTION: Look up – for even now He is moving towards you. He will pick you up and put you back on your feet again.

Drew me back into His way

'... he restores my soul ...' Psalm 23:3

A Syrian shepherd, Faduel Moghabghad, claims that in shepherd country there are many private gardens and vineyards, and if a sheep wanders into one of these private plots, it is forfeited to the owner of the land. In his view, therefore, the phrase 'he restores my soul' in Psalm 23 has reference to the way the divine Shepherd brings us back and rescues us when we stray into forbidden and dangerous places. One of our hymns, you might remember, contains some lines that reinforce this view: 'Put His loving arms around me, Drew me back into His way.' Sheep wander and get lost for many reasons, but mainly through heedlessness and inattention.

Some of us get lost the same way. Like sheep, we take a series of steps, none of them seemingly important, but each one increasing our distance from the Shepherd. The little tufts of worldliness that lure us on will, unless we are careful, leave us lost and forlorn. How easy it is to find ourselves in Satan's territory, not because of deliberate intention, but through a series of inattentions. 'The descent to hell', said someone, 'is so gradual that many do not suspect the road they are following is a downward path.' How encouraging then, to know that when, by our heedlessness, and inattention to God's ways, we stray into Satan's domain, the divine Shepherd does not leave us to our own devices, but constantly seeks our deliverance and restoration.

REFLECTION: We can be assured of this, God will always be willing to restore if we are willing to be restored.

Paths of righteousness

'He guides me in paths of righteousness for his name's sake.' Psalm 23:3

One translation puts it: 'He leads me in the paths that are right.' Another says: 'He leads me in the right way.' The Hebrew word for 'paths' means 'well-defined or clearly-marked trails'. Sheep, as everyone knows, are stubborn and self-willed creatures. If left to themselves, they will almost invariably leave a well-defined trail and wander off in a direction of their own choosing. An experienced shepherd, of course, is well aware of this, and tries to offset this tendency by going ahead of his sheep and making himself as visible as possible.

We, too, are stubborn and self-willed creatures – we prefer to go our own way and do our own thing. 'All we like sheep have gone astray; we have turned every one to his own way' (Isa. 53:6, RSV). As someone has said: 'It is by no mere whim on God's part that He has called us sheep. Our behaviour patterns and life habits are so much like those of a sheep that it is well-nigh embarrassing.' This desire that we have for self-determination, however, has got to be curbed or else the results will be disastrous. We prefer our own way even though it may lead us straight into trouble. If self-interest is primary then the result is self-destruction, for the self-centred soon become the self-disrupted. This is an issue that we must come to grips with right now, for unless we learn how to give up our self-centredness, we will fall into serious trouble – no matter how loving and concerned is our Shepherd.

REFLECTION: Our civilisation teaches us self-interest as the primary motivating force in life but Jesus teaches us to die to self.

Only one way

'... paths of righteousness ...' Psalm 23:3

'O ne of the characteristics of a radiant Christian', says J. Oswald Smith, 'is a willingness to put his personal life and affairs into the hands of Jesus Christ – without qualification and without reservation.' This is what Christ refers to when He talks about taking up the cross daily. It means being prepared day by day to put self-interest to death and to say, 'No longer my will, but yours be done.' Jesus followed the way of His Father right to the very end. When confronted by the cross, He was greatly tempted to follow His own desires and take the way that seemed best to Him, but came through the struggle to say: 'Father ... not as I will, but as you will.'

God's way is not just a way, or even the best way – it is the Way. The reward of following the Lord's path, rather than our own self-determined ways, is that we shall be led from one good pasture to another. An efficient shepherd always tries to keep his sheep on the move, thus avoiding over-use of the land and enabling his sheep to continually enjoy wholesome, fresh forage.

Be assured of this – God wants us to move with Him day by day to discover new insights and fresh revelation as He opens up to us the glories of His precious Word. Expect God to show you some new insight day by day. Faith is expectancy – according to your expectancy be it unto you.

REFLECTION: Are you faithfully following your Shepherd Leader into good pasture?

What is revival?

'... if my people ...' 2 Chronicles 7:14

There is, I believe, no greater issue facing the Church of Jesus Christ at this time than the subject of Holy Spirit revival. And there is no greater passage in the whole of Scripture that shows the way to revival than 2 Chronicles 7:14 – a statement so seemingly simple yet so positively staggering in its implications: '... if my people, who are called by my name, will humble themselves and pray and seek my face and turn from their wicked ways, then will I hear from heaven and will forgive their sin and will heal their land.'

The great Welsh revivalist preachers of past centuries used to refer to this verse regularly in their preaching. Many Christians can recite it at the drop of a hat. It is God's final and finished formula on the subject of revival; His recipe for a spiritual awakening. In the truest sense of the word *revival* is an unusual and extraordinary movement of God's Spirit that marks it off as being vastly different to the normal sense of God's presence in the Church. It is not just a spiritual trickle, a rivulet or even a river; it is an awesome flood of God's Spirit, a mighty Niagara that sweeps everything before it. Evangelism is the expression of the Church; revival is an experience in the Church. In evangelism the preacher calls on people to get saved; in revival people often call on the preacher to tell them how they can be saved.

REFLECTION: Evangelism is the expression of the Church; revival is an experience in the Church.

Relaxing the spirit

'Let us then approach the throne of grace with confidence ...'
Hebrews 4:16

T he central part of us is the spirit: the motivating centre of
our personality. How do we go about relaxing the spirit for
prayer? 'How did you like the aeroplane flight?' was asked
of a nervous man who had just flown for the first time. 'It was all
right,' he said, 'but I never did put my full weight down.' We cannot
enjoy an aeroplane journey, or this larger journey through life,
unless we learn to put our whole weight down. There can never be
complete spiritual relaxation unless that relaxation rests ultimately
in the love and goodness of God. A relaxed spirit is one that knows
and affirms this fact – God loves me and when at times He denies me
the thing I ask, it is only because love and goodness in Him decided
that I am not ready for it, it is not His will for me, or He will give me
something better.

The three Hebrew young men of Daniel's day said, 'God ... is
able to deliver us from the burning fiery furnace ... but if not ...
we will not serve thy gods' (Dan. 3:17–18, AV). They did not rest
their confidence in immediate deliverance but in the ultimate love
and goodness of God. That is what produces a relaxed spirit. When
at the depths of your being you hold and maintain the conviction
that God always wills your good then you are ready to be engaged in
the kind of praying that changes the world.

**REFLECTION: Let us put our whole weight down on the
ultimate love and goodness of God.**

Begin with Scripture

'... I Daniel, understood from the Scriptures ...
So I turned to the Lord God ...' Daniel 9:2–3

Time spent with the Bible is usually the best preparation for prayer. A short meditation on some fragment of Scripture quickens the spirit of devotion and primes the heart in readiness for contact with God. George Muller, founder of the orphanages in Bristol, claimed that one of the greatest discoveries of his Christian experience was the way in which meditation on the Scriptures prepared him for deeper communion with the Lord.

Once you have read the Word of God you have done what a pilot does when he tunes up his engines preparatory to the commencement of a flight. The Word has started your thinking and your aspirations going in the right direction. It has aligned you with the will of God and where the will of God is done the power of God can come. So *come to the Word expectantly.* Expect it to speak to you and it will. I am amazed at the number of Christians who open their Bibles, peruse its pages, but expect nothing to surprise them. They are seldom disappointed. Faith is expectancy – according to your expectancy be it unto you. *Come prepared to surrender to the truth it unfolds.*

One of the secrets of getting the best out of the Bible is contained in the word 'obedience'. To the extent that you are willing to obey, to that same extent will God's will be revealed. As you obey so He reveals and your spirit soars heavenwards in praise and prayer.

REFLECTION: You might like to meditate on the full prayer of Daniel (9:4–19).*

---

*For a selection of Bible-reading aids, visit our website: **www.cwr.org.uk**

Whose thoughts?

'... so are my ways higher than your ways and my thoughts than your thoughts.' Isaiah 55:9

I know of some Christians who come to their morning quiet time without a Bible and just sit and think of anything that comes to mind. One couple told me, when I asked them if they had a daily quiet time, 'Yes, we sit and smoke for a quiet half-hour after breakfast.' They were sincere people, but living defeated Christian lives, because they depended on the pitiable substitute of nicotine instead of the endless resources of God. I showed them how to go into a quiet time with God's Word, and when they learned to breathe God thoughts deep into the inner recesses of their being, they found they no longer needed nicotine, and relinquished the smoking habit.

If you begin your quiet time without a Bible and just sit enclosed with your own thoughts then you are likely to go off on a tangent, or become self-engrossed. Unless our thoughts are constantly corrected by God's thoughts then our thoughts go off in all directions, or mull around on themselves. So before attempting to get through to God in prayer start your quiet time by meditating on His Word. You will know it is inspired, for you will find it inspiring. You will know that God is in it for God will come out of it. This means that you will get to God, not through the medium of your own conceptions, but through the medium of God's revelation of Himself. His thoughts become your thoughts. You are ready for anything.

REFLECTION: The Bible, unlike any other book in the world, contains the *full* revelation of God for our lives.

Use a notebook

'Write down the revelation and make it plain ...'
Habakkuk 2:2

This idea was given to me by an old Welsh miner many years ago, just after I was converted. 'Keep a notebook when you go into your prayer time,' he said, 'it's easier to manage than prayer lists, and provides a more efficient record of your prayer vigils. On one side of the page write down all the things you want to bring before God, and on the other side the things God may say to you, or any specific answers to prayer you may have been given.' At first I thought his idea much too mechanical to be of lasting spiritual benefit, but when I began to put it into practice I found it helped to deepen my relationship with God in a way that is impossible to describe.

We all know of occasions when something pops into our mind that we know we ought to bring before God in our personal prayer times. But unless we make a note of it there and then we may find that when we come to pray, the matter has slipped our minds. A prayer notebook would have captured that fleeting thought or idea and recorded it so that it would not have been forgotten. Similarly, when we hear of a prayer that has been answered, unless it is recorded there and then we may find ourselves forgetting the issue in our personal prayer time, and thus make no special point of expressing our praise and gratitude to God for the answered prayer.

REFLECTION: 'I have found the words of Confucius to be wise and powerful: "The faintest ink is better than the finest memory."'

Help or hindrance?

'Now go, write it before them in a table, and note it in a book ...' Isaiah 30:8, AV

I remember sharing the idea of using a notebook some years ago at a church where I was invited to speak on the subject of 'Building an effective prayer life'. One man was concerned that a notebook would inhibit his prayer times. I sympathised with his point of view because whilst aids and techniques are useful they must never become so binding that they restrict our personalities and thus reduce our effectiveness in prayer. However, some time later I received a letter from this man, saying that, although the idea I had presented about the notebook had not appealed to him, he became increasingly intrigued by the idea and had adopted it into his prayer life.

This is what he wrote: 'I rejected the point you made about the notebook, but I see now that I did so because deep down I was afraid of anything that demanded discipline in my life. God spoke to me about this and, as I began to discipline myself to record specific prayer requests, specific answers, and the things God said to me, I found that instead of losing the sense of spontaneity in prayer, which is part and parcel of my make-up, it has enabled me to have a more effective prayer life than ever before. The floods of prayer now have a channel to run down and I know the channel is growing deeper and deeper every day.' It goes without saying that a notebook, such as this, should be carried with you everywhere you go.

REFLECTION: Unless we make a note of what God says to us we may find that when we come to pray, the matter has slipped our minds.

One in Christ

'... that all of them may be one ...' John 17:21

I n the Early Church the gulf between Jew and Gentile was a very wide one. Peter, being a strict Jew, had to undergo a shaking of his nest before he was prepared to launch out and minister to the Gentile congregation gathered in the house of Cornelius. The shaking came in a vision that God gave him. When God said, 'Rise, Peter; kill, and eat,' the command helped to shatter his bigotry, and from here on he rises above his prejudices to be the means in God's hands of bringing the Holy Spirit to the Gentiles.

Later when Peter is questioned by the leaders of the Church in Jerusalem as to why he went to a Gentile congregation, he recounts the vision God gave him and tells what happened when he began to speak to those assembled in Cornelius's home: 'As I began to speak, the Holy Spirit fell on them just as on us at the beginning ... If then God gave the same gift to them as he gave to us ... who was I that I could withstand God?' (Acts 11:15,17, RSV). The entire episode in the house of Cornelius was indeed a shattering one for the Early Church. It forced them to examine their attitudes, check their preconceived ideas and be open to change. The time has come for us to do something similar. We must examine our hearts and distinguish between principles and prejudices, between man-made traditions and unchanging truths of God. The next great step in Christendom is the demonstrating of Christian unity.

REFLECTION: In a world and an age seeking unity, we Christians have little moral authority unless we can demonstrate to unbelievers that despite our differences we are 'all one in Christ Jesus'.

Christian fellowship

'... that all of them may be one ...' John 17:21

How can Christians come together unless we agree on everything? We do not make that a prerequisite of fellowship in a home. The home can be united in spite of differences in temperament and belief. The one thing that binds us together is the fact that we are children of the same parents. So it is in the family of God. Let that suffice. The differences are needed so that they can become growing points. The music of the Hindus is based on melody and not on harmony as is Western music. A Hindu hearing some negro-spiritual singing said, 'What a pity they can't all sing the same tune!' Had they done so it wouldn't have been harmony. The very difference made for richness!

Someone has said, 'The measure of our maturity can be and is measured by the breadth and depth of our capacity for fellowship with other Christians. We are as mature as our fellowship.' So if we cannot fellowship with other Christians, even though they belong to other denominations, we reveal our immaturity. What then is the basis of Christian fellowship? Only one thing. Everyone who belongs to Christ belongs to everyone else who belongs to Christ. The basis of our fellowship is not around this doctrine or that doctrine. It is around Christ. God fellowships with you not on the basis of you being worthy of that fellowship, but because of who He is. You are to fellowship with everyone because of who you are – a lover of Christ.

REFLECTION: Christ must come first, and the unity of His Body must take priority over any denominationalism.

The Father's house

*'In my Father's house are many rooms; if it were not so,
I would have told you.' John 14:2*

Jesus knew full well how men and women longed for some sure word concerning the curtained future; He knew that the question of what lies beyond the grave was something that weighed heavily on their souls; He understood the concern and feelings of their hearts when they contemplated death. How could Christ, with such a heart of compassion, have remained silent when He was the only One in the world who could pierce the veil and enlighten people on what lay beyond? How could He withhold the truth when to utter it would bring such solace to troubled souls? He, being who He was, simply had to speak out, to say, 'If it were not so, I would have told you.' Not to have done so would have been unthinkable.

Can you imagine Columbus after having discovered America wanting to keep the matter to himself? Or Captain Cook after exploring New Zealand wishing to leave the world ignorant of his findings? Both of these situations are unthinkable given the character and ideals of the men concerned. Likewise, it is unthinkable that Jesus, having spent eternity past in the presence of His Father, would not want to tell His followers something of the glories of that wondrous world. He says in effect, 'If seventy years of life, more or less, is all you could expect, I would be frank with you and urge you to make the most of it, but in My Father's house ...'

REFLECTION: Our hope of heaven is as certain as the words of Jesus.

Seeing the invisible

'So we fix our eyes on not on what is seen, but on what is unseen. For what is seen is temporary, but what is unseen is eternal.' 2 Corinthians 4:18

Heaven should never be far from our minds as we make our way through this world. Some might respond to this by saying: Surely the constant consideration of heaven will interfere with work we have to do here on earth. Well, of course it can, but what I am talking about is a balanced view of the matter – not too little and not too much. My reading of Christian history has brought me to the conclusion that the Christians who did most for this world in which we live were those who thought a good deal about the next. It could be argued, and argued successfully I think, that Christians who never allow themselves to think of the world that lies beyond are largely ineffective in this.

If the truth be known, most of us go through life with our eyes cast downwards. We neither look nor long for heaven. Those whose eyes are never lifted up to see what lies ahead should not be surprised if they find the things of earth becoming more important to them than heaven, time becoming more important than eternity. It will enable us to hold onto things loosely, knowing that they are merely temporal. I think it was Cardinal Newman who said, 'Only those work with full effectiveness for the new Jerusalem below who see the New Jerusalem above. They make it after "the pattern which has been shown to them on the mount".'

REFLECTION: The constant remembrance that we are bound for 'a city whose architect and builder is God' will help us keep matters in perspective.

Between two gardens

*'Cursed is the ground ... It will produce thorns and
thistles ...' Genesis 3:17–18*

Why is it that, generally speaking, we do not walk
through this world with the prospect of heaven central
to our thinking? One reason could be that we reckon
we can have heaven now. A large percentage of believers appear to
hold the view that being a Christian means we will no longer have to
wrestle with problems or struggle with our finances and that we will
never get sick. Now let me say right away that I have seen too many
miracles not to believe in them, and I am convinced that many of
us are slow to avail ourselves of the resources of the abundant life
found in Jesus Christ. God is willing to bless His people; indeed He
delights in it. I have seen Him work miracles in my own life and
expect to see Him do the same in the future. That said, however, our
view of the Christian life will be an unbalanced one if we think that
life in Christ means that we never have to face problems or struggle
with difficulties.

When Adam and Eve were expelled from the Garden of Eden,
God put a 'Celestial Bouncer' at the entrance to stop them getting
back in. Now we live outside the garden in a world that is cursed
because of sin. Another garden awaits us, but that lies up ahead.
Meanwhile we must live in a garden that, though still quite beautiful,
has thorns and weeds. Those who ignore this fact have a very
unbalanced view of Christianity.

**REFLECTION: The 'wonderful world' we inhabit is still fallen
– it is a world for which we were not designed.**

Humble yourself

'Humble yourselves, therefore, under God's mighty hand, that he may lift you up in due time.' 1 Peter 5:6

What does God mean when, in talking about humility, He commands us to humble ourselves? I believe that what He has in mind primarily is a willingness to judge and evaluate ourselves, not by the standards of others, but by the standards of God's Word, the Bible; to come under its authority and submit to its truths. It is not possible to understand what humility is unless we are prepared to lay our lives alongside the Bible. One of the alarming trends in today's Christian society is the disappearance of the truly biblical Christian. I refer not so much to respecting the Bible as God's Book, or even carrying a Bible to church. I am thinking of those who fail to bring their lives under its authority, to see it for what it is – God's infallible Word – and live by its standards, eager to obey its commands. Such Christians are fast disappearing. We need the attitude that will not stand in judgment over the Scriptures but will sit under them in humility.

Listen to what God, speaking through Isaiah, says: 'This is the one I esteem: he who is humble and contrite in spirit, and trembles at my word' (Isa. 66:2). I am not suggesting that the phrase to tremble at God's Word means a literal physical trembling. It means, I believe, that we value the Word of God so highly that when we realise we are in violation of it our soul trembles within us.

REFLECTION: How many of us can honestly say that we tremble at God's Word?

Revival praying

'During the days of Jesus' life on earth, he offered up
prayers and petitions with loud cries and tears ...'
Hebrews 5:7

Praying for revival is not just ordinary praying. It is unhurried praying, not just saying words with a breathless eagerness to get it finished. It is passionate praying – prayer that is not afraid to draw upon one's emotions, to cry out to God, with tears if that is the way one feels. Someone has said that 'we will not see revival until we can't live without it'. God goes further in this matter of prayer by saying: 'If my people who are called by my name shall humble themselves and pray and seek my face ...'

If we are honest we are often more interested in seeing the hand of God at work than we are in seeing His face. We want to see the sick healed, we want to see supernatural events taking place, but revival praying puts as its priority a new vision of God, a new understanding of Him; to know God for Himself, who He is, and not just for what He can give. Revival praying is where we are drawn into a new relationship with Him, where intimacy with God becomes the most important thing. When did you last get down before God and pray with fervour and passion? And with a desire not simply to see a spiritual renaissance but to know God more deeply, to see His face. That's the kind of praying that brings revival. Generally speaking, *we do not pray enough, we do not pray passionately enough, not perseveringly enough, not persistently enough.*

REFLECTION: Is there a prayer group for revival in your church? If not, join one that might be in the area, or you could start one.

It's down to you

'The prayer of a righteous man is powerful and effective.'
James 5:16

I t is a lot to believe that we can witness a turn of the spiritual tide in our land, when we see Christianity declining and thousands drifting away from the mainline churches, but we must put our whole weight upon it. We must humble ourselves before God, pray more in private and in groups, claim the help of God to cut out everything in our lives of which He disapproves, plead for His grace and ask Him to flood our churches with His power.

Are you willing to pray more and join a group praying for revival, or to start a prayer meeting? You can be sure of this: God would not call us to pray if our situation were unredeemable. It would be wonderful if the whole Church in the United Kingdom would heed this message but the history of revival shows that when a proportion of God's people meet His conditions He moves in answer to their prayers. In Wales it was a small praying group who were used by God to usher in revival. You could be the vanguard of a mighty move of the Holy Spirit if you are willing to pay the price. Drawing closer to God may not guarantee we see corporate revival (that must be left to God's sovereignty) but one thing is sure: *you yourself will be revived.* And your action along with others will bring us closer to the great outpouring of the Holy Spirit for which so many are longing.

REFLECTION: You could be part of the vanguard of a mighty move of the Holy Spirit.

Security

'We love because he first loved us.' 1 John 4:19

Identity depends on three things – a sense that one is unconditionally loved, a sense of one's value and a sense of meaning and purpose. Those three elements can well be described by these alliterative words – *security, self-worth and significance.* By *security* I mean the positive feelings that flood the soul when we know that we are loved and loved unconditionally. Everyone longs to be loved – with a love that will never be taken away. The more conscious we are that we are the objects of that kind of love the easier it is to face up to life and rise above all its problems. Years ago Frank Sinatra sang: 'You are nobody until somebody loves you.' How true. The more aware I am that God loves me – and loves me unconditionally – the easier it is for me to do my daily tasks and relate well to others.

People have often said,' My problem is that I don't love the Lord enough.' My usual response to that statement is: 'No, that is not your problem. Your problem is you don't know how much the Lord loves you.' Our love for Christ is not something we manufacture in our hearts; it is the consequence of His love for us. His unconditional love touches the capacity to love in our hearts, and we find ourselves giving love for love. And that kind of love must flood our souls if we are to function the way we were designed and experience deep inner security.

REFLECTION: The kind of love for which our souls crave is divine love – love that goes on loving us no matter what.

Self-worth and significance

"'For I know the plans I have for you," declares the LORD, "plans to prosper you and not to harm you, plans to give you hope and a future."' Jeremiah 29:11

B y *self-worth* I mean a sense of being valued. At first it may appear that the distinction between being loved and being valued is nonexistent. Think of it like this: When we are loved by someone, we feel cherished; when we are valued by someone, we feel worthwhile. Seeing how worthwhile we are in someone else's eyes contributes greatly to our own sense of worth. One of the statements I learned when studying adolescent psychology was: I am not what I think I am; I am not what you think I am; I am what I think you think I am. A child comes to sense how much he or she is valued not by what the parents think, but by what *the child thinks* the parents think of the child. Often I have talked to young people whose parents loved them, but sadly somehow the message that they valued them did not get through. Hence they valued themselves not as their parents saw them but as they perceived their parents saw them.

By *significance* I mean a sense of meaning and purpose. Every single person on the face of this earth has a purpose in being here. We are not just meteorites on our way across the universe to burn out on the edge of some gravitational field. We are men and women made in the image of God with the signature of God in our souls. No one has a purposeless existence, let alone a child of God.

REFLECTION: In relationship with God we are unconditionally loved, highly valued, and our lives have total meaning: security, self-worth and significance.

What is sin?

*'They cried out to the L*ORD* and said, "We have sinned;*
*we have forsaken the L*ORD* ..."' 1 Samuel 12:10*

We misapply the word *sin* when we attach it to such things
as adultery, fornication, lying, stealing and cheating.
These are really *sins*, the branches rather than the
root. Sin is essentially self-dependency and self-sufficiency, trusting
in one's own resources rather than in God's resources. Dick Keyes
says: 'Sin is not always expressed in conscious animosity toward
God. More often it is a polite relegation of God to irrelevance.
Nevertheless it is still an expression of man's cosmic rebellion against
his Maker – man taking his stance in independence from anything
greater than himself.' I doubt whether anyone reading these lines is
consciously hostile towards God. But how many of us have relegated
Him to irrelevance, giving Him a certain place in our lives, but not
the central place? We put self-interest before God's interests. We pay
lip service to the fact that Christ is the source of true satisfaction,
yet we continue to drink at lukewarm, bacteria-infected wells of our
own making because we like to be in control of the water we drink.
That is relegating God to irrelevance.

Although Christians, we allow our thinking to drift towards
the notion that our security, significance and worth depend on
our performance, our status, our expertise, our accomplishments.
We tend to search for a deeper level of confidence than God,
something we can see, something we can touch, rather than the
invisible God. So foolishly we step off the Rock onto the shifting
sands of self-dependency. And that is the essence of sin.

**REFLECTION: God says He is enough – the One who can hold
us. But we are unsure, so we become self-dependent and sinful.**

What is repentance?

'Godly sorrow brings repentance that leads to salvation and leaves no regret, but worldly sorrow brings death.'
2 Corinthians 7:10

*R*epentance is not regret. Regret is being sorry for oneself, deploring the consequences of one's actions. *It is not remorse.* 'Remorse', says one writer, 'is sorrow without hope at its heart.' The great Early Church Father Tertullian said that remorse is an emotion of disgust. It eats its heart out instead of seeking a new heart. *Repentance is not reformation.* Some people seem to think all that is required is a change of lifestyle for the better, to turn over a new leaf. Amendment is substituted for the atonement. *Repentance is not reparation* (making amends). Like Zacchaeus, anyone who truly repents will, where possible, make amends to the person or persons he or she has wronged. But reparation is one thing, repentance another.

If our repentance contains only the elements of regret, remorse and reformation, and if we are sorry not that we have misplaced our dependency but that we have lost our inner peace or simply feel guilty, then our repentance is incomplete. Repentance literally means 'change of mind'. A good starting point is to think of it as *a change of mind about where life is found.* Life, *real* life is only found in Christ. Charles Colson says that repentance is the ultimate surrender of the self which is the ongoing submission of our lives into God's hands. Whenever we feel ourselves moving away from dependency on Christ and lean on other things, then we must recognise that our misplaced dependency is sin, confess it, and repent of it.

REFLECTION: God asks us to repent not so we conform to His laws but that we receive His love and live in intimate relationship with Him.

Love with a 'stoop'

'Let us then approach the throne of grace with confidence ...'
Hebrews 4:16

Grace is a characteristic of the Deity which is quite close to love (and mercy) but yet deserves to be seen as different and distinctive. On one occasion I heard an elderly Welsh preacher make this memorable remark: 'Grace is a word with a "stoop" in it; love reaches out on the same level, but grace always has to stoop to pick one up.' An anonymous writer had a similar thought in mind when he said, 'Grace is love at its loveliest, falling on the unlovable and making it lovely.' Grace, then, is God's kindness conferred upon the undeserving; benevolence granted to those who have no merit; a hand reaching down to those who have fallen into a pit. The Bible tells us to believe that on the throne of the universe there is a God like that.

When we read about grace in Scripture it is interestingly always in connection with those who have a special relationship with God. The grace of which the Bible speaks – which is sometimes termed 'special grace' or 'saving grace' – is reserved for the elect, in other words, those God foreknew would be brought into a special relationship with Himself through His Son, Jesus Christ. This is why we should distinguish 'grace' from 'mercy' or 'goodness', which, as Scripture tells us, is given to all: 'The LORD is good to *all*; he has compassion on *all* he has made' (Psa. 145:9, emphasis added). Grace cannot be bought, earned, deserved or merited. If it could, it would cease to be grace. Grace flows down as pure charity, falling on the unlovable and making it lovely. Amazing!

REFLECTION: Illion T. Jones, a Welsh preacher, said that: 'The word "grace" is unquestionably the most significant single word in the Bible.' Because of God's grace I am saved.

APRIL 20

Removing our mask

'Therefore each of you must put off falsehood ...'
Ephesians 4:25

Removing our mask of pretence is risky, but it is equally risky not to remove it. To keep trying to be what others expect us to be or want us to be, without ever coming to any real self-understanding, leads not to growth but to spiritual immaturity. The truth is, the harder we try to please everyone, the more certain it is that we will please no one. You must be yourself – in Christ. Dr Paul Tournier was once asked just how open one should be. He replied, 'Be prepared to say it all, but say only what you feel God is leading you to say.' Wise advice. Being prepared to say it all relieves us of our fear of exposing ourselves or being exposed, so that we can respond to another in loving honesty without the fear of saying too much. In being free to say it all, we are also free to be silent when we should be. So often we want to share our strengths but not our weaknesses.

Once, a woman shared with me about a matter that brought her great discouragement. It so happened that something similar had happened to me around the same time, and I took the opportunity to share with her my discouragement. She was overcome and said, 'I never thought you could be discouraged.' Later she said that my frankness brought her great hope, and out of it God ministered to her need. Christ ministered to this woman out of my weakness not out of my strength!

REFLECTION: Pretending to be somebody we are not is an exhausting and deceitful business.

Deep longings

'O God, you are my God, earnestly I seek you; my soul thirsts for you ...' Psalm 63:1

G od has built into us a desire for relationship with Him, which if not satisfied leaves us open and vulnerable to other sources of satisfaction. If God is not satisfying our souls we will seek something else to satisfy us. It is here that our personal problems begin. This desire for relationship with God is described in the Bible by many words – *desire, hunger, longings,* but perhaps the most descriptive of these words is *thirst.* The Bible often uses this word to describe the desire God has given us for Himself.

In his book *The Pleasures of God,* John Piper tells of reading this statement in Henry Scougal's *The Life of God in the Soul of Man:* 'The soul of man ... hath in it a raging and inextinguishable thirst. Never does a soul know what solid joy and substantial pleasure is, till, once being weary of itself, it renounces all property [and] gives itself up to the Author of its being.' John Piper comments that as he read those words, 'There was in me an immense longing to give myself up to God, for the quenching of this "raging thirst".' Our hearts thirst for something that earth cannot satisfy. God created mankind with a desire to relate to Him and others. Men and women fundamentally are relational beings. We desire to reach out for the kind of relationship that enables us to feel good. Nothing satisfies so much as relationship. We yearn for someone to care for us, to satisfy the deep longings of our soul.

REFLECTION: Augustine said: 'We were made by God, and made for God, and our identity will never be fully complete until we relate to God.'

A look in the mirror

'But we all, with unveiled face, beholding as in a mirror
the glory of the Lord, are being transformed into the same
image from glory to glory ...' 2 Corinthians 3:18, NKJV

The only place we can truly see ourselves as we are is in Christ. Christ is the mirror of God. We look at Him, and we see God reflected in Him perfectly. He is also the mirror by which we look at ourselves. He reflects a perfect likeness of the image that falls upon Him. We can look into the mirror of Christ and say with truth, 'That is the person I am.' This revelation for some of us can be appalling because the comparison shames us, and we can thank God that He saves us from seeing the truth all at once.

So then, let us look at ourselves in Christ. Look into the mirror of that amazing love and then contrast it with yourself. The first thing that strikes any man or woman who does this is an awareness of how much we are taken up with ourselves. It is from this that Christ would deliver us. He wants us to crucify that arrogant, dominating self and having crucified it, replace it with His own unselfishness. Do you have faith for this to happen? Draw close to Him and He will draw close to you. Open your whole being to Him, and He will open His whole being to you. And never forget that the life of God comes fully into us as it is allowed to go freely through us. In the words of the hymn, 'Freely to all ourselves we give, Constrained by Jesus' love to live, The servants of mankind.'

REFLECTION: As we look to Christ we are both shamed by the contrast but also gloriously transformed into His likeness of selfless love.

Your spiritual drive

'For Christ's love compels us, because we are convinced that one died for all, and therefore all died.' 2 Corinthians 5:14

J ust look at the life of the apostle Paul after he met with Christ on the Damascus road. Wherever he went he met with opposition, sometimes having his blood shed in the course of preaching the gospel, yet his passion for spreading the message of Christ's love never once seems to have dimmed. Permit me to ask you this personal question: What drives you? What makes you tick? If your life could be stripped down right here and now to its irreducible minimum what is the motivating force that drives you forward in your Christian pilgrimage?

Sometimes I look back to the early years of my ministry and my heart is ashamed. I was several years into my ministry before I realised I was more taken up with the cause of Christ rather than with Christ Himself. That realisation resulted in a fresh vision and a new anointing moving upon my life. One of the saddest things to behold, in my opinion, is a Christian who is content with practising the duties of the Christian life and relying on them to bring satisfaction to the soul rather than a dynamic and passionate relationship with God. Our souls are capable of great passion – we see this in great music and great art. Clearly when we look into the pages of the New Testament we see that the apostle Paul was a man who was burning up with the fever of God's love. The love of Christ was the secret of his spiritual drive.

REFLECTION: Am I more taken up with the cause of Christ, with working for Him, than with Christ Himself?

The purpose of living

'Having loved his own who were in the world, he now showed them the full extent of his love.' John 13:1

The purpose of living is this — *to love as we are loved*! When it comes down to it this is what life is all about: *loving involvement with God and loving involvement with others*. And it is here where we fail the most. Loving involvement with God of course carries no problems, but what about loving involvement with others? Even Christians can be difficult to relate to sometimes. Those involved in Christian ministry discover all too often that God calls us to move towards people who are guaranteed to hurt us.

So what can we do to avoid such hurts? We can arrange our relationships in such a way that we get close enough to people to be affirmed by them but not close enough to be hurt by them. But then that is a failure in love. In effect we are saying to God: I am not sure that your resources are strong enough to hold me in this situation so I will protect myself from any possible hurt through superficial relationships. And let's face it — that basically is a lack of trust. Loving well is when, though our own hearts may be hurting and we may be in the deepest pain, we can still move towards others without self-protection. It may not be easy but it is always possible. Never forget that. Our Lord not only lifts the standards to almost unbelievable heights but He also provides the power by which we reach up to them.

REFLECTION: When you gaze upon the face of someone you have hurt and you see hurt but no rejection in that look, you have just had a glimpse of the face of Jesus Christ!

Prayer and the Holy Spirit

'... we do not know what we ought to pray, but the Spirit himself intercedes for us ...' Romans 8:26

If we do not pray, we faint. Prayer opens us to God and to the resources of the Holy Spirit. Like a watch, life has a tendency to run down. It needs rewinding. Prayer rewinds the springs of life by opening our spirits to the Holy Spirit. You don't have to tamper with the hands of a watch to make them go round if the mechanism is fully wound. They go round of their own accord. Likewise, when we are in touch with God through prayer then the Holy Spirit supplies the energy we need to get through every day. And not merely get through, but sail through – victoriously. Paul says: 'The Spirit helps us in our weaknesses' (Rom. 8:26). Some translations use the word 'Helper' rather than 'Counsellor' in John 14:16 and that is precisely what the Holy Spirit does – He *helps*. Never is the Holy Spirit more helpful than when He helps us pray.

Once I went through a dark period when prayer lost all its appeal. I continued preaching and writing in a kind of mechanical way, and no one seemed to notice any difference. My words were carefully thought out, my sentences studiously crafted, but they were not soaked in prayer. Then the Spirit drew near and challenged me about my prayer life. 'But I don't *feel* like praying,' I complained. 'Then I will help you,' He seemed to say. He did, and by His grace lit the flame of prayer once again in my heart.

REFLECTION: Our divine Counsellor helps us overcome any disinclination we may have to pray and even prays through us.

In the valley

'Even though I walk through the valley of the shadow of
death, I will fear no evil, for you are with me ...'
Psalm 23:4

The scene that these words conjure up in our minds is
that of evening time, when the shepherd leads his sheep
down the mountainside into the valley, where flickering
shadows lie across the trail. The sheep, because they are so timid
and defenceless, are usually frightened by this experience. But they
follow the shepherd and therefore are comforted. They will not fear
evil because the shepherd is with them.

Millions of Christians have been greatly comforted by this verse
as they have passed through the dark valley of death. It underlines
the fact that although death may be a dark valley, it is not something
to fear, but an experience through which one passes on the path to
a more perfect life. The Good Shepherd is well aware of our fear
of death and constantly seeks to reassure us that, for the Christian,
death is but a dark valley opening out into an eternity of endless
delight. He has told us: 'Surely I will be with you always – yes,
even in the valley of the shadow of death.' What a comfort – what
a consolation. Many Christians fail to enjoy life because of a morbid
fear of death – it overshadows all they think and do.

Can there be a release from such fears? Thank God – there can!

**REFLECTION: So long as we let ourselves be influenced by the
fear of death, we can never attain the freedom God intended.**

No fear in death

'Even though I walk through the valley of the shadow of death, I will fear no evil, for you are with me ...'
Psalm 23:4

When we come to analyse the fear of death, three elements can be identified. First, the fear of the physical act of dying. Second, the fear of finality. Third, the fear of judgment. Doctors assure us that what people normally call 'the agony of death' is felt much more by those who are watching than by the one who is passing away. Add to this natural phenomenon the supporting power of God's never-failing grace, and it is possible to look even this physical aspect of death quietly in the face and say, 'My enemy – you are not really the terror that you seem.'

Then there is the fear of finality. No Christian need fear that death is equivalent to extinction, for Christ has said: 'I go to prepare a place for you ... that where I am you may be also' (John 14:2–3, RSV). Dr W.E. Sangster tells how, as a young boy living in the heart of London, he went for a walk one day and got lost. A kindly policeman took him to the police station. After waiting for what seemed like several hours in a dingy room, a stern officer came and took him down a dark passage where he saw his father waiting for him. Sangster said, 'It will not be different, I think, when I die. At the end of the dark passage my Father will be waiting.'

Finally, let us take the fear of judgment. Nobody who knows Christ should fear judgment.

REFLECTION: Death really has but one mission – to bring us into God's presence and give us an eternal place in our Father's house.

Discipline needed!

'... your rod and staff, they comfort me.' Psalm 23:4

S hepherds, in Bible days, carried very little equipment with them when they tended their sheep, but invariably they carried a rod and a staff. The rod was a club which was used for a number of purposes, but mainly to drive off wild animals or catch the sheep's attention. If a shepherd saw a sheep wandering from the path or approaching a potentially dangerous situation – such as poisonous weeds, or the edge of a precipice – he would hurl his rod slightly ahead of the sheep, thus startling it for a moment and causing it to scurry back to the safety of the flock. The rod therefore became an object of discipline, not to hurt or injure the sheep, but to direct it back into the way. Young shepherds would train for hours and compete with each other to see who could throw his rod with the greatest accuracy and across the greatest distance. The rod was what a shepherd relied on to protect both himself and his sheep whenever there was the threat of danger.

How many of us, I wonder, can go through the Christian life day after day without the need for some discipline? I can't – and I'm sure that is true of you also. Someone described the Christian life in this way: 'Dependence plus discipline equals dependable disciples.' Notice – dependence plus discipline … You can't be a dependable disciple without discipline. No discipline – no disciple. It's as simple as that!

REFLECTION: Discipline is good for us not bad. An undisciplined driver is a danger to himself and everyone else on the road.

The rod of discipline

'... God disciplines us for our good, that we may share in his holiness.' Hebrews 12:10

Observing the way in which a shepherd in Bible days used his rod to discipline his sheep and bring them back into the way gives us a glimpse into the character of God. Some Christians have such a distorted view of God that they interpret His disciplines as punishment, and fail to see that the reason why our heavenly Father disciplines us is not because He is angry with us, but because He loves us.

To understand God's purpose in disciplining us, it is necessary to observe the difference between two things – fear and respect. The Bible uses the word 'fear' in two ways: (1) as a form of anxiety, and (2) as a form of respect. As Christians, it is right that we have a deep respect for the Almighty, but we must see also that God does not want us to live out our days in anxiety, apprehension and dread. Some parents attempt to influence and discipline their children through the use of anxiety and apprehension, but God does not deal with His children on that basis. His disciplines follow a divine design that is calculated, not so much to punish our wrongdoing, but to promote our spiritual growth and maturity. How consoling this thought is – that when we disobey, God intervenes to correct us, not in anger, or with a desire to get even with us, but out of the deepest concern and interest for our spiritual development and wellbeing.

REFLECTION: God's dealings with us are not retributive, but remedial. We Christians are not under punishment, but under discipline – and the difference is vital.

Hand in hand

'... your rod and your staff, they comfort me.' Psalm 23:4

'It is the staff,' says Phillip Keller, 'that identifies a shepherd as a shepherd. No one in any other profession carries a shepherd's staff. It is uniquely an instrument used for the care and management of sheep. It will not do for cattle, horses or hogs. It is designed, shaped and adapted especially to the needs of sheep.' The staff was a slender pole with a little crook on the end, and was used for a variety of purposes. It was used to gently lift a newborn lamb and bring it to its mother when it had become separated. Also it was used to reach out and draw a sheep to the shepherd's side for physical examination, as timid and nervous sheep tend to keep as much distance as possible between themselves and the shepherd. The main use of an ancient shepherd's staff, however, was to guide the sheep. The tip of the staff would be laid against the animal's side, and the gentle pressure applied would guide the sheep in the way the shepherd wanted it to go.

One observer of the ways of a shepherd with his sheep says, 'Sometimes I have been fascinated to see how a shepherd will actually hold his staff against the side of a nervous or frightened sheep simply so that they are "in touch". They will walk along the way almost as though they were hand in hand.'

REFLECTION: Just as a shepherd walks alongside his sheep to comfort and to guide, so the Holy Spirit has come to comfort and guide us.

So very 'umble

'If my people who are called by my name shall humble themselves …' 2 Chronicles 7:14

How do we humble ourselves? Well, first let's think about what exactly humility is, for there are many fallacies in the Christian Church as to what constitutes this important spiritual quality. Some think, for example, that humility is self-effacement, but self-effacement can be a way of gaining face, like Uriah Heep in Charles Dickens' novel *David Copperfield*, who approached David Copperfield, wringing his hands and saying, 'I am so very 'umble, Master Copperfield … so very 'umble.'

In a church of which I was once the pastor I remember giving an address on the subject of humility and afterwards a woman came up to me and said, 'I did so much enjoy your address. Humility has always been a favourite topic of mine. In fact I regard it to be one of my best qualities.' Humility has several characteristics. First, it is a right estimation of yourself. You are not God but you are not a worm either. Humble people see themselves as they really are. Humility also has within it the fact of self-forgetfulness. The humble turn their attention from themselves to God; they rarely think about themselves at all. Again, humility recognises that without God we can do nothing. Those who are not humble foolishly believe that without them God can do nothing. Often what we think is humility is really nothing more than personal self-belittlement which has the goal of self-punishment or of hoping that someone will contradict them.

REFLECTION: Beware feeling proud of your humility.

Pride

'God opposes the proud but gives grace to the humble.'
1 Peter 5:5

D id you know that pride was the first sin ever to be seen in the universe? That's how the devil came into being. Once he was an angel of beauty and delight but he became puffed up by pride. Daniel Rowlands, a famous Welsh revivalist, said, 'We most resemble the devil when we are proud and we most resemble Christ when we are humble.'

'God who thrust out a proud angel from heaven', said Spurgeon to his students, 'will not tolerate a proud preacher either. God hides from the proud, you won't even feel Him near you.' He drew the attention of his students to this verse: 'Though the LORD is on high, he looks upon the lowly, but the proud he knows from afar' (Psa. 138:6).

Is it possible that that there could be more pride in the church you attend than in a comparable group of non-Christians? Pride in the fact you are saved and others are not, pride in your knowledge of the Bible, your ability to pray or preach? Pride or the lack of humility is one of the roots of sin. After all what is sin? Chop off the first and last letters and what are you left with? 'I' – the perpendicular pronoun as someone has called it. See it standing there on the page, 'I', tall and starched and stiff. Sin is really the ego standing up to its full height in the place which God has reserved for Himself – the centre of the soul.

REFLECTION: It is not possible to understand what humility is unless we are prepared to lay our lives alongside the Bible.

With you forever

'... I will ask the Father, and he will give you another Counsellor to be with you for ever ...' John 14:16

When the Holy Spirit visited them at Pentecost the dispirited disciples came alive again. Why? The answer is quite simple. Jesus had been *with* them, but the Holy Spirit was *in* them and would remain in them. There was no fear that *He* might go away. He would remain with them always. And what He was to them He is to us also – *a permanent presence*. In the Old Testament, we see temporary endowments of power for temporary tasks. In other words, the Holy Spirit came and went. Yet in John 14:16–17, Jesus announced that following His return to the throne in heaven the Holy Spirit's coming would be permanent. The idea of an occasional visitation is replaced by a permanent coming.

The Holy Spirit is a Counsellor who is available every day and all day. Human counsellors have to set aside special times to see people and often have difficulty in fitting everyone into their schedules. This, however, is not a problem to the divine Counsellor. You can approach Him any time of night or day, and though He may be involved at the same time in counselling thousands of your fellow believers, He will give Himself to you as if you were the only one on the face of the planet. And you don't have to look for Him in any other place than in your own heart. The Holy Spirit is not only the divine Counsellor but a dependable Counsellor. He is available to you and me – permanently.

REFLECTION: The Holy Spirit is a Counsellor who is available every day and all day.

Muddling along

'... I will ask the Father, and he will give you another Counsellor to be with you for ever ...' John 14:16

It is the night before Christ is to be crucified, and He is closeted with His disciples in an upper room in the sacred city of Jerusalem. The air is heavy with the atmosphere of imminent events. The Passover has been celebrated, Judas has just left, and suddenly Christ announces that He is soon to leave this world and return to His Father in heaven.

Their stomachs must have churned within them as they heard their Master say He was going away. For over three years He had been their Teacher, their Confidante and their Guide. He had comforted them when they were sad, inspired them in times of doubt, and encouraged them whenever their footsteps began to flag. He had been to them a Counsellor par excellence. But now He was going. How were they to handle things in His absence? What were they to do when they didn't know which course of action to take? Who was to be their inspiration and guide?

Another Counsellor is to take His place, He informs them – the blessed Holy Spirit. The Spirit came, as we know, at Pentecost, to be to the disciples all that Jesus was – and more. And He has remained in the world to be our Counsellor too. But how dependent are we on His counsel? How often do we draw on His resources? Sadly, all too seldom and too little. God has appointed a divine Counsellor to assist us, yet so often we prefer to muddle along on our own.

REFLECTION: Are you muddling along or walking in the Spirit?

Another Counsellor

'... I will ask the Father, and he will give you another Counsellor ...' John 14:16

Note the word *another*. Without that word we have no point of comparison; the word 'Counsellor' would be unanchored. Counsels us how? And to do what? He counsels us in the same way and with the same principles that Christ followed when He counselled His disciples. The Spirit's counsel was to be the same as Jesus' counsel. In the very nature of things it could not be different.

In Acts 16:6–7, the terms 'Holy Spirit' and 'Spirit of Jesus' are used interchangeably: 'having been kept by the Holy Spirit from preaching the word' (v.6), and 'the Spirit of Jesus would not allow them to' (v.7). The Holy Spirit seemed to the disciples to be the Spirit of Jesus within them. They were one. The counsel given to every believer by the Holy Spirit will accord with the counsel given to the disciples by Jesus when He was here on earth. If God is a Christlike God, then the Spirit is a Christlike Spirit. There are many matters about which I know little or nothing, but one thing I do know about is counselling as I have been involved in it for over forty years. When I meet a counsellor I can usually tell what school of thought he or she belongs to by listening to that person talk. It is the same with the Holy Spirit. I can tell what school He comes from. It is the 'The Jesus School of Counselling'. He counsels in the same way as Christ.

REFLECTION: Our heavenly Father has given us the Holy Spirit to be our Counsellor yet how much do we avail ourselves of His resources?

Return to Pentecost

'All of them were filled with the Holy Spirit ...' Acts 2:4

Whenever I think of the Church returning to Pentecost there comes to mind the story of Billy Graham who, as a young Youth for Christ evangelist, held a city-wide tent crusade in Los Angeles, California, somewhere around the middle of last century. Thousands of people came to Christ during that crusade, many of them Hollywood film stars. A minister who belonged to a liberal church in the city wrote in the local paper, 'Billy Graham has put the church in Los Angeles back 100 years.' When he heard that, Billy is said to have responded, 'Oh dear – I was really trying to put it back 2,000 years.'

At Pentecost, a high-voltage burst of spiritual energy and supernatural power flowed into the midst of those early disciples such as had never been known before. In a comparatively short time it affected the whole nation, spilling over eventually to other nations, even as far as Europe. When the Church witnesses the same degree of power that was present at Pentecost and that power spreads to whole communities, even to a nation as it did in the 1904 Welsh Revival, then and only then can it be said to be revival. People would suddenly become aware of God's presence even deep down in the mines and cry out to be saved. Three main characteristics of revival are: an intense palpable and extraordinary sense of God's presence, a deep desire to be rid of all sin and a powerful impact on the wider community.

REFLECTION: The Church of the future should be based on the Church of the past.

Just a carpenter

"'He's no better than we are," they said. "He's just a carpenter ..."' Mark 6:3, TLB

This statement is one of the most intriguing statements they could have made about our Lord. He might have been so many other things – a farmer, a fisherman or a builder. But no, Jesus was a carpenter. And the more I think about it the more I find a sublime fitness in that fact. For a carpenter *makes* things. Barns, children's toys, doors, tables, chairs. Jesus as a carpenter must have made them all. Long before He was crucified on a cross and the nails held the Carpenter, the Carpenter held the nails.

I wonder as He hammered the nails into wood – did He realise that one day men would hammer nails into Him. In a sense Jesus was a carpenter, a maker of things before He came to Nazareth. He who wielded axe and plane and hammer in the tiny village of Nazareth once laid down the timbers of the universe. And He was a maker too after He left Nazareth.

When the day came that He took off His apron for the last time, put away His tools and closed the door of the carpenter's shop behind Him forever, He did not cease to be a carpenter. Only His materials were different. He worked not with wood but with men and women. The woodworker became a wonder worker, transforming the lives of men and women. And to His disciples He said, 'Come, follow me and I will *make* you fishers of men' (Matt. 4:19, my italics).

REFLECTION: This humble carpenter built much more than doors or ploughs or yokes. He rebuilt the lives of those who, stained by sin, yielded to His claims.

A motley bunch

'Brothers, think of what you were when you were called.
Not many of you were wise by the world's standards; not
many were influential; not many were of noble birth.'
1 Corinthians 1:26

I want to suggest three things about this Carpenter of Nazareth that causes Him to be such a wonder. Firstly – He is a carpenter who selects the most unlikely materials. Most carpenters like to select the best wood they can when making something. But not this one. Just look at the disciples He chose, for example. What a motley bunch. I once did a study of the Twelve and I came to the conclusion that they represented all the points of the psychological compass.

There was Simon Peter, bluff, blundering, arrogant, impetuous, even foul-mouthed at times, and Judas, the betrayer, whose heart became open to Satan. The disciple Matthew had been a tax gatherer, the type of person who was hated by the Jews. When you look at the other disciples there doesn't seem much to qualify them to become the future leaders of the world's greatest enterprise – the Christian Church. But Jesus does not hesitate to enrol them in His school of discipleship. If there is one thing I have noticed in my long life it is that Christ does not always choose the well adjusted, the best educated or the sophisticated to accomplish His purposes. I have found the words of the apostle Paul encouraging: 'But we have this treasure in jars of clay to show that this all-surpassing power is from God and not from us' (2 Cor. 4:7).

REFLECTION: Many who lacked the benefits of a loving home,
a good education, a fertile mind and so on learned that there is
power with God to turn stumbling blocks into stepping stones.

Shaped for service

'No discipline seems pleasant at the time, but painful.
Later on, however, it produces a harvest of righteousness
and peace for those who have been trained by it.'
Hebrews 12:11

The Carpenter of Nazareth not only selects the most unlikely materials but spends time carefully shaping and fashioning them. Whether we are unlikely material or not, every one of us once selected has to be shaped. And the shaping process is not easy to bear, but it has to be done. How do you respond to the shaping process I wonder?

The Carpenter of Nazareth puts you on His bench, and the plane, the saw and the chisel go to work and as He comes up against the knots and the flaws, soon the shivers of wood fly in all directions. Often it is not a pleasant experience when God shapes us for service in His kingdom, but we will not be able to arrive at our full potential without it.

There is an old saying that though God loves us as we are He loves us too much to let us stay as we are, and He works on us in ways that sometimes we wish He loved us less. St Augustine, one of the early Church Fathers, discovered this when God began to work in his life and such were the challenges he went through that one day he cried out: 'O Lord love me less.' C.S. Lewis said that we cry out for and indeed have a loving God. His love however will not let us remain less than we can be. Christ sees in us more than we can see in ourselves and will work to bring that out.

REFLECTION: 'You haven't been made; you are still under construction.'

Set apart

'May God himself, the God of peace, sanctify you through and through.' 1 Thessalonians 5:23

The Carpenter of Nazareth not only selects the most unlikely materials, and carefully shapes them but He also sanctifies them and sets them aside for His purpose. The word 'sanctified' has several meanings; it means dedication, separation and cleansing. The vessels in the ancient tabernacle had to be set apart specifically for God's use. In the same way, God wants us not simply to decorate His world but to change it. He desires to set us apart to that special purpose He has for every single one of us. Before we were formed in our mother's womb He saw us and planned our destiny. Everything He has allowed in our lives has been because He foresaw how He could turn it to good and work to refining our characters, deepening our sensitivity to Himself and sharpening our effectiveness in His service.

Nowadays as I look back over my life, I view the times of difficulty, the doubts, the trials, the reverses, betrayals, and I thank God for every one of them. I have learned more from the hours of suffering than from the moments of triumph. Jesus Christ wants to use you at every point of your life here on earth. Remember He is out there striding ahead of you and He is looking back over His shoulder and saying to you, 'Come on … Follow me … I will make you into someone whose service for Me will bring great glory to My name.'

REFLECTION: 'I pray O Master let me lie/As on thy bench the favoured wood/Thy saw, thy plane, thy chisel fly/Make me into something beautiful – and good.' (George MacDonald)

The quality *par excellence*

'Holy, holy, holy is the LORD Almighty ...' Isaiah 6:3

Y ou cannot help but notice that God is portrayed in the Bible as uniquely and awesomely holy. In fact, there are more references to the holiness of God in Scripture than there are to any other aspect of His character. But what do we mean when we say God is 'holy'? There are three thoughts underlying the word 'holy'. First, the idea of separation, of being withdrawn or apart. Second, brightness or brilliance. Third, moral majesty, purity and cleanliness.

It is interesting that those who came into direct contact with God in the Old Testament were inevitably overwhelmed by His moral majesty. Isaiah went into the Temple to pray at a time when his people were in grave difficulties. I feel sure that whatever answer Isaiah thought he would get as he opened up his heart to God, it was not the one he received. He was given a vision of a holy God that shook him to the core of his being. Why should this be? I think it was because the reality of God's holiness is one of the main lessons we are taught in His school, the divine prerequisite for understanding what is in the heart of God, the most important qualification for learning from the Lord. Sadly, we don't hear much about the holiness of God in the modern Church. But, just as it was in ancient times, so today, the fear of the Lord is, as the psalmist so beautifully put it, 'the beginning of wisdom' (Psa. 111:10).

REFLECTION: Do you really know what it is to serve a *holy* God? Have you ever received a vision of His moral majesty and purity?

Great is Your faithfulness

'Your love, O LORD, reaches to the heavens, your faithfulness to the skies.' Psalm 36:5

H ow wonderful it is, in an age when unfaithfulness is such a regular feature of life, to focus our gaze on those scriptures that point to the trustworthiness of our God. The one before us today is quite wonderful, but consider also these: 'O LORD God Almighty, who is like you? You are mighty, O LORD, and your faithfulness surrounds you' (Psa. 89:8); 'If we are faithless, he will remain faithful, for he cannot disown himself' (2 Tim. 2:13). For God to be unfaithful would be to act contrary to His nature, and if He ever were (we are only speculating because He could never do so) then He would cease to be God.

We are told God's faithfulness extends to the skies. This is the psalmist's picturesque way of expressing the fact that far above all finite comprehension is the unchanging faithfulness of God. He never forgets a thing, never makes a mistake, never fails to keep a promise, never falters over a decision, never retracts a statement He has made, and has never breached a contract. Every declaration He has made, every promise He has given, every covenant He has entered into is vouchsafed by His faithful character. This is why Christians all around the world can say with confidence, '… his compassions never fail. They are new every morning; *great* is your faithfulness' (Lam. 3:22–23, my italics).

REFLECTION: As you read or hear God's Word, can't you just feel the energy that flows from the Scriptures buttressing your confidence in Him?

Pray in Jesus' name

'... my Father will give you whatever you ask in my name.' John 16:23

W
e should give attention to the words of Jesus which state, 'And I will do whatever you ask in my name, so that the Son may bring glory to the Father. You may ask me for anything in my name, and I will do it' (John 14:13–14). What does praying in Christ's name really mean? It means more than just attaching the formula to the end of our prayers and saying, 'This I ask in Jesus' name' for, quite clearly, the formula could easily be attached to prayers that are crudely and utterly selfish.

It means praying according to the *character* of Christ, or praying prayers that He would pray if He were in our shoes. God can only answer prayer if the prayer is in accord with the Spirit of Jesus Christ. Don't try to get God to do anything that is not Christlike. He can't do it for it is impossible for God to do anything that is against His own nature. Prayer is not trying to get God to do our will, but it is the bringing of our will into line with God's will.

When we pray in the name of Jesus we are asking that we might be so caught up in the Spirit of Christ, whose sole aim was to do the will of His Father, that we will pray the kind of prayers that put God's will as the highest priority in our lives, even though it may run counter to our own plans and desires.

REFLECTION: Praying in Jesus' name is not a magic formula for personal gain but a magnificent obsession with God's will.

Prayer as self-surrender

'... not my will, but yours be done.' Luke 22:42

Kagawa, the great Japanese Christian, defined prayer in one word – 'Surrender'. He was right. It is the surrender of our selfish desires in order that we might lock into God's desires – the giving up of self-interest in order to find an eternal interest. If we fear to surrender our wills to God in the event He might deprive us of something we feel is beneficial to us, or that we might lose our ambition, then we are greatly mistaken. Prayer is the wire surrendering to the dynamo; the child surrendering to education; a branch surrendering to the vine. A branch, if not surrendered to the vine, but cut off and on its own is not free, or fulfilled, but dead. A person who doesn't surrender to God isn't free; he is futile.

Learn, therefore, to pray your prayers in the Spirit of Jesus Christ. Prayers that are undergirded by biblical principles. Prayers that put God first and self second. Prayers that Jesus would pray if He were in your shoes. To pray such prayers will not demean your personality but direct it – to God's ends. It is not a passive surrender but, as someone described it 'alert passivity'. It is a passivity that awakens the whole being to the right kind of activity. The surrender is but a step to real mastery.

REFLECTION: Prayer is the will to die on the level of an empty, selfish, defeated, ineffective, short-circuited life, and the will to live on the level of a victorious, full, effective and abundant life.

Choose to be thankful

'Praise the LORD, O my soul; all my inmost being, praise his holy name.' Psalm 103:1

D o you find it difficult to think of things for which you can be grateful? Then open up your Bible to Psalm 103. You can't help but feel that as the psalmist writes he is experiencing what one writer has called 'the spontaneous overflow of a swelling heart'. 'But I don't always feel like that,' I have heard people say, 'and surely to praise God when you don't feel like it is hypocrisy.'

Let's look at that argument a little more closely. Notice how the psalmist begins: 'Praise the LORD, O my soul.' See what he is doing? He is charging his soul to praise the Lord. He is saying, in effect, I am going to use my will to stir up my mind to focus on reasons why I should praise the Lord. I may not feel like doing it but I am going to do it anyway!

We can choose to praise God whether we feel like it or not. We don't have to wait until something happens that evokes praise in our heart; we can by an action of our will stir our minds to contemplate the goodness of God, and when we do that, a law of the personality goes into action, namely that what we think about will soon affect the way we feel. I have never found it to fail.

REFLECTION: No matter how difficult things are you have a choice to praise Him or not praise Him, to thank Him or not thank Him.

Remember

'Praise the LORD, O my soul, and forget not all his benefits ...'
Psalm 103:2

I t's sad when Christians wait until they feel like praising rather than using their wills to command their minds to focus on reasons for praise. Stirring his mind to action brings up a number of reasons for the psalmist to praise – eight in fact: divine benefits, forgiveness, healing, redemption, love and compassion, satisfaction and renewal. He begins by charging his soul not to forget God's benefits and soon, as his mind goes to work to identify those benefits, his emotions follow his thoughts like little ducks follow their mother on a pond. And when after 22 verses he comes to an end, you feel that it is either his pen or his parchment that have run out and not his stream of praise. And it all started with a charge to his soul not to forget the Lord's benefits.

How quickly we forget! We forget past mercies and blessings and we are all the poorer because of it. We would be much calmer and more confident in the presence of new troubles if we had remembered vividly the old deliverances; if we had kept them fresh in mind and been able to say, 'The God who delivered me then will not desert me now.' Many Christians keep what they call a 'Gratitude Journal' and when they need to remind themselves of reasons to praise they open it up, and then praise rises because it must.

REFLECTION: 'His love in times past forbids me to think/ He'll leave me at last in trouble to sink.' (John Newton)

He redeems the situation

'... in everything give thanks; for this is the will of God in Christ Jesus ...' 1 Thessalonians 5:18, NKJV

The apostle Paul in his letter to the Thessalonians tells us to rejoice always; and that in everything we ought to give thanks. In everything? Yes. In everything. Does that mean we are to thank God for the bad things that happen to us – sickness, accidents, infirmities, and so on? Paul would say, 'Yes!' Everything means everything.

If Romans 8:28 is true (and I believe it is) then God only allows into our lives those things that He can turn to good. I take that to mean that if God foresees that a certain situation could arise which He was unable to turn to good then He will not permit it to happen. No matter what happens to you God is committed to working good out of it and because of that it is possible to thank Him for everything that happens to you. You are not thanking Him for the evil, but for the good that He is going to bring out of the evil, for the way He is going to redeem the situation and bring something out of it that redounds to His glory. If you find it difficult to come to grips with this concept, then don't worry. When something happens to you that you feel is evil and you cannot find it in your heart to give God thanks for what has taken place, then start by giving Him thanks for His presence in the situation.

REFLECTION: One thing is sure: those who have cultivated an attitude of giving thanks in everything are those who have a deep, settled peace in their soul and a confidence towards the future that nothing will be able to shake.

The root of sin

*'When the woman saw that the fruit of the tree was good
for food and pleasing to the eye, and also desirable for
gaining wisdom, she took some and ate it.' Genesis 3:6*

Oswald Chambers says, 'The root of sin is the suspicion that
God is not good'. Until I read that, I had always believed
the root of sin was rebellion. Chambers, however, sees
deep into Satan's strategy, and goes right to the heart of the situation.
Satan understood better than Eve herself how her personality was
constructed. He knew that once Eve entertained a doubt about
God's goodness, that doubt would lead to disobedience. It is easier to
disobey God when the mind entertains a doubt that He is good.

G. Campbell Morgan described the process of temptation like
this: Appealing to the intelligence of the woman, the enemy created
an aspersion which was calculated to change the attitude of her
emotion and so capture the final citadel, the will. Satan insinuates
a doubt into Eve's mind concerning the goodness of God. Once that
doubt is entertained, it soon affects the way she feels about God in
her emotions. Then doubting God and disliking God (because of His
limitations on her freedom), the next step is disobedience towards
God. This is how the personality functions: What we think greatly
affects the way we feel and how we feel determines the way we act.
Our will does not function in a vacuum; it is greatly influenced by
what we think and how we feel. Doubting God leads to disliking
God; disliking God leads to disobeying God.

**REFLECTION: An absolute belief in the goodness of God is a
tremendous weapon to enable us to overcome temptation.**

Dignity and depravity

'So the LORD God banished him from the garden of Eden ...'
Genesis 3:23

What we call the Fall, when Adam and Eve disobeyed God, is no myth; it is a grim and awful fact. Strange though it may seem, however, the doctrine of the Fall and original sin is one of the most flattering to humankind. The Fall both flattens and flatters us, pointing at one and the same time to our depravity and our dignity. Blaise Pascal, the French mathematician and Christian philosopher, said: 'What a chimera is man! What a contradiction! Judge of all things, feeble worm of the earth. Depository of truth; sink of uncertainty and error! The glory and scandal of the universe!' Our dignity is that we are made in God's image; our depravity is that we carry in our personalities a fragmented version of that image.

Having decided to live independently and rebel against God, Adam and Eve were cut off from union with Him. They once reflected so gloriously the divine image but now became broken lenses reflecting broken light. Now the knowledge of God is limited, the emotions degraded and the mind corrupted. Intelligence becomes bounded by its own limitation as it was severed from infinite knowledge. The emotions become dwarfed as to their capacity and tainted by sin. The will, a magnificent ruin, became perpetually attempting to secure mastership and yet will never succeed because it has lost its own spring of action – and its own Master.

REFLECTION: There is a way back to God but it lies in another direction – not via Eden but through Christ.

Ruined relationships

*'To the woman he said "... Your desire will be for your
husband, and he will rule over you."' Genesis 3:16*

The Fall disrupted Adam and Eve's relationships not only
with God but also with each other. Many a commentator
has puzzled over this verse but one of the best explanations
is by Gilbert Bilezikian: 'The woman's desire will be for her husband
so as to perpetuate the intimacy they had prior to the Fall, but her
nostalgia for the relationship of love and mutuality that existed
between them before the Fall, when they both desired each other
will not be reciprocated by her husband. Instead of meeting her
desire he will seek to rule over her. In short the woman wants a mate
and she gets a master. She wants a lover and gets a lord, she wants a
husband and gets a hierarch.'

Prior to the Fall, knowing that they were loved and loved
completely, Adam and Eve then gave to each other the same degree
of love that God poured out to them. The love that God had begotten
in them, by the vision and experience of His love for them, widened
in their hearts to embrace each other. They related perfectly to each
other and to God. Once they doubted the divine love, however, and
took of the forbidden fruit, the doubt they had of God's love began to
show itself in their relationship to each other. They remained alive
with a desire and a capacity for love but were left disconnected from
God and from each other.

**REFLECTION: Adam and Eve were unsure of each other,
insecure in their relationship with God and also with each
other. Isn't that often the same in relationships today?**

Ruined emotions

'He answered, "I heard you in the garden, and I was afraid because I was naked; so I hid."' Genesis 3:10

L ook at the impact the Fall had on Adam and Eve's emotions. God designed Adam and Eve as reactive beings. He gave them the ability to think and their thinking, in turn, produced certain emotions within them. When they were in fellowship with God, then you can be sure they felt only positive and pleasant emotions, like happiness, joy, peace and security. Once they had rebelled, they experienced new emotions. Three of those emotions can easily be identified. First came guilt and shame. This can be seen in their attempts to cover up their nakedness with leaves from the trees of the garden.

Other emotions they would have felt are fear and anxiety. A third stream of emotions was that of anger and resentment. These emotions can be recognised in the way they shifted blame to each other. We often displace our anger onto others. Feeling angry is not comfortable, so we like to spread it around and dump it on others as much as we can. These three streams of emotions are still the main culprits in the human heart to this very day. Underlying all negative emotions is self-centredness and self-interest. Emotions that show love are emotions that are more other-centred than self-centred. All negative emotions arise because of the absence of love. Where love is not, other emotions flow through the personality.

REFLECTION: Where love is, fear is not. Where love is, anger is not. Where love is, guilt is not. Adam and Eve's emotions were like God's until the Fall when they became unlike God's.

The response of Jesus

'... I love the Father ...' John 14:31

A striking example of using situations to advance God's purposes is seen when the Pharisees challenged Jesus about the Sabbath. 'At this, the enemies of Jesus were wild with rage, and began to plot his murder' (Luke 6:11, TLB). How did Jesus react to that most difficult situation? A few days later, we are told, He decided to spend the whole night in prayer. What His thoughts were during that night of prayer, we can only conjecture, but I can't help feeling that, although He knew that He was destined to die at Jerusalem, it must have been borne home to Him that night in an even more powerful way. He saw clearly that the opposition to His ministry would eventually culminate in His death. So before that happened, He decided that this would be the moment at which He would choose the men who would continue His ministry.

When day broke, He promptly proceeded to select the Twelve. Here is a perfect example of what happens when God works in someone whom He loves and who loves Him. Such was Christ's love for His Father that He had absolute trust in the Father's will. He knew that God loved Him so much that He would allow nothing in His life unless it furthered the purposes of their partnership. And in the same way, God wants to set up a similar partnership in your life and mine.

REFLECTION: God pleads for our absolute confidence and trust, so that whatever happens we know that out of it will come a purpose that is wise and good.

Becoming a fruitful Christian

'... live a life worthy of the Lord and ... please him in every way: bearing fruit in every good work ...' Colossians 1:10

Effectiveness and fruitfulness in the Christian life don't *just* happen: they come and continue as a result of careful planning and pruning. 'Every branch of mine that bears no fruit, he takes away, and every branch that does bear fruit he prunes, that it may bear more fruit' (John 15:2, RSV). There is no way that we can be effective disciples of Christ except through relentless pruning – the cutting away of non-fruit-bearing suckers that sap our energies, but bear no fruit. Our Father, the Gardener, knows that it is possible to have luxuriant growth with no fruit, and so the useless non-fruit-bearing growth must be cut away.

Life depends as much upon elimination as it does upon assimilation. With many of us, much of our life is overgrown with useless things. God has many pruning knives, and with some of us He may have to use them all. When He prunes, however, He does so with the utmost tenderness and care, and He will not permit anything to happen to us unless it accords with the purposes which He planned for us before the world began. So be open to Him in the days that lie ahead, for He needs your consent and cooperation if He is to do a perfect and complete job. Let Him prune you from mistakes to mastery, from despair to delight and from blunders to beauty. And when the pruning process feels painful, remember that the knife is in good and reliable hands. Your *Father* is the Gardener.

REFLECTION: It is often only when we are willing to give up, that we are able to give out.

Lacking in passion?

'To him who loves us and has freed us from our sins by his blood ... to him be glory and power for ever and ever! Amen.' Revelation 1:5–6

We focus now on what we have to do in order to bring our personalities back into correspondence with the divine design and thus ensure that our souls do more than survive, they thrive.

The first thing to do is to acknowledge that you are a longing being and that your longings can never be fully satisfied except in a deep ongoing relationship with Jesus Christ. If you do not acknowledge this then you are driven to try and meet your longings in other ways. When you do acknowledge your longings you get in touch with the fact that you are a thirsty yearning being. Focus on that fact; feel the thirst. Our desire to know God and enjoy Him depends on how aware we are of a lack in our life.

Don't be satisfied with the mere duties of the Christian life. One of the saddest things to see is a believer remaining content with practising the duties of the Christian life and relying on them to bring satisfaction rather than a dynamic and passionate relationship with Jesus Christ. Why is it, I often ask myself, that many Christians I meet have so little passion in their lives? Clearly they are not in touch with their longings. The only satisfying relationship with God is a passionate one.

Only in a passionate relationship with God will your longings for security, self-worth and significance be met.

REFLECTION: Read Revelation 1:1–8. Feel the passion of the writer. Are you passionate about Christ? Does He fill and thrill your soul to the exclusion of all else?

You have been charged!

'"Therefore I bring charges against you again,"
declares the LORD.' Jeremiah 2:9

The reality of how foolish we are without the wisdom that comes from God is brought home to us forcibly in Jeremiah 2:4–13. In this remarkable part of Scripture God is bringing charges against His people, and is so concerned about a certain matter that He calls in the heavens to come and look at what His people are doing (v.12).

What is it that troubles the Almighty to such a degree that He talks like this? He tells us in these words: 'My people have committed two sins: They have forsaken me, the spring of living water, and have dug their own cisterns, broken cisterns that cannot hold water' (v.13). 'Can you believe it?' the Almighty seems to be saying. 'My people are extremely thirsty yet walk right by the water I provide for them, pick up a shovel and go out into the desert to dig a cistern. And the cisterns they dig spring leaks every time. They get a mouthful of water and then it's gone. Then they go and dig another one.'

Why would people walk past a 'spring of living water', go out into the desert, and try to slake their thirst by drinking from a cistern containing dirty, lukewarm water? It doesn't make sense. The only answer is that human thinking, left to itself, is so utterly foolish and rebellious that it is sure it can find satisfaction for the thirst in the soul by some means other than God. It can't, but it believes it can – hence it is foolish.

REFLECTION: Do I look to things other than the living God to satisfy my thirst?

'The happiness of being free'

'Then the Lord said to Satan, "Have you considered my servant Job?"' Job 1:8

Because God has endowed us with a power that He Himself possesses – the power to choose – each of us is able to determine our character and decide what kind of person we want to be.

In our reading today we see Satan standing in the presence of God and being asked, 'Have you considered my servant Job? There is no-one on earth like him; he is blameless and upright, a man who fears God and shuns evil.' Clearly God found great delight in Job's decision to respond to the gifts He had given him with an attitude of thankfulness. It is this freedom to choose what kind of people we want to be that gives us the ability to delight the heart of God.

If He had to wring gratitude out of us what kind of pleasure would that give Him? Job's freedom to choose to delight God also, of course, gave him the ability to sadden Him. C.S. Lewis said that God gave us this free will because although free will makes evil possible so it is also the one thing that makes love and joy or goodness worth having. As we read the book of Job we realise that there were times when Job's statements must have saddened God, but his conclusion would no doubt have gladdened Him. Our wills can work against God or with Him. How good it is for both humankind and God when the will works with Him.

REFLECTION: The happiness which God designs for us is the happiness of being free, freely choosing to accept Christ and follow Him and to love others. This delights the heart of God.

True peace of God

'Peace I leave with you; my peace I give you. I do not give to you as the world gives. Do not let your hearts be troubled and do not be afraid.' John 14:27

P eace. It's something most people want above all. Peace in their homes, in their families, in their work situations. Peace in their minds. Peace is the third quality of the Spirit and Christians must possess it in order to become Christlike in character. This is more than peace of mind: it is peace of spirit. A woman once told me, 'I turned to religion [note: religion, not Christ] to obtain peace of mind. Although it helped me greatly it couldn't compare with the experience I discovered in transcendental meditation.' The fact that she was looking for peace of mind showed the shallowness of her quest. You cannot have peace of mind unless you have something deeper – the peace of God. It is a peace that begins in the spirit.

Peace of mind is the outcome of the deeper peace in the spirit. You cannot have peace of mind if there is conflict in the spirit. As one preacher put it, 'To know the peace of God you must know the God of peace.' To tinker with the mind and leave the depths untouched is unproductive. It only produces a peace that goes to pieces. True peace comes from adjustment to reality, which can only come from adjustment to God. Peace of mind breaks down if the worm of doubt is eating at its centre. When calamity comes peace is shattered. Christian peace flows out of a right personal relationship with God and His Son the Lord Jesus Christ.

REFLECTION: Only God's peace is real peace. Do you know His peace?

He has gone ahead

'You prepare a table before me in the presence of my enemies.' Psalm 23:5

W hen David referred to a 'table', he was not thinking of an indoor banquet, but of the high, flat-topped plateaus where the sheep were taken to graze in the summertime. Prior to taking his sheep on to this higher ground, a caring and concerned shepherd would go up alone to see if there were any wild animals or any poisonous weeds and, if so, plan his grazing programme to either avoid them or take whatever steps were necessary to eradicate them. The sheep arriving on the high tableland would not, of course, realise it, but they owed their safety and security to the fact that the shepherd had gone before them to prepare for them a 'table' in the presence of their enemies. There are vipers' holes from which the poisonous snakes emerge to bite the noses of the sheep. In addition to these dangers around the feeding ground, there are holes and caves in the hillside in which live wolves and jackals.

The bravery and heroism of the shepherd reaches its highest point as he works to close up these dens with stones, confront and kill the beasts with his long-bladed knife. It has been known for a shepherd to lose hundreds of sheep in one day by failing to take the necessary precautions in this matter. The way God protects and cares for His children as they go out into the world is a grander and more wonderful thought than that of seating them at an indoor banqueting table.

REFLECTION: God provides safety and provision in the very midst of trouble and danger.

Consider Him

'Consider him who endured such opposition ...'
Hebrews 12:3

A shepherd, more often than not, has to go through a good deal of personal sacrifice and danger in order to prepare the 'table', or feeding ground, for his sheep. He may have to endure loneliness, privation, hunger and sometimes even physical injury in his efforts to make the feeding ground safe for his sheep. Many a shepherd comes back from such an expedition covered in cuts and bruises. Just as a good shepherd sacrifices himself for the sake of his sheep, so has Christ, the Good Shepherd, gone to the utmost lengths possible to bring His sheep into a place of spiritual contentment and security. Unfortunately, we forget all too easily just what was the personal cost to Christ in preparing the table for His redeemed people.

When next you come to the Table of Communion – which is really a feast of thanksgiving in remembrance of His tender love and care – ask yourself: do I fully appreciate what it cost my Lord to prepare this table for me? And what did it cost? It cost Him His life. As Christmas Evans, one of our great Welsh preachers, picturesquely put it: 'Never did any shepherd climb a mountain as dangerous and as challenging as Mount Calvary. There on its summit the Good Shepherd drew sin to battle, overcame all its forces, silenced forever the voice of the archenemy of our souls – and by so doing has prepared for us a table in the presence of our enemies. Come and be fed ...'

REFLECTION: Consider Christ's sacrifice to prepare for your salvation.

Peace from irritation

'You anoint my head with oil ...' Psalm 23:5

S heep, we are told, are especially irritated by flies and other winged parasites which buzz around their heads and make their lives a misery. *The Handbook of Bible Times and Customs* lists over twenty varieties of flies that can be found in the Middle East. 'Sheep are especially troubled by nose flies,' says one shepherd, 'for they buzz around the head of a sheep attempting to alight on the damp mucous membranes of the sheep's nose.' So irritating can be the effect of nose flies that sometimes a sheep will beat its head against a tree or a rock in order to find relief. An alert shepherd, when he sees this taking place, bathes the sheep's head in olive oil. This results, almost immediately, in a dramatic change in the sheep's behaviour. Gone is the frenzy and restlessness and soon the sheep begins to quietly graze or lie down in peaceful contentment.

Perhaps at this very moment you are facing an endless bombardment of irritations and difficulties that are causing you to become downcast and fainthearted. Draw near to Jesus – your heavenly Shepherd. Spend some moments in quiet prayer and contemplation. Let Him bathe your hurts in the soothing oil of the Spirit. Then rise and go your way in the knowledge that no matter how frustrating life's circumstances and situations the divine Shepherd is only a prayer away.

REFLECTION: When you feel like beating your head on a wall, lay it instead in the hands of Jesus for Him to bathe your irritation with His peace and love.

Peace instead of torment

'... the mind controlled by the Spirit is life and peace.'
Romans 8:6

W hen worn down by the anxious and tempting thoughts that buzz around inside our heads, we must not only focus our gaze upon Christ but we must also come to Him in petitionary prayer. In talking over the years with people who were plagued with evil thoughts, I have been surprised at the number who have told me that they have never actually come to God and asked directly for His help. James reminds us that we do not receive simply because we do not ask (James 4:2).

How, then, do we ask? It can be done in your own words or in the words of an appropriate hymn. You can say something like this: 'Father, lay Your consoling hand on this forehead which is oppressed with irritating and evil thoughts. Help me now by breaking their hold upon me, and release me from their grip. In Jesus' name.'

It must be understood, of course, that as well as praying, you, too, must accept some responsibility in this matter. It's no good praying, 'Lord, deliver me from this evil thought', and then wallowing in it in your imagination. God will do His part, but you must also do yours. Some Christians make it their daily petition to ask God for the anointing of the Spirit upon their minds. Coolness in place of heat, and peace instead of torment are the rewards of those who are swift to turn to the Shepherd and invite Him to minister to them in this way.

REFLECTION: You need have no fears that His supply of oil is limited in any way. He draws from a cup that never runs dry.

Do you pray?

'... if my people, who are called by my name, will humble themselves and pray ...' 2 Chronicles 7:14

Y ou may say, 'I do pray.' But do you? How much? How sincerely? When, for example, did you last stay up late just to pray? When did you rise early simply to pray? It is prayer that opens us to God's power. All around us the power of God is flowing and it comes in at the place of prayer. A little prayer and a little of that power gets through. A lot of prayer and a lot comes through. Fervent believing prayer causes it to come in like a flood. How selfish sometimes are our prayer lives?

It's interesting how when our family is in trouble or our needs cry out to be met we can develop a passion in prayer that is not there for those who may be outside our small circle. A lot of our praying is shot through with self-interest, our concerns, our needs, and so often everything that comes up has a self axis. Me! Me! Me! It's surprising the strange ideas that some Christians have in relation to prayer. I have met many who view it as nothing more than just reciting what we call the Lord's Prayer. Although it is an important framework for understanding what prayer is all about and has been a blessing to the Church universal when said corporately, if we think that when we have recited the Lord's Prayer that is the end of the matter then we are just fooling ourselves.

REFLECTION: Prayer to the Christian is like training to an athlete – sometimes enjoyable, sometimes difficult but always essential for strength and stamina.

Turning

'... if my people who are called by my name will ... turn from their wicked ways ...' 2 Chronicles 7:14

God has a further challenge for us – He asks us to turn from our wicked ways. The people of God with wicked ways? Surely it means silly ways, careless ways perhaps. The Bible says *wicked* ways and when God uses the word He means it to be understood in its original sense – 'sinful and iniquitous'. What are these wicked ways, these Spirit-quenching things that block the path to revival? Well, God is not specific about them so we are left to some degree of speculation in regard to their precise nature.

Permit me to give you some examples based on Scripture of what I think can be listed as the wicked ways of the people of God. When we allow our spiritual condition to remain lukewarm and complacent – that is a wicked way. When we hold bitterness and resentment against a group or an individual and refuse to offer the same degree of forgiveness that Christ has given to us – that is a wicked way. Unforgiveness kills the spiritual life; it is a wicked way. When we neglect the reading and study of the Scriptures – that is a wicked way. When we withhold our tithes and offerings from God – that is a wicked way. What about such things as continued moral failure, lying, low expectations of holiness in oneself and others, indifference to the winning of others to Christ, loss of temper, idolatry, gossip, hypocrisy, pretence ... the list could go on and on. Let us turn from our wicked ways.

REFLECTION: The word 'ways' suggests behaviour that has become settled and established.

Where to pray

'... Jesus ... went off to a solitary place, where he prayed.'
Mark 1:35

I f it is possible find a quiet place to which you can withdraw
and where you can feel secure from interruption. Jesus said,
'... when you pray, go away by yourself, all alone, and shut the
door behind you and pray to your Father secretly' (Matt. 6:6, TLB).
There are times, of course, when Christians are to pray together (see
Matt. 18:19) but Jesus is talking here about individual prayer, not
corporate prayer. And the secret of effective praying as individuals is
to pray in secret. All Christians need to have, if possible, a quiet spot
in which to pray, for such a spot will gather spiritual associations
which will quicken their imagination whenever they go there, and
will call them to prayer even when inclination ebbs.

Praying with friends, or with your family, is a necessary and vital
part of prayer, but to build up your personal relationship with Christ
you need to spend time with God *alone*. I realise, of course, that for
some, the finding of a quiet place to pray is almost an impossibility.
Those who live in overcrowded homes, or share a room with a non-
Christian in a college or university, will find it difficult to find a
private spot in which to pray. Difficult, but not always impossible.
It's amazing how the Lord leads His children towards appropriate
private spots and places once He sees within them a desire for
intimacy with Himself.

REFLECTION: Try to find a place to pray without distractions.

15 WAYS TO A MORE EFFECTIVE PRAYER LIFE

The secret chamber

'Hannah was praying in her heart ...' 1 Samuel 1:13

A commuter who was the only Christian in a large family said, 'As soon as the train pulls out of the station I climb the stairs in my soul to the sacred chamber of my imagination where I picture myself meeting with the Lord Jesus.' Admittedly it took him some time to learn the secret, but with patience and perseverance you, too, can learn to build a chapel in your soul. It's astonishing how real a secret chamber can be, built within the heart by imagination and consecrated thought.

Charles de Foucauld lived a hermit's life in the deserts of North Africa. He was sometimes invited by the French officers to their Mess where the officers told stories that passed the bounds of propriety. Rather than leave the Mess he learned to sit still and withdraw into the secret chamber of his soul. When he was asked if he felt upset by some of the stories passed around he said he never heard them because he was in his own 'oratory'. That kind of oratory any man or woman can, with determination, build within his or her own soul.

It should not be forgotten, also, by those whose prayer life is hindered because of lack of privacy, that it is always possible to go for a walk with Jesus. Christmas Evans, one of Wales' greatest preachers, tells of walking along the base of Mount Snowdon one evening and entering into such a spiritual tête-à-tête with the Lord that it transformed his whole being.

REFLECTION: It is possible to be alone with the Lord in the midst of a crowd.

Relaxed and receptive

'Then King David went in and sat before the LORD ...'
1 Chronicles 17:16

Y ou will not go far in prayer if you approach it with a tense
spirit as though you were going to force God to give you
what you ask. The spirit of prayer should be what someone
described as 'alert passivity'. Alert passivity means that while your
spiritual, mental and physical sensibilities are awake and alert to
God yet they are relaxed and receptive. In order to put yourself
in an attitude of alert passivity you must first begin with the body.
So take a moment to relax physically.

As the body becomes tied up with physical tensions so the mind
becomes tied up with mental tensions. Learn to focus your mind on
God. Draw from Him the strength and power you need. See yourself
linked to Him through the sacrifice of His Son on Calvary. He is
your God and you are His child. You are an heir of God and a joint
heir with Christ. To every cell of your being, say, 'I put you at God's
disposal. He is now in every cell, bathing them with His gentleness,
reinforcing every weakness, coordinating all parts and making them
into a beautiful whole.' And to the nerves: 'O nerves, the carrier
of so many negative messages, I now set you to work on the job of
reporting better news – your God comes, comes with the good news
of calm, poise, confidence and redemption.' Open every door of your
being to Christ – give Him all the keys and He will come in.

**REFLECTION: It is difficult to be spiritually receptive if we
are physically or mentally tense.**

The high-water mark

'God is love.' 1 John 4:8

Three things are told us in Scripture concerning the nature of God. First, 'God is *spirit*' (John 4:24), which means He has no visible substance. Second, 'God is *light*' (1 John 1:5), which means no darkness can dwell in Him. In Scripture darkness stands for sin, evil, death, and so on. Third, 'God is *love*', which means the energy that flows out from His Being is that of infinite, eternal beneficence. The text 'God is love' has been used as a slick statement yet often without much understanding of its meaning.

When John wrote the words 'God is love' it was the first time in history that the declaration had been made. People had believed that God was love, and had speculated about His benevolence, but now the categorical statement is laid down for all to see. These words, in my judgment, are the high-water mark of divine revelation; nothing more needs to be said for nothing greater can be said. Often I create a mental picture for myself of the angels peering down from heaven as John wrote those words and then, when they had been written, I imagine them breaking into rapturous applause and saying to each other, 'They've got it. They've got it! At last they see that God is love.' And a sigh of deep satisfaction and great joy would have filled the portals of heaven because the greatest truth about God had now been made crystal clear. The implied was now inscribed.

REFLECTION: Read Ephesians 3:14–19 – and use this as a prayer for yourself and for others.

The cross's magnetism

'But I, when I am lifted up from the earth, will draw all men to myself.' John 12:32

Focusing on the fact that God is love causes our own love to flame in response. Seeing the love God has for us, our own heart responds with love. We give love for love. We cannot help it. Let's be done with the idea that love for God is something we work at. It is expressed in good works, of course, but it *begins* in contemplation of how much we are loved. Often I tell people that they cannot love until they have been loved, and they cannot serve until they have been served. We love because God *first* loved us. Our souls must receive love before they can give out love.

Those who did not receive much love from their parents may protest and say, 'I can't love God because my soul was never properly prepared to love; my parents didn't love me.' That is a problem, I agree. However, it is not an insoluble problem. No one who stands at Calvary and sees Jesus dying for them on that tree can ever argue that because they were not loved by their parents they cannot now receive God's love. If they really believe that then they are saying that God's love is obstructed by the adverse influences of human conditioning. God's love will flow into us only if we let it and if we really want it. To desire it is like the touch of the hand on a roller blind; instantly the spring rolls up the blind and the sunlight flows in.

REFLECTION: Just to really *want* God's love is enough; He will do the rest.

A prod towards perfection

'... what does the LORD your God ask of you but to fear the LORD your God ...?' Deuteronomy 10:12

T he *first* thing God called Israel to do when He announced that they were to be His special people and live the way He wanted them to live was not to love Him, serve Him or keep His commandments, but to *fear* Him. Loving Him, serving Him and keeping His laws were of great importance, of course, but the very first thing God asks of them is reverence and fear. How does all this relate to the love of God – the essence of His nature? When thinking about God, it is wise to see love and holiness as intertwined; not to do so can lead sometimes to serious error.

Many in today's Church present the love of God in such a way that it has given rise to the saying 'God loves me as I am.' When I have heard people say this and have questioned them, I have found the idea in many minds is this: 'God loves me as I am, and whether I go on from here or I stay the same, it makes no difference to His love for me.' That is entirely true, but it is not the entire *truth*. Because God is love, He loves us as we are, but because He is love and He is holy, He loves us too much to let us stay as we are. We can be secure in the fact that God loves us just the way we are, but the holy love of God calls us to move ever closer to Him, and cries out, 'Be holy, because I am holy' (Lev. 11:44).

REFLECTION: Could the security I feel as I rest in God's love turn to smugness and complacency? Though I am 'accepted in the Beloved' that doesn't mean God doesn't want me to come closer.

Doubts about the faith

'... so that your faith .... may be proved genuine and may result in praise, glory and honour ...' 1 Peter 1:7

There was a time – a dark period in my Christian life – when I had serious doubts about the faith myself. Then I read this: 'Doubt is the other side of faith. No one should worry if there are doubts. They are messages that tell us to turn the coin and we will find the other side to be true.' That statement brought about a revolution in my soul. The more I pondered it the more I came to see that I should not worry about my doubts but see them as the vestibule through which I must pass in order to enter the temple of truth. What destroys faith is our unwillingness to confront our doubts and allowing them to harden into unbelief.

First we see that doubts are the common experience of most Christians. We must accept the fact that doubts will come, and not think them to be a sign that we do not have faith. Second, Satan is a tempter. The art of doubting is natural to us in our fallen condition, but Satan often works on our doubts and tempts us to unbelief. Third, we must continue to believe in the face of our doubts and pray. Fourth, it takes time to overcome some doubts and this is why perseverance is a quality that every Christian must cultivate. George Macdonald said, 'A man can be haunted by doubts and find that he grows thereby because of them.'

REFLECTION: It may not be everyone's experience, but it has certainly been mine, that every deep spiritual assurance I have in my soul has been preceded by varying forms of doubt.

When doubts arise

'Consequently, faith comes from hearing the message, and the message is heard through the word of Christ.'
Romans 10:17

Permit me to share with you the way I have dealt with the doubts that have arisen (and sometimes still do) in my Christian life and experience. Whenever doubt comes I remind myself that to doubt is not to sin.

Next, I pray over the matter, asking the Lord to give me His help in overcoming my doubts and using them as stepping-stones to a deeper faith. Just as a bone becomes stronger after it has been broken and knit together again, so as I have prayed over my doubts I have found myself becoming, as Ernest Hemingway put it, 'strong at the broken places'. Finally, I bring all my doubts to the judgment bar of Scripture where God has provided for us so many 'infallible proofs'. My counselling experience has shown me that those who defect from the Christian Church because of doubts are those who have indulged their doubts and have not laid them against the certainties of the Word of God. It is vital for Christians to understand that God has condescended to our weakness by giving us the Holy Scriptures, which are stored with powerful truths and concepts able to quench the fiery darts of the devil. So many Christians complain of spiritual doubt while all the time they do not use the secret weapon which God has put into our hands – His holy and infallible Word.

REFLECTION: When doubts arise, persevere through them by following the principles I have just delineated, that you may become 'strong at the broken places'.

Sharing our faith

*'For Christ's love compels us, because we are convinced
that one died for all, and therefore all died.'*
2 Corinthians 5:14

I have often been asked: 'I have known the presence of God in
my life in a real and vital way, but now, for some reason, it
seems to have ebbed away. Why is this?' There could be many
reasons, but I have often found that a major cause is a failure to
share what they know of God with others. If there is no outflow, the
inflow automatically stops. It is a law of life that whatever is not used
atrophies or dies.

Professor Henry Drummond talks about some fish caught in the
dark waters of the Manunoth Caves in Kentucky, USA, in which
it was found that although they had eyes, they could not really see.
No one quite knows how they got into the caves, but there in the
darkness, where no natural light ever penetrated, eyesight became
superfluous. Now, of course, we must not push this too far and
suggest that if we do not work at sharing God's love and presence
with others, we will lose our salvation, because that is not what
Scripture teaches. It is a fact, however, that the more we share what
we have received, the more we will have to share. In my teenage
years I was challenged by Revelation 22:17, 'The Spirit and the bride
say, "Come!" And let him who hears say, "Come!"'. When I read it,
the Spirit said to me: 'You have been a hearer – now say "Come".' I
went out and won my first soul to Christ.

REFLECTION: Don't be a hearer only.

Four steps in sharing

'We are therefore Christ's ambassadors, as though God were making his appeal through us. We implore you on Christ's behalf: Be reconciled to God.' 2 Corinthians 5:20

Many people are hesitant to share the love and presence of God with others because they do not know how to go about it. The best salesmen act as though the thing they are selling is of great importance to them and they do not push too hard, for they know this might produce an unfavourable reaction. I dislike exceedingly the idea of 'selling religion' but we can learn four simple steps in their approach when explaining our faith: 1. What is it? 2. What will it do for you? 3. Who says so? 4. How can you get it? I commend these four steps to those of you who find difficulty in sharing with others what God has shared with you.

What is it? First, clear away misconceptions and point out what it is not. It is not being joined to a religion, but being joined to a Person – Christ. What will it do for you? You will find forgiveness, freedom, reality, a sense of inner unity and of 'coming home'. Who says so? Christ does – through His Word and through the testimony of multitudes of His followers. How can you get it? By repenting of sin – not just wrong habits and actions, but the basic sin of self-dependency – depending on self rather than on God. I recommend these four questions as a framework for sharing Christ with others. They have worked for me and for many others. I have a conviction they may also work for you.

REFLECTION: We must be careful not to present Christ as a commodity but as our loving Lord and sacrificial Saviour.

What a tranquilliser!

'I have loved you with an everlasting love ...' Jeremiah 31:3

H ow little real love there is for God,' comments Arthur W. Pink, a noted theologian. He suggests that the reason for this, and the resulting low level of spirituality in today's Church, is that our hearts are so little occupied with thoughts of the divine love. Since God is eternal, it follows that His love also is eternal. This means that God loved us before earth and heaven were called into existence. This is the truth proclaimed in Ephesians 1:4–5, where we are told that we were chosen in Christ before the creation of the world. What a tranquilliser this is for our hearts! If God's love for you had no beginning then it has no ending either. It is from 'everlasting to everlasting'.

Another thing we need to know about the love of God is that it is a *holy* love. This means that His love is not regulated by whim or caprice or sentiment, but by principle. Just as His grace reigns not at the expense of righteousness but 'through' it (Rom. 5:21), so His love never conflicts with His holiness. This is why John says that God is *light* before he says that God is *love*. And this is why, too, the Almighty never lets us go unchanged. He loves us too much for that. His love is pure, holy and unmixed with maudlin sentimentality. God will not wink at sin, not even in His own people.

REFLECTION: 'The better we are acquainted with His love – its character, its fullness, its blessedness – the more will our hearts be drawn out in love to Him' (Arthur W. Pink).

Made in His image

'So God created man in his own image ...' Genesis 1:27

The pattern God followed when He made the first human pair was 'in our image'. Mankind was unlike anything that had ever been created before. Nowhere do we read that God put His image in the beasts or any other part of creation. No other animal in creation could relate as God relates, think as God thinks, feel as God feels and choose as God chooses. Only human beings have the image of God written into their very constitution. God took dust in His hands and as a result we bear the divine image. No other creatures of God are handmade. We are unique. It means we are superior to all other creatures. And no other creature was told to rule over anything. To put it in its simplest form, being made in God's image means that when the Almighty designed the first human pair, He saw something of Himself reflected in them.

'God created us', said Philip Yancey, 'so that when he looked upon us he would see reflected something of himself.' But just *how* are we like God? God is a being who relates, thinks, feels and chooses. These same capacities were written into Adam and Eve at their creation. They could relate like God, think like God, feel like God and choose like God. They were limited, of course, in the expression of these abilities (only God is unlimited), but the possession of these four characteristics constitutes the essence of the divine image.

REFLECTION: Surely it is one of the most staggering truths in the whole of the Bible that we are made in God's image.

Designed to relate

'The Lᴏʀᴅ God said, "It is not good for the man to be alone. I will make a helper suitable for him."' Genesis 2:18

Men and women have been so designed that they are capable of entering into a relationship with God and with one another. The very first person to whom Adam related after his creation was God. However, God points out something that was *not* good. Adam seemed perfectly secure in his singleness. We never read of him making any complaint that he was lonely. But in order for God's image to be fully revealed in him as a relational being, he needed someone like himself to whom he could relate – someone with skin on! God has designed us to relate not only on a level with Him but also on a level with other human beings. After Adam had named all the animals, it would have occurred to him that for every animal in creation there was a mate. Was it at that moment, I wonder, that he began to realise something was missing in his relationships – that no matter how well he related to the animals, he was created for another type of relationship, a far superior one, with someone like himself?

The moment Eve was created and brought to Adam was the moment the image of God as a relational being was for the first time seen on the earth. Adam now had someone to whom he could relate on the same level as himself, someone he could speak to, see, and touch. The image of God as a relational being was complete.

REFLECTION: Adam was designed to relate not only to God but also to someone like himself – a thinking, choosing, feeling being – with skin on!

Maturity in marriage

'... we will no longer be infants ...' Ephesians 4:14

David Mace said, 'There are no unhappy marriages – only marriage partners who are immature.' Many people go into marriage hoping that in some way it will help them overcome their emotional immaturity. But marriage, in itself, doesn't solve our emotional problems. It merely gives them a new arena in which to work. An emotionally immature person is not suddenly made mature upon entering marriage. Those magic words spoken at the altar do not suddenly make you grow up emotionally. One of life's tragedies is the fact that people grow up physically and reach the age when they can legally be married but they never grow up in their emotions. Such a person is still a child whose life is characterised by sheer childishness, selfishness, temper tantrums, or I-want-what-I-want-when-I-want-it attitudes. This is why it is often said, you are not really ready to be happily married to another person until you are happily married to yourself! One of the basic traits of a mature person is being able to control his emotions whatever they may be, and not let the emotions control him.

The apostle Paul advises in 1 Corinthians 13:11 '... when I became a man, I put away childish things' (NKJV). The English words 'put away' in this text come from a Greek work *katageo* which means to disconnect or render inoperative. You move towards greater maturity in your emotional life when you *make up your mind* to stop acting childishly and deal with life's issues on a more adult level.

REFLECTION: Becoming mature involves many aspects of life but often boils down to one element – a decision.

The love of Jesus

'When they hurled their insults at him, he did not retaliate; when he suffered, he made no threats. Instead, he entrusted himself to him who judges justly.' 1 Peter 2:23

In our Lord's heart burned and blazed a love that needed no self-protection. Thus He continually exposed Himself to the possibility of His love being unreciprocated. How could Jesus love so well? What was His secret of being able to move towards others without self-protection? The relationship He had with His Father made Him the most secure man who ever lived. He never had an identity crisis. He knew who He was, why He was here, and also that, though He could not depend on the love of other human beings He could rest securely in His Father's love – a love that would never be taken away. Thus, He could move towards others in the knowledge that though they might hurt Him, they could not destroy Him. The strength of His Father's love flowing through Him enabled Him to keep on loving. The love that flowed towards Him on a horizontal level might be tainted with failure but not the love that came down to Him from above. Relationships are the clearest window through which we can look to see the condition of our souls; relationships can speak to us about how deeply we are trusting God.

What is true about our heart's direction with another human being will reveal what our hearts truly feel towards God: confident trust or constricting self-protection?

REFLECTION: Do you relate to God and others on the basis of a trust in Him to look after your deepest welfare so that you are free to fully love others as Jesus loved?

Be yourself

'But the fruit of the Spirit is love, joy, peace, patience, kindness, goodness, faithfulness, gentleness and self-control.' Galatians 5:22–23

There is no one else in the world who can present the gospel to others in exactly the same way that you can. God doesn't want you to be another Billy Graham or a Luis Palau. He wants you to be yourself. You are as different from anyone else as one blade of grass from another, and, for that reason, you are most attractive and effective when you are yourself. To be real is to be attractive, and you are least attractive when you try to be somebody else.

When I say 'be yourself', I am not saying that you take no steps to improve yourself. We owe it to God to change our bad habits for good ones, and to allow the fruit of the Spirit to be revealed in our lives and characters. Do you have the personality of an extrovert? Fine. Use it for God, but watch that you don't become overbearing and manipulative. Are you an introvert? That's fine too. But work on improving your conversational and relationship skills. One preacher put it: 'No matter how clear or obscure your message, your personality shines through.' So learn to rest in God, and recognise that as His life flows through the particular temperament and individuality which He has given you, you can share the faith with others in a unique and wonderful way.

REFLECTION: God can pour His truth into us all as we are; and as we each contribute our own uniqueness, anointed by the Holy Spirit, He will produce a composite picture of His love and purpose for the world.

The value of time

'Don't waste your time on useless work ...'
Ephesians 5:11, The Message

We must not become obsessive about it, but our lives will be lived with greater effectiveness for God if we learn to value the minutes, the hours and the days the Almighty gives us. This resolve must become an integral part of our daily thinking: 'Time is valuable and I dedicate myself to spending my time as wisely as possible to the glory of God.' The Christian who wants to make the best use of his or her time must have a keen awareness of its value. The reason time should be regarded with great importance is that it is God-given. We all have the same amount of time. God gives it to all, equally. Time cannot be bought, no matter how rich you are. And no matter how poor, you won't receive less. Every one of us has sixty minutes to the hour, twenty-four hours to the day and seven days per week.

However, perhaps the greatest reason why time should not be wasted is because it is irrevocable. I noticed this advertisement: 'Lost, yesterday, somewhere between sunrise and sunset, two golden hours, each set with sixty diamond minutes. No reward, they are gone forever.' Someone said: 'Yesterday is a cancelled cheque. Tomorrow is a promissory note. Today is the only cash you have. Spend it wisely.' So budget your time. The best way to use money is by budgeting. It is the same with time.

REFLECTION: If we plan each day with God, then we won't need to spend so much time fretfully re-examining our decisions. After all, time is not ours, but His.

Dealing with pain

'... Christ suffered for you, leaving you an example ... When they hurled their insults at him, he did not retaliate ...'
1 Peter 2:21–23

How do Christians deal with pain? They are like the apple trees which, when slashed produce finer and bigger apples. 'For some reason', said a horticulturalist, 'the trees bear better fruit when slashed and wounded in this way. So we slash them into added fruitfulness.' So, my dear Christian friend, remember, the next time you are on the receiving end of an unpleasant situation or event, the 'slash' can become a reason for greater fruitfulness. Are you, at this moment, a victim of someone's bitter and sarcastic tongue? It hurts, doesn't it? One can retaliate, of course, but recrimination is no way forward: it only increases the bitterness. Here's a better way – if you can do it: let the tongue-lashing slash you into fruitfulness.

Let no one think that what I am advocating is easy. No one likes to be treated with sarcasm and contempt. But the nearer we get to the spirit of Jesus Christ, and the more closely we inspect the principles of Scripture, the more we discover that there is a *better* way than retaliation – the way of making events make us. We may feel the pain, but instead of wasting it in revenge or self pity, we accept it and let it help us become better in character and conduct and more like Jesus. Pain that has no purpose in it is fruitless, it simply ends in suffering – and no more. But pain which has a purpose contributes to the growth of the personality and greater spiritual fruitfulness.

REFLECTION: Our reaction to pain can make us better or bitter.

Managing the emotions

'In your anger do not sin ...' Ephesians 4:26

J ust like a warning light in a car, problem emotions such as anger, fear and guilt signal that some maintenance work is needed and we need to look at what is going on inside us. Here are a few suggestions I have found helpful for dealing with problem emotions. First, face and feel your emotions. Don't pretend they are not there. Christians struggle with this issue because Christian teaching says we should put away things like anger, lust and malice (Col. 3:5–10). Whenever we experience these feelings, because we wish they were not there, we can so easily deny their presence. But you can't begin to deal with any negative emotion unless you first admit that it exists. Second, discover the cause. Whenever a problem emotion arises in your life – anxiety and fear, guilt and shame, anger and resentment – ask yourself such questions as these: 'What is the possible goal that is being thwarted in my life at this time? What is the actual block to that goal?'

Wise Christians understand that negative emotions tell them something about themselves. They allow their emotions to alert them to the need for some fundamental changes in what they are pursuing. Third, decide to express emotions in harmony with biblical principles. This does not mean giving free reign to feelings, 'letting it all hang out'. Maturity means managing those feelings so that they are expressed appropriately. You have God's promise of help in this. Draw on it.

REFLECTION: **Emotions may influence us, but they should not rule us.**

Being in relationships

'If it is possible, as far as it depends on you, live at peace with everyone.' Romans 12:18

To be is to be in relationships. We come to a sense of our identity, who we are, in a relationship. Clyde Narramore says, 'We don't know who we are until we know whose we are.' To be fully human and fully alive we must know something of how to relate. Our maturity as Christians is best seen in the way we relate. I know people who thought they were spiritually mature because they knew their Bibles well. They could quote Scripture and knew the answers to many of the questions put to them about the Bible, but they were not good at relating, and hence they were immature. The core of our maturity as Christians is visible in the way we relate.

'Christianity', says one author, 'is probably compromised more in our relationships than any other thing.' God uses people to help refine people. God wants to make us like Jesus, and one of the ways He goes about doing that is to put us with people who might rub us the wrong way. The finishing touches will be made when we see Christ, but the major shaping of our characters takes place here and now – through our relationships. Do you realise that the people you work with and relate to are handpicked by the Lord to expose your temper, your pride, your stubbornness and so on? Make a list of all the people you don't get along with and ask yourself, 'What is God trying to show me about myself through them?'

REFLECTION: Where do we find a better place to put into operation the principles of Scripture than in close relationships?

Existing for non-members

'The Lord's message rang out from you ... your faith in God has become known everywhere.' 1 Thessalonians 1:8

Many churches today resemble the local golf club. Their common interest of course happens to be God rather than golf, but they see themselves as religious people doing religious things together. They concentrate on the benefits of membership and have never understood, as Archbishop William Temple said, that 'the Church is the only co-operative society in the world which exists for the benefit of its non-members'. Temple was using a hyperbole of course as he would be the first to agree that Christians do have a responsibility to each other to love one another and encourage one another. But, that said, far too many churches are totally introverted.

One writer I came across who has his finger on the pulse of 21st-century charismatic Christianity said, 'For many people today church is about (1) obtaining financial prosperity, (2) securing a personal 'breakthrough' and (3) finding the key to getting your prayers answered.' He added, 'I'm amazed we don't end up every service by singing four verses of "It's all about me, Lord, it's all about me".' I have said before that if the local church had done its job in the way it should be done then large areas of the world would be evangelised by now. What an indictment that is against us and how it ought to send us to our knees in fervent believing prayer for God to deepen our passion for souls and give the world the impression that in the Father's house there is not just bread, but enough to spare.

REFLECTION: Ask God to deepen your passion for souls.

Extravagant love

'Then Mary took a pint of pure nard, an expensive perfume; she poured it on Jesus' feet and wiped his feet with her hair.' John 12:3

The reason Jesus said the story of Mary and the outpoured perfume would be told everywhere for all time (Matt. 26:13), I believe, is because He wants to keep drawing our attention to the fact that the most important thing in our lives is not our grasp of doctrine, important though that is, but how passionate we are in our love for Him. The scribes and Pharisees were of all people the most highly educated in the Scriptures at that time. They believed God's Word and taught many of the right things, priding themselves on their strict adherence to the Old Testament Law, and yet the picture dear to Jesus, the one He held close to His heart, the one that brought a tear to His eye and a smile to His face as He moved towards the cross, was that of Mary. Because, I reiterate, what touches Jesus' heart is not so much what we know but how much we love. The scribes and Pharisees were fighting over theology but Mary was kneeling at His feet. And that to Him was beautiful. That's why this story of Mary has its place in the Word of God. And He said, '… wherever this gospel is preached … what she has done will also be told …' (Matt. 26:13).

As far as we know, Mary never did very much: she didn't cast out demons like the disciples, she never worked miracles. All she did was to love the Saviour and it was the way she loved Him that made the difference: she loved Him passionately, extravagantly, lavishly.

REFLECTION: How much will it cost you to abandon your inhibited approach, to be extravagant and say, 'Lord, I love You!'?

No denial of reality

"'For I know the plans I have for you," declares the LORD ...'
Jeremiah 29:11

I have concluded that there are three things in our lives of which we need to become aware and repent, if necessary on a daily basis. The first is our failure to trust God's love. Instead of basking in the security that His love brings us we turn to others. If love is not forthcoming from them, we are not above manipulating them to give us the love that really we ought to be drawing from God. A second thing is our failure to believe God's evaluation of our worth. In Christ God esteems us as being equal to His Son for we are called Christ's brothers (Heb. 2:11–12). Sadly, far too often we fail to believe the worth we have in Christ by God's grace and through faith in Him.

The third thing we need to be ready to repent of is our failure to see any meaning or purpose in our lives. When we stop seeing our life from God's point of view – an eternal perspective – then we begin to wonder how much purpose there is to our being in this world. God has a purpose for every life. You are a person of destiny no matter how things may appear to you. If you are a Christian, the Spirit of God is at work in your life, making you different from every other Christian in the universe.

Not to believe these three things is a denial of reality. When we move away from accepting them repentance is the only way back.

REFLECTION: There is a point to your being here on this earth, and there is something God wants to achieve through you – something He can achieve through you alone.

Practise faith

'Master, we've worked hard all night and haven't caught anything. But because you say so, I will let down the nets.'
Luke 5:5

One great writer on the subject of prayer, said: 'A person's prayer life is only as strong as that person's faith in God.' Because faith is essential to effective praying we must put this important word under the spiritual microscope and examine it in detail. Faith is simply trust – it is confidence in the ability of God to do what He promises to do in His Word. Corrie Ten Boom labels faith as a 'fantastic adventure in trusting Him'. The dictionary defines faith as 'trust in the honesty and truth of another'. If we are to be effective in prayer then we must believe. God is honest in what He says in the Bible. The Bible contains many references to faith. There is saving faith spoken of by Paul in Ephesians 2:8. There is the 'gift of faith' again spoken by Paul in 1 Corinthians 12:9.

The great apostle also speaks in Ephesians of the 'unity in the faith' (Eph. 4:13). The faith of which I am now speaking, however, is what some describe as *simple* faith – the innate ability to *trust*. John Bisagno, speaking of simple faith, says, 'Don't get the idea that if you can only muster more faith, you will be effective in prayer. Faith is not some mysterious commodity to be sought after. You do not need more faith: you need to learn to appropriate the faith you already have ...' Faith can be described as follows: it is the willingness to act on God's Word with complete abandonment and total trust.

REFLECTION: We do not need great faith in God, we need a little mustard seed of faith in a great God.

Faith and prayer

'And without faith it is impossible to please God ...'
Hebrews 11:6

God delights in faith. The Scripture says, '... anyone who comes to him must believe that he exists and that he rewards those who earnestly seek him' (Heb. 11:6). The greatest thing we can do to please God is believe Him! I have suggested earlier that it is important to read the Word of God before we pray, but another reason for this is because the reading of God's Word quickens our faith. 'Faith cometh by hearing,' says Paul, 'and hearing by the word of God' (Rom. 10:17, AV).

God's Word produces faith, and faith produces power for prayer. Prayer, faith and the Word of God are directly related. They strengthen one another. So when you pray, begin to exercise the muscles of your faith by committing yourself more and more to what God has promised you in His Word. Step out in faith, as Peter did on the water. You may feel yourself sinking at times, but don't worry – the Lord will be on hand to deliver you. The more you exercise your faith the more expert you will become in the art of prayer. You see it is not enough to simply ask God for things, we must *believe* for them also. Jesus said, 'Therefore I tell you, whatever you ask for in prayer, believe that you have received it, and it will be yours' (Mark 11:24). If you are sure that what you ask is according to God's Word then don't just ask for it, *believe* for it.

REFLECTION: The initiative is in heaven. Only your unbelief can stop it coming out.

Goodness and mercy

'Surely goodness and mercy shall follow me ...'
Psalm 23:6, NKJV

A s I look back over my life, I can remember many events which I viewed at the time as calamities. I can recollect one particular occasion – during 1968 – when, as I looked forward into the future, things looked so black that I considered leaving the ministry. Now, with hindsight, I can see that the hour of darkness was one of the great turning-points in my life, and moved me, not toward a lesser ministry, but a wider one. Goodness and mercy followed me, and turned what looked like despair into a door of greater opportunity. Such is God's skill at turning tragedy to triumph that He brings good out of evil. It is my belief that God does not engineer what we might describe as 'calamities' or 'disasters', but that they happen as the consequence of sin, ignorance or carelessness.

'Many a life', says one writer, 'has been saved by the *Titanic*. The track of westbound ships across the Atlantic was shifted further south, away from the dangerous icefields, and the obsolete Board of Trade requirements with regard to emergency lifeboat accommodation were stringently revised.' This is often the way it is in life – disappointment, tragedy and grief teach people a great deal. In the Christian life, however, this is not often the way it is – but always the way it is. God follows hard on the heels of every event and circumstance in our lives, not only teaching us a great deal, but working to turn every loss into a gain.

REFLECTION: God's goodness and mercy is greater than any trouble that may befall us.

JUNE 29

But God

'Surely goodness and mercy shall follow me ...'
Psalm 23:6, NKJV

D avid's phrase is an utterance of faith. It can be said only by
someone who looks beyond the events and circumstances
of life and has implicit confidence in the One who is
ultimately in control. David believed that no difficulty or dilemma
could come into his life without eventual good emerging from
the chaos. If you can get hold of this truth and absorb it into your
life as a working principle, then it will transform your attitude to
everything. Never again will you be at the mercy of circumstances.
In Acts 5:40–41 we read an astonishing statement: '... when they had
called in the apostles, they beat them ... Then they left the presence
of the council, rejoicing ...' (RSV). Rejoicing? Over injustice? How
is it possible to rejoice over an injustice? Because they believed,
with David, that the last word was not with men, but with God –
'goodness and mercy' would follow them and turn the situation
to their advantage. When you can rejoice over injustice, you are
indomitable.

Another verse from Acts reads thus: 'Because the patriarchs were
jealous of Joseph, they sold him as a slave into Egypt. But God ...'
(Acts 7:9). That phrase, 'but God', is at the end of every injustice – He
has the last word. And just as God used the injustice done to Joseph
to feed the Egyptian people and his own family, so He transforms
every injustice, every sorrow, every bereavement, every tragedy.

**REFLECTION: Christianity may not explain everything, but it
most certainly transforms everything.**

I'll never leave

'... and I will dwell in the house of the LORD for ever'.
Psalm 23:6

The thought that comes through in this final phrase of the psalm is clearly this – I am so utterly contented with being under the care of my loving Shepherd that I have no wish to have my circumstances changed – I want things to stay this way forever! Phillip Keller's rugged translation of this final phrase may offend the purists, but to me it states fairly accurately what was in the psalmist's mind. 'Nothing will ever make me leave this outfit! It's great!' And to that I add a hearty Amen!

Dr E. Stanley Jones, when referring to the subject of life after death, remarked: 'Only life that is eternal is really life: every other kind of life has the seeds of death in it.' George Bernard Shaw once said, 'I don't want to have to live with George Bernard Shaw for ever.' We can hardly blame some people for not wanting to live with themselves for ever, because they are poor companions to themselves now. A lot of people dislike themselves, and thus to spend eternity with a self you dislike is not a happy prospect. But suppose you have a self that is transformed into the image of Christ – and not only changed into His image, but joined to Him inseparably – what then? Ah – that is different! That is more than existence – that is life. Remember, eternity is not just living for ever – it is living with Jesus forever. That's what makes the difference.

REFLECTION: Eternal existence is only desirable because it will be in the presence of eternal love.

More effective prayer

'... when you pray ...' Matthew 6:5

A new convert to Christianity said that whenever he got down on his knees and tried to talk with God his mind went blank. As a result he was growing increasingly frustrated in relation to the matter of personal prayer. I explained that our rate of progress in the Christian life is greatly determined by our power *in* prayer. If we don't pray then we don't grow spiritually – it's as simple as that. The important thing is to develop a system or an approach to prayer that is suited to your temperament and personality. There is no way to get on in the Christian life without the disciplined practice of prayer. The way to grow 'in Christ' is to talk with Him: to talk with Him daily and to talk with Him for more than just a few moments.

Some use printed prayers. Others memorise a sequence of words which they use at the beginning and the end of the day. Others, convinced that prayer is only meaningful when it is spontaneous, pray only when they *feel* like praying. But the most important practice of the Christian life cannot be left to the unpredictability of feeling. Every Christian needs to establish for themselves a systematic approach to prayer – one that is simple and uncomplicated yet flexible enough to allow for individual spiritual growth. When you pray you are like an electric bulb in the socket, full of life and power. When you don't pray, you are like that bulb out of the socket – lifeless.

REFLECTION: If you know how to pray you know how to live, if not then you merely exist.

Breathe a prayer for help

'... but Satan stopped us.' 1 Thessalonians 2:18

When a tiger attacks a victim the first objective is to slit the throat of his victim with his sharp claw. When the victim is no longer able to breathe, he is finished. Satan, the enemy of our souls, seeks above all to cut off our spiritual breathing because he knows that when this is accomplished we die of our own accord. As you seek to develop greater prayer effectiveness be alert to the fact that the devil will do everything in his power to discourage you and divert your attention to other things. He doesn't mind how many committees you sit on, how many sermons you preach, how much evangelistic literature you pass out, how many meetings you attend, providing you spend little or no time in prayer.

So, send up a little prayer right now, asking God to help you see that you are beginning something which will make all the difference between weakness and strength, between defeat and victory. You will find that the more you pray the more you grow in spiritual things. You can never be better in life than you are faithful in prayer. We can do more than we think and accomplish things beyond our abilities when we pray. Many Christians think of themselves as reservoirs with a fixed capacity, but if we are men and women who give ourselves to prayer then we are more than reservoirs – we are rivers. We are attached to infinite resources and therefore we have boundless possibilities.

REFLECTION: Prayer tones up the whole life. If prayer lags, life sags.

Establish a definite time

'Very early in the morning ... Jesus ... prayed.' Mark 1:35

S ome Christians complain that their busy lives leave them no time to pray, but as it has been said, 'If you are too busy to pray, then you are busier than God intended you to be.' So build a fence around a certain part of the day and reserve it for contact with God through prayer. The best time to pray is in the morning when your mind is fresh and the day is still before you. The psalmist said, '... in the morning I lay my requests before you and wait in expectation' (Psa. 5:3). Don't try to find a time for prayer – *make* time. If you go through the day trying to fit a prayer time into your schedule you will fail. Make it the first priority after you awake from sleep to keep a prayer appointment with the Lord. We need not, and should not, limit our prayers to such appointed moments with God. We can pray anywhere – in the street, on the way to work, travelling in a bus or train. But these spontaneous and unpremeditated prayers must be seen as *extras*.

Growth and development in the Christian life demand firmness with ourselves in relation to fixed and definite times for prayer. Those who practise daily contact with God through prayer are often amazed how easily they transcend worries and fears and resentments, and live on a higher, more positive, level. The answer is quite simple: it's the result of being shut in with God.

REFLECTION: When we deprive ourselves of a regular contact with God through prayer we remove ourselves from the power that makes for effective Christian living.

Lifted by prayer

'... O LORD; you bestow glory on me and lift up my head.'
Psalm 3:3

A traveller tells of journeying through the Panama Canal. He says, 'The great sea gates were closed upon us. We, who had sailed the oceans, were blocked, shut in, helpless, our freedom gone. But lo, we felt a great lifting, great fountains were opened up from beneath, and to our astonishment that great ship was lifted 35 feet in just seven minutes. Then the gates opened and we glided out on a higher level, out on the bosom of Lake Gatun.' The morning prayer appointment does that – it shuts you in with God, the door closes upon you and you seem so enclosed, so helpless. And then God's infinite resources begin to bubble up from within, you are lifted silently, powerfully, effortlessly, without noise or strain, on to a higher level. The door opens and you glide out on to a higher level of life.

William R. Inge reminds us: 'It is quite natural and inevitable that if we spend an average sixteen hours of our day in thinking about the affairs of the world, and only five minutes in thinking about God ... this world will seem two hundred times more real to us than God.' Blaise Pascal, once declared, 'Nearly all the ills of life spring from this simple source, that we are not able to sit still in a room.' What, if in that stillness we meet with God? Would not all our fears, our hesitancies, our doubts, be hushed in the quiet of God?

REFLECTION: Experience has shown that unless one has a regular organised time for prayer then it loses its energy, its force and its power.

Keep that appointment

'Three times a day he [Daniel] got down on his knees and prayed ...' Daniel 6:10

Y our prayer times will not always be full of vitality and spiritual excitement. At times, prayer can seem like drudgery. If our prayer times were conducted solely on the basis of feeling, then our moments of communion with God would be few and far between. We must learn to pray and keep our appointment with God whether we feel like it or not. If we have an engagement with a friend, or a business appointment, we keep it, regardless of our feelings – sickness or emergencies apart. We would regard someone as lacking in common courtesy if he or she cancelled an engagement with a friend, just because they 'didn't feel like it'. Are we to be less courteous with God?

I have found that one of the most common misunderstandings is the view that prayer is only effective when it arises from an eager and excited heart. Nothing could be further from the truth. Many of the great saints of the past who have written on the subject of prayer believed that great waves of feeling belong only to the early stages of discipleship.

This does not mean, of course, that the higher you rise in the levels of discipleship the less feeling will be involved. It means rather that the more experienced you become in prayer the less dependent you will be on feeling, and the more dependent you will become on faith. Faith, not feeling, measures the efficacy of prayer.

REFLECTION: Faithfulness in prayer produces prayers of faith.

The prayer of Jabez

'Jabez cried out to the God of Israel, 'Oh, that you would bless me and enlarge my territory!' 1 Chronicles 4:10

According to some research one of the least read books of the Bible is the first book of Chronicles. That's because the first nine chapters are taken up with the family tree of the Hebrew tribes. This formidable list of names has made even the bravest of students turn back. Yet, as with all difficult passages of Scripture, there are rewards for pressing through. And one of them is to come across this little known prayer of Jabez which consists of just 29 words. Before it there are names, and after it there are names, but tucked away in between is this amazingly simple but powerful prayer. There was something about Jabez that caused the historian to pause. You can search the Bible and you will not find Jabez mentioned anywhere else. Clearly his prayer caught the attention of the writer of Chronicles: 'Oh, that you would bless me and enlarge my territory.' He was not being selfish in that prayer, he was simply asking for what he believed God wanted to give him.

God is at work in our lives. Don't be afraid to ask Him for things, especially His grace. It's here for the asking – and the taking. Was Jabez' prayer answered? Most definitely. When he asked, God heard his prayer. The following five words are some of the sweetest in the Bible: 'And God granted his request' (v.10). When you ask for needed grace be assured of this: your prayer will always be answered.

REFLECTION: To know that grace is there in abundance is one thing, but to ask for it is another.

Christian realism

'We are hard pressed on every side, but not crushed;
perplexed, but not in despair ...' 2 Corinthians 4:8

This is a tough world – a world still reeling from the effects of the Fall. Not to recognise or understand this means our expectations will be higher than they should be and our disappointments deeper than they need be. The prospect of heaven is something we should always keep before us. It helps us gain a right perspective on everything. Some believe we can have heaven now: 'Health and wealth until the day we die.' This is nonsense, of course, and quite unscriptural. Yes, God does answer prayer in the way we desire and does work miracles – but not always. Sometimes He lets His people suffer. And it is no good saying the ones who suffer have no faith. That is a cop-out. And a cruel cop-out.

The Church needs a theology of suffering to balance its theology of miracles. We live in a world for which we were not designed – hence we experience a marred joy. By that I mean that even in our happiest moments we will experience a degree of sadness that arises from the fact we are in a fallen environment. At our best moments we are aware that what we are experiencing is not the fullness of what we were made for. This is not negative thinking; it is realism. And facing the reality does not diminish the joy; rather, it helps prevent us pretending that what we have is better than it is. This is Christian realism – a factor missing in many sections of today's Church.

REFLECTION: Paul knew there was a better world to come,
and the prospect of that helped to embolden him.

Groaning within ourselves

'... we ourselves ... groan inwardly ...' Romans 8:23

Even the most casual observer of the Christian life ought to be convinced that we were not made for the kind of world in which we live. We were designed for better things. However, because sin has entered this fair creation, we live now in a fallen world. And until that better world comes along we yearn for what we do not have. The apostle Paul tells us that the whole creation groans (Rom. 8:18–27). Everything that lives is subject to disease, death and decay.

Have you sung the hymn 'All things bright and beautiful' recently? It is a lovely hymn but the woman who wrote it was not looking at the whole of creation, just some of it. She was being selective for the purpose of the hymn. However, Paul, when he looked at creation, looked at it as a whole. Some of creation is 'bright and beautiful', but sin has made other parts of it downright ugly. But not only does creation groan; we do also. 'We ourselves,' says the apostle Paul, 'groan inwardly' as we wait for sin and its effects to be banished from the universe. Note it is we who are indwelt by the Spirit who groan in this way. Unbelievers don't share this experience. The Holy Spirit sensitises our souls to the fact that down here there is something wrong with almost everything. It is this groan that keeps us balanced, knowing that perfection cannot be brought about by human methods.

REFLECTION: To have peace and joy and yet groan inwardly is a tension with which Christians have to live.

JULY 9

Comfort from the promise

'You will grieve, but your grief will turn to joy.'
John 16:20

Throughout the Church's history God's people when faced by life's problems have drawn comfort from the promise of heaven. How, for instance, did slaves in America endure their afflictions? The Negro Spirituals, as they are called, give us the clue. They sang often of the prospect of heaven. The promise that one day we will be with Jesus in a perfect world has a powerful effect on our lives in the present and enables us to cope with difficult situations because it gives us that most precious of all ingredients – hope. It is like a doctor saying to a woman in labour, 'Hold on, the baby you long for will soon be in your arms. Now you feel pain but soon you will feel pleasure.' Awaiting us in heaven is a happiness that is beyond description.

Paul longed to get to heaven but because his presence was more necessary on earth he was willing to stay (Phil. 1:23–24). One preacher I heard remarked, 'Paul was eager to go but willing to stay. We are willing to go but eager to stay.' Paul often used the prospect of heaven to help him overcome the trials of this life. Think, for example, of these words: 'I consider that our present sufferings are not worth comparing with the glory that will be revealed in us' (Rom. 8:18). A friend of mine says, 'Here on earth there is something wrong with everything. In heaven there will be nothing wrong with anything.' Here we sojourn; there we belong.

REFLECTION: We will carry out all the work that concerns God's purposes on this earth with skill and thoroughness, because by faith we have the perfect always in view.

Led by the Holy Spirit

'... because those who are led by the Spirit of God are sons of God.' Romans 8:14

In some Christian circles to talk of being guided by the Holy Spirit brings an adverse reaction, as if it were a strange and superstitious thing to be led of God, directly and first-hand. But 'he,' said Jesus, speaking of the Holy Spirit, 'will guide you into all truth' (John 16:13). It is the Spirit who helps to clarify the issues that puzzle us and assists us in seeing clearly the next step we must take. All of us, I am sure, can remember moments in our life when we dropped to our knees in confusion and cried out, 'Lord, what shall I do now?' And all of us too, I imagine, can remember moments when through the Holy Spirit's ministry of guidance that prayer was answered.

Without weakening our personalities and thus making us overly dependent, the divine Counsellor remains at hand to bring clarity and illumination to our minds whenever we need it. That guidance, of course, comes in different ways – through Scripture, through circumstances, through sanctified reasoning or through the Spirit speaking directly to our hearts. But whichever way it comes, the end is always the same – light for the way ahead. If we lose the sense of being led by the Spirit we become victims of our circumstances. Then we are circumstance-directed instead of Spirit-directed. Guidance by the Holy Spirit is the very essence of Christianity because if there is no sense of leadership we will have little sense of God as our Father.

REFLECTION: If we are not being led by God how can we claim to be His sons and daughters?

Mission requires submission

'He guides the humble in what is right and teaches them his way.' Psalm 25:9

A ll of us, as Christians, must walk through the world with a sense of mission. 'The significance of life', I have read, 'is determined by the significance of what it is identified with and what it represents.' A sense of mission brings a sense of submission. Instead of making you proud and cocky it has the opposite effect. You feel awed and humbled. You want to walk softly before God. You are on what has been called 'the adventure of humility'. The whole thought of guidance, whether it is occasional or continuous, strikes at the citadel of the personality and demands the surrender of self-sufficiency. That is why some find the subject of guidance intimidating; they don't like the idea of giving up their independence. If we are to be guided, then there must be a shifting from self-will to God's will (Psa. 25:9). That will, not your own, becomes supreme. God's will becomes your constant frame of reference.

Guidance should not be a spiritual luxury for a few souls; it should be the minimum necessity for every Christian. It gives mission to life. It's surprising how many Christians there are who, though they know God, know little about His guidance, either occasional or continuous. Hence their impact upon life is feeble. Guidance, I say again, is the very essence of Christianity. But the divine Counsellor's concern for us is the same as Christ's concern for His disciples – to guide and not to override.

REFLECTION: God wants to guide us yet at the same time create initiative in us.

Five forms of guidance

'But when he, the Spirit of truth, comes, he will guide you ...' John 16:13

The task facing the Holy Spirit of giving us guidance is similar to that of every thinking and concerned parent. To lead us and at the same time produce initiative in us is a task worthy of divine wisdom. 'Many parents are benevolent tyrants', says a child psychologist whom I know, 'who snuff out all initiative and personality in their children. Guidance must be such that each person is guided into a free, self-conscious, choosing, creative personality.' These are the general routes to guidance: first, guidance according to the character of Christ. We know who God wants us to be like – He wants us to be like His Son. Anything Christ would not do we should not do.

Second, guidance through His Word. He makes the Bible come alive to us, and throws a beam of light on the path ahead. Third, guidance through circumstances – putting us in situations where the circumstances indicate the direction in which we ought to go. Fourth, guidance through the counsel of good and godly people. Fifth, guidance through the direct whispering of the Spirit within us. Some look on this method as strange and mysterious. It is capable of being abused, I admit, but it is a form of guidance that is clearly laid down in Scripture. Some call it 'the inner voice'. However, we must always be sure that the inner voice is the Spirit's voice, not our own voice.

REFLECTION: It is necessary for Christians to receive divine guidance as we make our way through this world because we are carrying out purposes that are not our own.

Know the Spirit's voice

'The Spirit told Philip, "Go to that chariot and stay near it."' Acts 8:29

How do we recognise the voice of the Holy Spirit when He speaks to us? 'My sheep know My voice,' Jesus told His disciples categorically (John 10:3–5). When I go to the telephone and hear my mother's voice, I know immediately who is speaking. I know it is not my sister or my secretary, for I have heard that voice thousands of times during the course of my life. 'Ah,' you say, 'but a voice in your ear is a lot easier to discern than a voice in your soul.' Granted, but there is a way to tune in to the voice of the Spirit and learn to hear His accent in your soul. Train your spiritual ear to *listen*. When the king complained to Joan of Arc that he never heard the voice of God, she replied, 'You must listen, then you will hear.' '... Samuel said, "Speak, for your servant is listening"' (1 Sam. 3:10).

There are two main reasons why people fail to hear the Spirit's voice: their spiritual ears are untrained or they are unwilling. Many of us don't want to listen to the voice of God because we are afraid that if God reveals His will to us, it will be disagreeable. When you commune with God, give as much time to listening as you do to talking. At first you will not be able to distinguish the voice of the subconscious from the voice of the Spirit, but in time the differentiation will be possible.

REFLECTION: Sometimes the Spirit booms so loudly in the soul that His voice is unmistakable. But usually He speaks quietly, and to a soul that sits quietly before Him.

A visit to Korea

'Then the temple of the LORD was filled with a cloud, and the priests could not perform their service ... for the glory of the LORD filled the temple of God.' 2 Chronicles 5:13–14

I n the almost sixty years I have been a Christian I have seen some wonderful things happen and sat through some thrilling meetings. The most memorable of these was in Pusan, South Korea, in the late 1970s. I was conducting a crusade there and was invited to speak at a 5am prayer meeting where I was told 5,000 Christians met to spend time with God before setting out on their day's work. Just after the meeting began the Holy Spirit fell in a way I have not experienced before or since. The Koreans have a wonderful way of what they call 'praying in concert', when everyone prays out loud asking God for whatever is on their hearts. Then after they have prayed they lift their voices in powerful praise.

It was during this prolonged time of praise that I heard a Korean woman speaking words of praise to God in the Welsh language. I clearly understood what she was saying. In perfect Welsh she was praising God in words that when translated said this: 'Thank You, Lord, for the gift of Your salvation ... for giving Your Son for us on the cross of Calvary ... For the gift of Your Holy Spirit ...' and so on. The effect on me was so great that I felt goose bumps coming up on my flesh as I stood surrounded by these thousands of worshipping Koreans, praising God in their own language – and some, no doubt, in other languages inspired by the Spirit as well.

REFLECTION: Have you experienced such an atmosphere of God's presence? Do you long to?

Breath vocalises

'All of them were filled with the Holy Spirit and began to speak in other tongues as the Spirit enabled them ... Then Peter stood up ... raised his voice and addressed the crowd.' Acts 2:4,14

On the Day of Pentecost we are told the disciples were all filled with the Spirit and began to speak ... They were men and women with new voices. The same Spirit enabled the vacillating disciple Simon Peter to stand up and preach a sermon that convinced 3,000 people to become followers of Jesus Christ. Just imagine it – one sermon and 3,000 people are won to Christ. Nowadays, even with the same Spirit available to us, in some places it takes 3,000 sermons to win one soul to Christ!

Christians, someone has said, are like trumpets; they are not much good until breath is blown into them. Certainly the breath of God that blew over Wales in 1904 caused thousands of men and women to lift their voices in praise and glory to God. They would pray and sing God's praises for hours and miners could be heard singing the great hymns of the faith in the cages that carried them from the pit bottom to the surface. It's wonderful to hear some of those hymns still being sung at football matches, but how much more wonderful it would be to see churches filled with men and women who were vocal for God both in both prayer and praise.

The great John Wesley when he lay dying in the East End of London was said to lament the fact that he could no longer travel on horseback across the land using his lungs to preach the glorious gospel of Jesus Christ.

REFLECTION: Could I be more vocal for God both in prayer and praise?

The punctuality of God

'When the day of Pentecost came, they were all together in one place.' Acts 2:1

The timing of God is seen everywhere in Scripture. It's a favourite theme of mine. Not only did Jesus come to Bethlehem on time, but He went to the cross on time also. Jesus revealed Himself in Scripture as a Man with a mission, moving towards a predetermined hour and, as He moved through the world, He seemed to have His eye on an unseen clock. On several occasions, it is reported in Scripture, He declared His time had 'not yet come'. Then there came a time when, 'Jesus ... looked towards heaven, and prayed: "Father, the time has come. Glorify your Son, that your Son may glorify you"' (John 17:1).

He came right on time at Pentecost too. When Jesus went away from this world to take His place at the right hand of His Father, He told His disciples not to leave Jerusalem but to wait there for the gift His Father had promised – baptism with the Holy Spirit. And there they waited. But nothing happened, day after day, until the tenth day when suddenly the Holy Spirit arrived. And 'All of them were filled with the Holy Spirit and began to speak in other tongues as the Spirit enabled them' (Acts 2:4). Why can we say that He arrived at just the right time? Because the tenth day coincided with the Feast of Pentecost, when crowds would be jostling in the streets and filling the Temple. With all this going on in Jerusalem, it was just the right moment for the Holy Spirit to come!

REFLECTION: Have you asked God to come again in power into your life and your church?

Stories of revival

'... more and more men and women believed in the Lord and were added to their number.' Acts 5:14

W hen revival came to Wales in 1904, there was an extraordinary sense of God's presence throughout almost the whole of the Principality and it lingered for some time afterwards. There are stories of blaspheming miners struck down by God's power, and then after surrendering their lives to Christ rising to find that so deep was the work of the Spirit in their hearts they no longer wanted to swear. This sometimes created problems for those who directed the pit ponies that hauled the tiny trucks of coal from the coal face to the cages that came down to the pit bottom, for their instructions to the ponies were often given through swear words. Many of those who were converted in this way tell how they had to teach their horses a new language.

As one wag put it, 'On such occasions down there in the bowels of the earth even the horses knew there was revival!' During the days of the Welsh Revival people could be heard crying out again and again in their native language, 'O God make me clean.' There was a respect for law and order. In the Welsh valleys throughout 1904 crime figures dropped and for some months many magistrates found they had no cases to consider. They were presented with white gloves as a symbol of the 'clean' communities. In the Hebrides revival, men out on the fields, others at their weaving looms, were so overcome by the sense of God that they were found prostrate on the ground.

REFLECTION: Revival, wherever it happens, usually has an ethical overspill into the world.

The body in trouble

'Is any one of you sick? He should call the elders of the church to pray over him and anoint him with oil ...' James 5:14

Today we think about how a physical problem can affect the spirit. I once counselled a woman who felt abandoned by God. But her problem was actually rooted in a physical malfunction. Though the problem was not a spiritual one it had a negative effect on her soul.

Another man I counselled said his spiritual life was being adversely affected by bizarre thoughts which he believed to be the result of attacks by the devil. Again I recommended a medical check-up. This revealed a small tumour which his doctor said was affecting his body's chemistry and consequently the functioning of his brain. The problem was resolved when the tumour was removed.

Let me give you one further illustration. A woman once asked me to pray for her child who had been diagnosed by an evangelist as being 'demon possessed'. Apparently he had raced around the church one night when this evangelist was preaching, and he had declared that the boy must have a demon. I have learned not to jump so readily to conclusions. When I talked to the child I was certain that he was not possessed and once again suggested a medical check-up. The child's doctor diagnosed brain damage which he said was causing hyperactivity. Medical intervention helped to solve this problem too.

We should thank God for medical skill, but not forget to thank Him too for the healing resources of Christ.

REFLECTION: And when we are ill we should also remember that today's text advises us to call on the elders for prayer. It need not be the doctor *or* the Church. It can be both.

Repentance

'Produce fruit in keeping with repentance.' Matthew 3:8

W hat are we to do about our 'wicked ways'? God says we are to *turn* from them. A synonym for the word 'turn' is 'repent'. Some Christians may feel that deciding to discontinue what God calls 'wicked ways' is enough. It is not. Once we admit that we are in need of change in our lives there must be a moment of deep repentance before we can move on in our relationship with God. To recognise something as wrong and resolving not to do it again is good but not good enough. We must take care of past violations by repenting of them. There can be no deep ongoing relationship with the Lord until we know how to act over the wrongs of the past. When our Lord spoke to the church at Ephesus, He reprimanded them because they had left their first love (Rev. 2:4). How was the situation to be corrected? They were to *remember* from where they had fallen, *repent* and *return*. Someone has described this as the Three Rs of Relationship. They were to look back to the position from which they had fallen, repent of it and return to God in deep humility of heart.

The Bible is replete with texts that stress the importance of repentance. People think repentance is feeling sorry for your sins. But that is not what the word is about. The Greek word for repentance is *'metanoia'* which means a change of mind resulting in a change of direction and behaviour.

REFLECTION: Repentance begins not by waiting to feel sorry about our sin but seeing how wrong it is and making up our mind to turn in a new direction.

Delighting in His will

'Here I am – it is written about me in the scroll –
I have come to do your will, O God.' Hebrews 10:7

C.S. Lewis in his *Screwtape Letters*, says that the routine of adversity, the gradual decay of youthful loves are what wear Christians down. He points out also that suffering is probably not an obstacle to Christians since human beings have been told it is an essential part of redemption. Screwtape rues the man who feels that every trace of God has vanished and asks why he has been forsaken and yet still obeys. Was it not obedience that kept our Lord persevering to the end?

What keeps you in the path of righteousness? Are you kept there by a fear of hell, or can you say, 'I delight to do Your will, O my God' (Psa. 40:8, NKJV)? What is the secret of not just doing one's Christian duty but delighting in it? Those who love delight to serve. They have come to know God in Jesus and behind the dictates of conscience stands a loving person. To them sin is not just a broken rule; it is a wound in His heart. Goodness is not merely duty well done; it is a direct and deliberate serving of the Beloved and hence a joyous delight. If you go to a lover of Jesus and say, 'Don't you get bored with going to church, reading the Bible, putting up with all kinds of persecution?' you will get an answer like this: 'You see, I love Jesus, and because I love Him, I delight to do His will.'

REFLECTION: Psalm 112:1 says this: 'Praise the LORD.
Blessed is the man who fears the LORD, who finds great delight
in his commands.'

Responding to God

'Blessed are the meek, for they will inherit the earth.'
Matthew 5:5

A number of things happen to us when we pray despite our lack of feeling and inclination. Firstly, *the meek submission of our will deepens our spiritual lives.* The human will is so self-centred and stubborn, that it wants its own way in everything. The more I make my will respond to God, the easier it becomes to take God's way in *everything.* When, by an act of will, we decide to spend time with God *even though we don't feel like it* we take the steps to break our will of its inherent self-centredness and thus train it to respond more to God than to our own carnal desires. The will, it seems, gets the message that God is first in my life and it is learning to respond more to God's way than my own way.'

Once we learn how to make our human wills submit to the divine will we have discovered one of the greatest secrets of the Christian life: one that opens our whole being to God's endless resources of life and power. Secondly, our resolution to engage in prayer greatly strengthens thought control. The more we practise thought control, focusing the core of our thought life, the imagination, on the things of Christ, the more expert we will become in the matter. When we confront every negative thought pattern, the thoughts that lead us away from the place of prayer, and stubbornly refuse to let them have their way, we take an important step toward mastery of our thoughts.

REFLECTION: Prayer does not depend on feelings but on faith.

Muscles of faith

'And without faith it is impossible to please God ...'
Hebrews 11:6

One great spiritual leader, Dr E. Stanley Jones, said, 'The one business of human living is to keep our wills coinciding with the will of God in self-surrender and constant obedience.' Committing ourselves to prayer when we don't feel like it develops powerful muscles in our faith. Just as physical exercise builds up muscles in the human body, so does praying against inclination greatly strengthen the tenacity of faith. Jesus placed great emphasis on faith. He never said 'Thy feeling hath made thee whole' but 'Thy faith hath made thee whole'. The old Welsh theologians used to say that 'faith develops only as it is exercised'. They claimed that everyone has a 'measure of faith' (Rom. 12:3) but we can only rise higher in the scale of faith as we use the faith we have. The more we use it, they said, the more powerful it becomes.

If a man or woman finds themselves in doubt about their ability to develop, and sustain, a systematic and methodical prayer life, let them undertake a planned programme of prayer for a month. Let them keep a daily appointment with God, even though they may not feel like it. Let them pursue the task with firmness and resolution. I would be greatly surprised if, at the end of the trial period, they did not discover such a joy and rapture that nothing, positively nothing, would in future keep them from the place of prayer. The experiment would end in an experience.

REFLECTION: Prayer is a form of spiritual exercise that produces strong and energetic Christians.

Difficult to forgive

'... forgiving each other, just as in Christ God forgave you.' Ephesians 4:32

T he desire to hold bitterness and resentment against someone who has injured us lies deep in the human heart. Unforgiveness, however, has serious spiritual and psychological consequences. Explain that forgiveness involves two things: (1) Wiping the slate clean in relation to the offence; and (2) Handing over to God the responsibility for discipline or punishment. It is important to make this clear, as some people say they are willing to forgive but not to forget. Next, suggest people make a list of the hurts and offences which need to be forgiven. This ensures that nothing remains hidden to come up at another time. Then encourage them to view these hurts and offences from God's point of view. Show them that God has been using hurts to improve their character, as the offences and injuries suffered by us become, in God's hands, the best 'teachers' for developing our characters and spiritual effectiveness.

Next, get them to reflect on what God has done for them: as we see the depth of God's forgiveness in our lives, it motivates us towards the forgiveness of others. Finally, show them that forgiveness is an act of the will. If we wait until we feel like forgiving, we may never do it. We must obey the command of Ephesians 4:32 and say, by an act of the will, 'I forgive this person in Jesus' name, just as Christ has forgiven me.'

REFLECTION: Is there someone you need to forgive?

Graduating in grace

'From the fulness of his grace we have all received one blessing after another.' John 1:16

To move on and mature in the Christian faith we must realise that grace has to be used before more is given. In John 1:16, the phrase 'one blessing after another' can be translated in several different ways. The New King James Version uses the words 'grace for grace'. J.B. Phillips' translation says: 'there is a grace in our lives because of His grace'. A number of translations use the phrase 'grace upon grace'. When I looked at this verse in a Welsh version I found a word that in English would be best translated as 'succeeding': 'grace succeeding grace'. This, I believe, perfectly captures John's meaning. We must use the grace God gives us in the present to be ready to use the grace which will then succeed it.

One preacher I know claims that we graduate in the use of grace. 'A man can't walk into a university', he says, 'and submit himself for a doctorate. He must be a Master first in his field of study. He can't walk in and submit himself for a Master; he must be a Bachelor first. It is only as you absorb learning at one level that you are able to absorb it at a higher level. So it is with grace. We advance. We graduate.' The point he is making is that if we do not avail ourselves of God's grace at one stage then we may not be offered further supplies at a later stage.

REFLECTION: The Christian life is like a path and we proceed along it one step at a time. Present grace must be used before future grace is given.

JULY 25

Demonstrate grace

'... God demonstrates his own love for us ...' Romans 5:8

During a programme on TV in which a group of people were talking about the amazing grace of God, one sceptic asked: 'If grace is so amazing why don't Christians show more of it?' There is enough truth behind that question to sting. Charles Swindoll says: 'Grace is not something simply to be claimed; it is meant to be demonstrated. It is to be shared, used as a basis for friendships and drawn upon for sustained relationships.' So often grace is stifled in relationships. We can be going along fine until someone upsets us, and then showing grace to that person is something we fail to do. We may prefer to avoid these issues, but not to confront them is to miss one of God's steps. God has created us as choosing beings. We can choose to be either gracious or ungracious. The next time you feel you have to disagree with someone remember you have a choice: you can disagree disagreeably or disagree agreeably.

'How is it', says one writer, 'that Christians called to dispense the aroma of grace instead emit the noxious fumes of ungrace?' We must face the fact that we Christians, generally speaking, do not reflect or relay to others the grace we have been given in the way we ought. Critics of Christianity rarely criticise Christ; their criticisms are reserved for the followers of Christ who so poorly represent Him. Friedrich Nietzsche said: 'In truth there was only one Christian and He died on a cross.'

REFLECTION: If grace is so amazing why don't Christians demonstrate more of it?

Missed grace

'Be careful that none of you fails to respond to the grace of God, for if he does ...' Hebrews 12:15, Phillips

What an interesting instruction we find in Hebrews 12: see to it that no one misses the grace of God. How can God's grace be missed? Instead of turning to the grace which God offers we can turn to temptation and end up soiling our soul. That's what it means to miss the grace of God. One possible result of missing or refusing the grace of God is the development of a bitter spirit. Another one is the possibility of falling into impurity. We need grace to live pure lives, and when that grace is missed or refused we become extremely vulnerable to temptation, especially impure thoughts or deeds. Most of us feel powerful urges, especially in the realm of sex. However, God has provided us, through His grace, with the strength to control these urges, and build a life in which morals regulate the appetites. If we miss the grace we will also miss the moral strengthening that comes with it.

The third possible consequence of missing or refusing the grace which God gives is that we can lose our reverence for the things of God. Esau did this because he was more concerned with the present than the future. One of the effects of God's grace is that it enables us to measure the things of time against the things of eternity. Esau failed by valuing food for his stomach more highly than his birthright (see Gen. 25:29–34). So let this solemn warning sink deep into your heart.

REFLECTION: Grace is always there to help you deal with every issue in a Christ-like way.

Loving confrontation

'... He will convict ... of sin ...' John 16:8, NKJV

An aspect of good counselling, and one which we see demonstrated both by our Lord and the Holy Spirit, is bringing important issues to a head through *loving confrontation*. This involves moving people away from symptoms on the surface to face the significant issues.

Look with me first at how Christ demonstrated this skill in His encounter with the woman at the well (John 4:1–26).How did Jesus get to the root problem in the heart of the Samaritan woman without seeming to invade sanctities? Did He say bluntly: 'Woman, you are living an adulterous life'? No, He pinpointed her problem in a more delicate way: 'Go, call your husband' (v.16). She replied weakly, 'I have no husband.' That was true, He acknowledged, recognising her honesty before touching the ugly areas of her life (vv.17–18). It was just a step from there to confronting her with the real issues for which she needed help, and soon her heart was open and exposed. Christ always saw past the trivial issues to the major ones, and never hesitated, though always respectfully, to bring the hidden things to light. Note the word *loving*. But if confrontation is to be successful, then it must be done in a way that shows a strong detestation of sin but respect for the person. Jesus models the way in which to do this. And so too, of course, does the Holy Spirit by revealing sin and guiding us in the truth.

REFLECTION: The Holy Spirit helps to reveal our failings and gives us the strength to overcome them so we are spiritually transformed.

Spiritual examination

'Search me, O God ... See if there is any offensive way in me.' Psalm 139:23–24

T he safest form of self-examination is that which is carried out in the presence of the Holy Spirit and under the guidance of the Spirit. Some Christians are always examining their hearts and thus become unhealthily introspective. Others never examine their hearts and become spiritually indolent and lethargic. Spiritual examination ought to be a regular activity. I know many Christians who examine their hearts every Sunday. They claim this is the best time, when work and other pressures can be dismissed from the mind. Whenever it is performed (and one can hardly get by with less than once a week), first invite the Holy Spirit to be present and to guide.

The whole purpose of self-examination is to identify the things that should not be in our lives and to bring them to God so that they may be uprooted. If the Holy Spirit is not invited to the moment of self-examination then it is possible that we could end up in a state of self-pity rather than contrition. The Spirit never moves us to self-pity; the Spirit moves us to repentance. Self-pity is an enemy of repentance because it is an attempt to remove the soul's pain by humanistic means rather than by entrusting oneself to God and His Holy Spirit. Begin with the prayer of the psalmist and wait before Him to see what He will make you conscious of. Then ask God for forgiveness and go out into the day – forgiven and cleansed.

REFLECTION: Spiritual examination ought to be a regular activity.

Calling sin, sin

'Woe to those who call evil good ...' Isaiah 5:20

One way by which sin seeks to enter our lives, and get past our guard, is through the use of euphemisms – calling a deadly or serious issue by a less offensive name. It calls a lie a 'fib', and stealing, 'scrounging'. It calls living a loose sexual life, 'love'. It calls having an affair 'having a fling'. A minister tells of a joint meeting of doctors, psychiatrists and ministers he attended. The purpose of the meeting was to see how the various professions could work together. There was a great deal of talk about premarital and extra-marital sexual relationships. The minister said, 'I knew, of course, what they were meaning by all that, but there was one old rural parson there who was confused by the terms, and couldn't keep up with the conversation. Finally he said, 'Pre-marital and extra-marital sexual relationships? Do you mean fornication and adultery?' Those plain, but biblical, words came like a bombshell to that highly-trained and sophisticated group of men.

We live in an age that likes to gloss things over with less challenging names, and that is one way in which society greases the path to sin. The Holy Spirit, however, works in the hearts of those who are His, encouraging them to see sin for the ugly thing it is and to stubbornly refuse to change the labels. A deadly thing is not made innocuous by a less distasteful name. Leukaemia is still leukaemia even when you call it 'a problem in the blood'.

REFLECTION: Call a spade a spade and not an agricultural implement.

Chasing God

'As the deer pants for streams of water, so my soul pants for you, O God. My soul thirsts for God, for the living God.'
Psalm 42:1–2

L earn to pant after God as did the psalmist. Some time ago I read the comments of Paul Weaver, who briefly reviewed a book called *The God Chasers* by Tommy Tenney. He said: 'I found the title particularly intriguing. After all, how can you chase God? I started reading the book and could not put it down. It challenged my life and whetted my appetite for more of God. *There is so much about God that I know so little about.*' What does it mean to chase after God? Or as the psalmist put it, to pant after Him? It means several things. It means realising there is so much about God that I know so little about.

The apostle Paul, a man who knew more about God than most, cries out in Philippians: 'I want to know Christ and the power of his resurrection and the fellowship of sharing in his sufferings, becoming like him in his death' (Phil. 3:10). Someone has said, 'The beginning of education is the realisation of your ignorance.' It is the same in the spiritual life. The beginning of spiritual development is the realisation of how little of God we know. Consider that, and let it whet your appetite to know more of Him. 'Panting after God' also means to make Him the soul's central focus. This means much more than attending church on Sunday, making sure you say your prayers before you go to sleep or occasionally reading a brief portion from the Scriptures.

REFLECTION: God's purpose is for us to know Him intimately, to gaze upon His face, knowing that as we do, our soul will find Him to be its delight.

Let God be God

'... any of you who does not give up everything he has cannot be my disciple.' Luke 14:33

I f the expression – 'let God be God' – is new to you then let me explain it to you. Our ego was never meant to be central to our personality – despite what modern psychologists say. We were made to have God at the centre of our beings and for the ego to revolve around Him. Thus we are designed not to be ego-centred but God-centred. To let God be God is to surrender our ego into His hands. I must emphasise that surrender does not mean collapse or loss of individuality. A truly surrendered person offers to God an alert self, no longer eager for its own way but for the way – a self knowing its place is second, and eager to serve the First. Everybody surrenders to something.

One writer puts it like this: 'Everyone goes into the shrine of the heart and bends the knee to something, something that has the place of supreme allegiance.' Can I ask what you bow the knee to? Some bow the knee to what others think of them. They don't act, they react. Others bend the knee to themselves. Self-interest is supreme. There are many other things – money, sex, ambition – which may be the centre of devotion. Each one of us must whisper the consent of abdication before grace can flow into our souls in all its fullness. You must say to yourself: 'I am not the one who is supreme. God is. I bow the knee to Him and to Him alone.'

REFLECTION: It is possible to give up lots of things without giving up the self. You see, that is where our life is – in the self. It must be surrendered.

Be kind

'And be kind to one another, tenderhearted, forgiving one another, even as God in Christ forgave you.'
Ephesians 4:32, NKJV

This is a verse I repeat to myself almost every day. Apart from its spiritual truth, I love the sheer cadence and rhythm of its language. I challenge anyone to improve on this sentence from Scripture. I regard it as a perfect piece of prose. And within it I hear the sweetest possible music – the music of the grace of God.

The verse is made even more beautiful by comparing it to the preceding verse which says: 'Let all bitterness, wrath, anger, clamour, and evil speaking be put away from you, with all malice' (v.31, NKJV). Now every one of those words is ugly. Put together, they remind you of when the dark clouds roll up over the sky, hiding the face of the sun and shutting off its warmth, causing the heart to shiver. But then, in the next verse (the verse I have taken as my text), it is as if the sun breaks through and sheds its warmth and light and the heart is cheered once again. Listen to it once more: '... be kind to one another ...' What a wonderful contrast! God be praised! However we look at it, this is a clear command of God. If we are Christians then kindness is not optional. We are expected to be kind. It's part of the Christian lifestyle. To be a Christian and not to be kind is an absurd contradiction. But, when you think about it, it's a sad fact that we ever have to be reminded of the need to be kind.

REFLECTION: 'I have regretted being unkind, but I have never regretted being kind.'

God is good

'For God so loved the world that he gave his one and only Son ...' John 3:16

I was brought up to believe that the root of sin is rebellion, but Oswald Chambers changed my mind when he said, 'The root of sin is the suspicion that God is not good.' He moved the primary issue from the will to the emotions. If I understand the personality aright, it is our thinking that affects the way we feel and our feelings that affect the choices we make. The thought that perhaps God is not good is powerful.

Oswald Chambers points out that in the Garden of Eden what produced the Fall was the fact that Adam and Eve did not believe God had their highest interests at heart, and that thought of not being considered by God produced emotions that brought about capitulation in the personality. Personally, I think it makes a lot of sense. We live today in a world where the data showing that God is good is not all that convincing. We see His majesty in creation, but God lets little babies be abused and, when we think of His permissive will, we realise He could have intervened if He had wanted to. And then there are times when God doesn't answer prayers, which causes us to wonder whether He is really as good as He says He is. Do you know what I do when I find these thoughts circulating in my being? I come back to the fact of the cross and dwell on the truth that a God who gave His Son to die for me has got to be good.

REFLECTION: Fix your thoughts on the cross and spend time thinking about the love God showed in giving His Son to die for us!

He knows best

*'But God demonstrates his own love for us in this:
While we were still sinners, Christ died for us.'*
Romans 5:8

I have met so many Christians who have pushed down their feelings of disappointment with God over something that happened in the past. They never deal with it but stuff it into the unconscious. We never bury an emotion dead – it is always alive. This is why we must face our emotions, feel them and wrestle with them, if necessary, until we come to the realisation that God knows best. Change the 'd' in disappointment to 'h' and what do you get? His appointment! Who amongst us has not met the difficult issue of thwarted plans, things not turning out the way one expected, and so on. God is all-powerful. But Christians know that, in the midst of the greatest catastrophe, we are called to believe that God has not lost His power and could intervene if He wished, but that He has allowed it to happen for an overall good and wise purpose. And it is tough believing that in the face of some situations which God allows. Our concept of God is crucial to our growth.

Many times in my life I have got upset with God and I have said, 'Lord, you don't love me.' But He has always come to me and bidden me gaze at the cross. And there, as I see how much I am loved, the scales fall from my eyes and my own love flames in response. Oh yes! A God who gave His life for me on the cross has got to be good.

REFLECTION: 'The answer I give to people who ask why God allows certain things is: I will wait until I get home to know the reason why and He will tell me Himself.'

Righteous indignation

'The wrath of God is being revealed ... against all the godlessness and wickedness of men ...' Romans 1:18

For many of us, wrath conjures up the idea of being out of control, an outburst of 'seeing red', a sense of wounded pride, or just a fit of bad temper. But God's wrath is never out of control, never arbitrary, never self-indulgent and never ignoble. These things may be true of human anger, but never of the divine. God is angry only when that anger is merited. Even among men and women there is such a thing as righteous indignation, though in my opinion it is more rare than we think.

I used to believe the difference between righteous indignation and human hostility was this: when someone was angry with me *that* was human hostility; when I was angry with someone else *that* was righteous indignation! That 'opinion' disappeared as I grew more mature, I hasten to add. All God's indignation is righteous. In love, as our Creator, He makes demands of us, and when we refuse to accept His way His wrath is the consequence. How can a God who is holy condone evil? How can the One who established the moral law remain impassive when that law is broken? Such a thing is impossible. It is precisely this adverse reaction to evil that the Bible has in mind when it talks about God's wrath. God cannot treat good and evil alike. He can look over it – look over it to the cross where it can be forgiven – but He cannot overlook it.

REFLECTION: The more we really understand the reason for God's wrath the more we want to praise and adore Him. And how grateful we are that we are forgiven.

Communication in marriage

'... Everyone should be quick to listen, slow to speak and slow to become angry.' James 1:19

C ommunication has been defined as 'the process in which two people share both verbally and non-verbally in such a way that their message is accepted and understood'. Communication in marriage consists of three components: talking, listening and understanding. Let's take them one by one. *Talking*: No marriage can grow or develop unless the partners take time to talk to each other. If a married couple are extremely busy with a growing family, or business demands, they should allocate certain times of the day for the purpose of just talking together.

The second component of communication is *listening*. Listening has been defined as 'not thinking about what you are going to say when the other person has finished speaking'. Many marriage partners concentrate so much on getting their point across in a conversation that they fail to pay attention to cultivating the art of listening. An invaluable device in building good communication techniques, particularly when you are discussing a relationship problem, is to practise listening to your partner without interrupting.

The third component of communication is *understanding*. Try to understand not just what your partner is saying but why he or she is saying it. In fact, gently asking your spouse to explain their actions in an atmosphere of loving acceptance can produce greater closeness. It is absolutely amazing how people change when they know they are understood.

REFLECTION: When you speak you create a world – a world of cosmos or a world of chaos.

The divine intention

*'For those God foreknew he also predestined to be
conformed to the likeness of his Son ...' Romans 8:29*

We were created by God to grow spiritually. We can live against that design or live with it. When we violate the law of growth that God has built into our make-up we violate ourselves. We become frustrated, unfulfilled and unhappy. To know consciously, or to feel unconsciously, that the central purpose of your life as a Christian – the thing for which you have been created – is not being fulfilled, or worse, violated, is to bring a sadness to the spirit which affects every part of your existence. No amount of marginal happiness can atone for this central dissatisfaction. If you are not thriving spiritually then you are a discontented person. This discontent will spread itself through all marginal forms of satisfaction and cause them to curdle and become sour.

It is my belief that as soon as the Spirit of God enters our life through conversion an energy is released in us which moves us towards the goal of spiritual maturity and makes us more and more like Jesus Christ. I love the Living Bible paraphrase of today's text which reads thus: 'For from the very beginning God decided that those who came to him – and all along he knew who would – should become like his Son ...'. God is so excited about Jesus that He wants to make everyone like Him – not in appearance, of course, but in character.

REFLECTION: Since growing and thriving spiritually is God's clearly stated intention, if we do not thrive then the fault is certainly not God's but ours.

A definition of love

'A new command I give you: Love one another. As I have loved you, so you must love one another.' John 13:34

The real problem behind our relationships is the same as that which first disrupted relationships in the Garden of Eden. It has to do with our confidence in the goodness of God. Once the foundation stone of God's goodness is removed from beneath us, we do not have a hope of building good relationships. The reason for this is that we must have complete trust in God in order to relate to others. Relationships sometimes hurt. People, being fallen human beings, can fail. In truth, the more we relate to people, the more we are guaranteed to get hurt. It follows then that we need supernatural support if we are to relate well to others because what often destroys relationships is the fear of getting hurt. When our relationships are governed more by a fear of getting hurt than by a desire to love, our relationships will be superficial. We will get close enough to people to be socially acceptable but not close enough to be hurt.

Whenever we are more concerned about our own welfare than we are about the welfare of others, we are not loving as we are loved. There are many definitions of what it means to love. Charles Finney said, 'Love is bringing about the highest good in the life of another.' A line in *Love Story* defined love as 'never having to say you are sorry' – idealistic but hardly realistic. One of the best definitions of love is this: 'Love is moving towards others without self-protection.'

REFLECTION: Consider again: 'Love is moving towards others without self-protection.'

The greatest challenge

'And be kind to one another, tenderhearted, forgiving one another, even as God in Christ forgave you.'
Ephesians 4:32, NKJV

This is where kindness is shown at its brightest and its best – in forgiveness. The word 'forgiveness' implies that there has been wrongdoing and Christians, like the rest of humanity, say and do wrong things to one another. Then comes the challenge to forgive and this is one of the greatest challenges of Christian living.

I had a tremendous test of this kind many years ago. A man who worked with me said some bad things about me and I resolved to make him sorry for what he had said. So I set out to make him squirm, and I was in a position to do this. But I found I couldn't pray with a disposition like this. I would try to pray but my words seemed to bounce back from the ceiling. We just cannot get through to God when we hold unforgiveness in our hearts. God wouldn't even listen to me, let alone answer me. I gave up my vengeful attitude and behaviour and the power flowed through my life again almost instantly. When people say, 'My problem is I can't forgive', I say, 'No, that's not your problem. Your problem is you don't know how much you have been forgiven. That's your problem.' When we see how much God has forgiven us, really see it, I mean, then the wonder of it is so powerful and motivating that we simply cannot hold back from forgiving others.

REFLECTION: Be honest – are you holding on to unforgiveness, even bitterness?

Forgive and forget

*'Be gentle and ready to forgive; never hold grudges.
Remember, the Lord forgave you, so you must forgive
others.' Colossians 3:13, TLB*

The famous psychoanalyst, Freud, said that 'the mind will return again and again to that which gives it pain'. But it need not do so when the things that cause it pain have been replaced by God's peace. Are you having difficulty in this area of remembering to forget? Have you been deeply sinned against? Has somebody slandered or libelled you or done you a terrible injury? Are you nursing in your heart the hope of revenge? Then I come to you in God's name and plead with you to deal with it in the way we are commanded to do in Scripture. However justified your resentment against another person, to harbour that resentment is to poison yourself. Be rid of that poison in God's name.

'Every Christian', someone has said, 'should be three things: a giver, a forgiver and a forgetter.' For now let me help you with the matter of being a forgiver and a forgetter. *If you want God to help you forget then you must first be willing to forgive. You provide the willingness and God will do the rest.* C.S. Lewis said, 'Forgiveness, a lovely idea until we have something to forgive.' It's not easy to forgive but here you can claim the special help of God. The fact that God has forgiven us is one of the most powerful inducements to forgiveness we can ever consider.

REFLECTION: To hold on to unforgiveness is a violation of the divine law (see our verse for today). You *must* forgive. And we can do it – in God's strength. We'll start to see how over the next two days.

How do I forgive? (1)

'The life I live ... I live by faith in the Son of God, who loved me and gave himself for me.' Galatians 2:20

I believe there are three things necessary in order to forgive and forget. First, *focus on how much you have been forgiven.* Think how extensive God's mercy has been in your life. You may think you have committed only little sins but, as someone has put it, there are no little sins, just as there is no little God to sin against. Nothing anyone has ever done towards you is as offensive as what you have done to God over the years by ignoring His claim upon your soul and refusing Him admittance into your life. Yet now He has forgiven you, washed all your sins in the blood of His Son, and written your name in the Lamb's book of life.

Take your time over this. Reflect on that fact that you have been forgiven until its truth penetrates deep into your soul. There is a story told of Thomas Chalmers, a great preacher of yesteryear, who one day when preparing a sermon on Paul's words was so struck by Paul's use of the word 'me' in our text that he began to apply it to himself. Such was the weight of meaning the words had for him that he ran out into the street and accosted the first passerby with the words, 'It was for me, for me, he died.' Ponder the depth of God's mercy towards *you.* Reflect on the great debt which you owed Him but which through His wondrous mercy has been cancelled.

REFLECTION: The more you can envision the sweep of God's forgiveness towards you, the more you will be able to extend the sweep of your forgiveness to others.

How do I forgive? (2)

'Be kind and compassionate to one another, forgiving each other, just as in Christ God forgave you.'
Ephesians 4:32

The second thing necessary to forgive and forget is: *deal honestly with any lingering resentments that may be in your soul.* No doubt some of you reading these lines will have gone through deep hurts and even deep horror. As you think now of that person who hurt you, abused you, slandered or libelled you, tortured you, rejected you, release the poison of bitterness in Jesus' name. Let it gush out before God and tell Him that you want to be free. Be prepared to go all the way with God on this. Don't settle for half forgiveness and say, 'I'll forgive but I will never forget.' Limited forgiveness is no forgiveness at all. If you find yourself pulling back over this matter of forgiving then it is probably because the wonder of the fact of how much you have been forgiven is still in your head and has not reached your heart. Focus again on how much you have been forgiven. And if you think that God is harsh in putting before you this alternative – forgive, or else – then realise that He has your best interests at heart. Your soul was never made to carry the poison of bitterness and resentment. Those are toxins in your personality.

Thirdly, *ask God to help you forget.* If you accept the responsibility to forgive then God will accept the responsibility to help you forget. You can bank on it. You do the possible, God will do the impossible

REFLECTION: You will never rise to be the person God wants you to be when bitterness and resentment are allowed to fester in your soul.

How's your father?

'As a father has compassion on his children, so the LORD has compassion ...' Psalm 103:13

J.B. Phillips, in *Your God is too Small*, says that our concept of God is invariably founded upon a child's idea of his father. If he is fortunate enough to have had a kind, indulgent and considerate father, then, when he becomes a Christian, he tends to project that same image on to God. But if the child has a stern, punitive parent, of whom he lives in dread, the chances are that his Father in heaven will appear to him as a fearful being. Some outgrow such a misconception, and are able to differentiate between the early 'fearful' idea and the later mature conception. But many don't. They carry a 'parental hangover' into their Christian life and *endure* rather than *enjoy* it because they are never quite sure that God has their highest interests at heart.

I wonder, is someone reading this who pictures God as tyrannical, judgmental, punitive or just plain disinterested? Ask yourself: where did I get this picture of the Almighty? Not from the Scriptures. Decide now to leave behind all misconceptions, and discover the true God – the God of the Bible. How does the Bible convey to us a clear picture of God's heart and character? Well, it is not just the Book, wonderful though it is, but what the Book says about God's self-revelation in the Person of His Son. We may catch glimpses of Him in the words He utters, but the only way God can be seen as He really is, is in the incarnate life of His Son.

REFLECTION: There was, and is, no other way for God to reveal Himself, in understandable terms, except through a human life – Jesus.

Our motivations

'Come, all you who are thirsty, come to the waters ...'
Isaiah 55:1

Since the Fall, everyone born into this world arrives with a deep sense of insecurity, inferiority and insignificance. No human love can give us what our souls long for; and bereft of a relationship with God, the best that earthly relationships (such as parents, friends and peers) can do is to make us feel only moderately secure, worthwhile and significant. We will never resolve the identity crisis in our souls until we know how to relate to the true God who alone can give us what our souls require – unconditional love and eternal meaning. We all long to get back to what was lost in the Garden of Eden. And our longings are the most powerful part of our personalities. Our longing fuels our search for meaning, for wholeness, for a sense of being truly alive. It is the most important thing about us, our heart of hearts, the passion of our life. And the voice that calls to us from this place is the voice of God.

This thirst in our souls, if not satisfied in God, lies behind most of the problems of the personality. The Trinity designed our inner beings for the most incredible joy and satisfaction; but when we do not experience a close and intimate relationship with the Father, Son and Holy Spirit then we become extremely vulnerable to those things that excite our senses, and we find ourselves living for them or depending on them to satisfy our soul.

REFLECTION: If we do not drink deeply of the water that comes from Christ, then we will turn easily to other sources of satisfaction.

Foolish people

'My people have committed two sins: They have forsaken me, the spring of living water, and have dug their own cisterns, broken cisterns that cannot hold water.'
Jeremiah 2:13

The Almighty, speaking metaphorically through Jeremiah, accuses His people of preferring to dig their own broken cisterns rather than rely in humble dependence on the Lord for their life. Because we believe the lie that we can find satisfaction for our souls apart from God there is now a blindness in our minds. Though it does not prevent us from understanding scientific laws, mathematics or any of the other things our educational establishments teach us, when we try to comprehend the moral and spiritual world, we reveal our mental failure. The Bible uses an interesting word to describe our mental failure to figure out the moral world. It is called folly or foolishness. A fool in Proverbs is not someone who is intellectually challenged. A fool is someone who *thinks* he knows where life is to be found, but doesn't.

There is something in all of us that hates the fact that apart from God we will never be able to satisfy the deep thirst and deep longings in our souls. Facing that truth requires that we adopt the position of helplessness – giving up our vain attempts to make life work without God – and helplessness is something our carnal nature abhors. We much prefer to be in control of the water we drink. And that is a strategy the Bible regards as foolish.

REFLECTION: How pained God must have felt as He observed His people spurning His offer of living water, free for the taking, and laboriously digging their own cisterns.

Our view of God

'I am the true vine, and my Father is the gardener.' John 15:1

'I am the true vine,' said Jesus, 'and my Father is the gardener.' Note the word 'Father'. Whatever needs to be done in your life, you are in good hands! Your *Father* is the Gardener. Some people base their view of God, the Father, on the mental images of Him which flow through their minds. However, no man or woman has the resources within themselves to discover, unaided, the true and living God.

Job asks: 'Can you search out the deep things of God?' (11:7, NKJV).The answer is plain – no! For what we find in our upward search for God is not God, but the projection of our thoughts into the heavens. We create God in the image of our imagination – and it is not a true image. Philosophical reasoning has searched in a dark universe for a philosophical God who isn't there. The God of the Bible can only be discovered by revelation. No one could ever imagine that the God of the universe would step out of heaven, come right down to earth, live in a human body and die on a cross to redeem us. A love like that just doesn't exist – not in the category of philosophy. But seeing is believing. The Creator, knowing that we could never come to Him, came to us and, through the revelation of the Bible, gives us the truth about Himself. And the truth is: He is not just omnipotent power but eternal Love.

REFLECTION: Jesus' own untroubled spirit arose, I believe, from the fact that He had complete confidence that His Father's purposes were wise, loving and good. And so must we.

Attacks of Satan

The God of peace will soon crush Satan under your feet.'
Romans 16:20

God uses *the attacks of Satan* to advance our progress and develop our spiritual effectiveness. Moffatt translates John 14:31: 'his [Satan's] coming will only serve to let the world see that I love the Father and that I am acting as the Father ordered.' Our Lord made even Satan serve! And when the Master has control of your life, He can do the same for you, and turn the attacks of Satan to your spiritual advantage. The secret of Jesus' power is contained in the words: 'the Prince of this world is coming. He has no hold on me' (John 14:30–31, Moffatt).

There was nothing in our Lord's personality through which Satan could gain an advantage – no sin, no self-pity, no bitterness, no self-centredness. The same cannot be said of us, for though we are *saved* sinners, there is still a lot of sinfulness and self-centredness resident in our natures. Despite this difficulty God, Christ and the Holy Spirit are working hand in hand to help us overcome our sinful nature; and such is the skill and wisdom of the Trinity that they can use even the attacks of Satan to further those purposes. Do you feel as if you are being attacked by Satan? Are you conscious of being the victim of strange diabolical pressures? Then take heart, God has promised that He will not permit Satan to inflict upon you more than you are capable of bearing (1 Cor. 10:13). As you draw close to Him, He will make the attacks of Satan *serve*.

REFLECTION: Christ was able to turn the efforts of Satan towards positive ends.

Job's hedge

'Have you not put a hedge around him and his household and everything he has?' Job 1:10

First, let me say that I believe that the Old Testament patriarch Job was singled out by God to become a classic example of unconditional faith in God (James 5:11), and that today's Christians should not walk around wondering if at any moment God is going to allow Satan to invade their lives with all kinds of disasters and catastrophes. Job, you notice, had a 'hedge' around him.

What does it mean – a 'hedge'? God, I believe, has providentially established a boundary of spiritual protection around every human life, for if not, Satan's power, being what it is, would eliminate every child born into the world. The Almighty God, protective of the life He creates, ensures that Satan does not have an open door into the human personality. If this were not so, there would be much greater chaos in human affairs than there is. Some people may, through dabbling with the occult or by consulting Satan in séances, break open that hedge. Then, of course, unless they repent and turn to Christ, they openly expose themselves to Satan and his power. In Job's case, God took away the protective hedge from around His servant so that Satan could enter his life in a way not normally permitted and inflict upon him the full extent of his strategies. Job, of course, came through victoriously, proving that it was possible for a man to serve God because he loved Him, and not for personal advantage.

REFLECTION: God is protective of the life He creates (see 1 Peter 1:3–5).

Battles produce muscles!

'... take your stand against the devil's schemes.'
Ephesians 6:11

W e need to keep in mind that Satan's attacks come under the strict supervision of the Almighty, and He permits only that which accords with His eternal purposes. The question is often asked: why does God permit the devil to have such power? Why, for that matter, didn't God eliminate Lucifer as soon as he had sinned and thus spare the universe from a good deal of chaos and suffering? We can never fully answer that question because, quite simply, we are unable to see into the divine mind. However, I have no doubt myself that the answer is partly because God, knowing the end from the beginning, knew that He could turn all Satan's efforts to advantage. Satan, therefore, has his uses.

One such can be seen in our Lord's life when He was confronted by Satan in the wilderness. Although it is not in the nature of God to tempt, He allowed Satan to try to take advantage of Jesus after His forty-day fast in the wilderness, and so attempt to bring about His downfall. But watch what happens. Christ, in His weakened condition, triumphs over the devil's repeated temptations and comes out of the wilderness in the 'power of the Spirit'. Notice, He went in *full* of the Holy Spirit (Luke 4:1), and came out in the *power* of the Spirit (Luke 4:14).What did Satan's attacks succeed in doing? They helped to turn mere fullness to power.

REFLECTION: Our Lord's spiritual tissues had been hardened in the struggle. When we stay close to Christ, then our own battles with the devil will have the same effect.

Take heart when tempted

'... when you are tempted, he will also provide a way out so that you can stand up under it.' 1 Corinthians 10:13

I have talked with many Christians over the years and I have noticed that those who appear to be immune from temptation, reveal, in private conversation, that their immunity was won through a series of spiritual battles. I know in my own life that temptations which would at one time have shaken me to the very foundation of my being, now have little impact upon me. This is not true of all temptations, but it is true of most. I have, as one writer put it, 'got into the habit of experiencing victory'. I say this, of course, in utter dependence on the Holy Spirit, for I am fully conscious that in this life we never achieve full immunity from temptation. To my delight and amazement, I find I am becoming fixed in goodness. Habit is now working for me where once it worked against me.

Those of you reading these lines who are struggling with some strong and fierce temptations – take heart. God is permitting you to be engaged in a battle with Satan which will not deprive you but deepen you. In His strength and power, you will emerge from this conflict with a refinement and a poise that you never thought possible. The battle will serve to show you that it is 'Not by might, nor by power, but by my spirit, saith the LORD of hosts' (Zech. 4:6, AV). You will rejoice, not in what you can do, but in what He can do within you.

REFLECTION: Then there comes a time, through humility, experience and conflict, when you outgrow many temptations of Satan.

Our greatest ally

'... holding on to faith and a good conscience.' 1 Timothy 1:19

The Bible explains that we have inherited from Adam and Eve a nature which has a bias towards evil. People murder, lust and a whole host of things. What happened in Genesis is still with us today. However, we ought never to run away with the idea that we are just helpless victims of depravity and are powerless to do anything about it. God has built within us a conscience, which is one of our greatest allies when we wish to fight against our innate depravity. Conscience never takes time off. It can, however, be easily stifled or smothered. It tells us we should do right, but it cannot always tell us what is right to do. The word *conscience* means 'knowledge with oneself' or 'complete knowledge.' Theologically it means more.

Archbishop Trench, one of Britain's great archbishops, defined conscience in this way: 'I know that God knows that I know.' Alexander MacDol, a Scottish preacher, said: 'Conscience is the supreme court of the universe set up in the human spirit.' Conscience is not an infallible guide. It needs sensitising, enlightening, reinforcing. Hugh Redwood, a journalist, said, 'Your conscience is a watchdog, but make sure you don't feed it sleeping tablets.' Conscience, guided by the truths of Scripture and energised by the grace of God, becomes a powerful spiritual force in the battle against inner corruption.

REFLECTION: We cannot let (a fallen) conscience be our guide, but we can allow a conscience based on Scripture to guide us.

The disease of sin

'... for all have sinned and fall short of the glory of God ...'
Romans 3:23

A s we see how the tempter came to Eve in Genesis 3, surely we must recognise that this is not just a story that comes to us out of the ancient past; it's as up-to-date as the temptation you faced last night, the temptation you may be feeling this morning ... The scene has changed, but the methodology has not. Adam and Eve had everything they needed back there in the garden, but there came a moment of temptation when one thought dominated their minds: Are we missing out on something? Is God keeping something from us? They failed to resist that temptation – the temptation to reach out and take something that was forbidden to them – and began a slide that affects every one of us to this very day.

Some theologians have likened depravity to a congenital disease. The predisposition is there from earliest infancy. It is infectious; no quarantine can effectively prescribe or limit its incidence. And it is fatal in its consequences. '... sin, when it is full-grown, brings forth death' (James 1:15, NKJV). The slide into depravity – the desire to run our lives on our own terms without recourse to God – has affected every individual who has ever been born, with the single exception of Jesus Christ. We all have within us the propensity to do evil and to disobey the Word of God because we doubt His goodness and rebel against His love.

REFLECTION: We can't help having the disease of sin, but we can combat it by drawing upon the grace of God that enables us to rise above its influence.

The quiet time

'... O LORD, you hear my voice; in the morning I lay my requests before you and wait in expectation.' Psalm 5:3

I know of nothing that promotes the awareness of God's presence in a believer's life more powerfully and effectively than the regular practice of a morning quiet time. Some have great difficulty with this, their lifestyle or circumstances prevent them from finding either the time or the place to be alone with God during the first part of the day. Don't feel condemned if your circumstances do not permit you to get alone with God until the day is well under way. He understands and will be there waiting for you whenever you can make it. The story is told of Susannah Wesley (the mother of John Wesley) that when she was deprived of privacy for her quiet time, she would lift her apron over her head and for a few minutes commune in prayer with God. When the children saw her do this, they would whisper to each other, 'Hush, mother is having her quiet time.'

Try also to be alone when you have your quiet time. It is good for married couples to share together in prayer, but everyone needs to spend some time alone with God if they are to cultivate their individual relationship with Him. Every Christian must try to have some time alone with Him at the beginning of day, even if it is only a few quiet moments. Savour those moments, they will provide you with a fountain in your heart at which you can slake your thirst throughout the day.

REFLECTION: Although 'the morning quiet time' seems an antiquated phrase it is still relevant today and even more important than breakfast!

The habits of Jesus

'But Jesus often withdrew to lonely places and prayed.'
Luke 5:16

T he New Testament tells us that Jesus felt the need of three simple habits: 1. He went into the synagogue to read 'as was his custom'; 2. He went up a mountain to pray 'as usual'; 3. He taught the people 'as was his custom' (see Luke 4:16; 22:39; Mark 10:1). These three simple habits of reading the Scriptures, spending time in prayer and sharing with others are as basic to the Christian life as 'two and two make four' is to mathematics. If Jesus couldn't get along without definite times for prayer, then how can we hope to? But how are we to make the best of our daily or regular times of prayer and contemplation? There can be no fixed rules, only suggestions.

Experience has shown that the best way to begin a quiet time is by reading the Scriptures. Then one might sit quietly in the Lord's presence and say: 'Father, have You anything to say to me?' Sometimes God may have something special and personal to say to you arising from your reading of His Word. Wait and see what He might have to say to you before moving on to a time of prayer for others and yourself. God not only delights to talk to us, but He is delighted also when we talk to Him. This is what prayer is, a conversation with God. So tell Him the things that are on your mind, the joyful things as well as the difficult things, and expect His answers.

REFLECTION: God has gone into His Word and so, when we read it, God comes out of it.

Partnership with God

'Remain in me, and I will remain in you.' John 15:4

An old Welsh miner told me that every day, following his quiet time, he would think of what he had to do that day and visualise the Lord being involved in every moment of it. 'I am in partnership with God,' he said, 'and I have learned to think of the responsibilities of the day not as "mine", but as "ours".' He ordered his day on the basis of a divine partnership. He went on to tell me that as he thought ahead into the issues of the day, he would talk to God about them in the same way that a man would talk to a business partner: 'What shall we do about this matter, Lord? There's another issue that will be coming up later in the day … how shall we handle that?'

The chief merit of this approach to practising the presence of God is that it highlights one of the greatest truths of Scripture, that of the divine–human partnership. Can you think of anything more wonderful in earth or heaven than the fact that the Almighty God, the Creator of the universe, takes an active interest in every single detail of our lives and is willing to team up with us? 'Christianity', said a missionary to China, 'is a secret companionship.' Just think of it, you need not go into any day alone, but arm in arm with that Secret Companion. Partnership with God does not mean that He dominates our personalities; His purpose is to guide, not override.

REFLECTION: The Lord relates to us in a way that is helpful and supportive while at the same time taking care not to snuff out our initiative and creativity.

The power of a wise word

'Death and life are in the power of the tongue ...'
Proverbs 18:21, RSV

The right word spoken at the right time can change a life, especially when that word has in it the ring of divine authority. Imagine a tool so powerful that with it you can elevate a person's spiritual vision, deepen his moral convictions and improve the quality of his service for Christ. A properly selected Bible text is that potent! Listen again to the writer of the book of Proverbs as he brings into focus the importance of a true and timely word:

'Everyone enjoys giving good advice, and how wonderful it is to be able to say the right thing at the right time!' (Prov. 15:23, TLB).

'Timely advice is as lovely as golden apples in a silver basket' (Prov. 25:11, TLB).

More often than not the timely word is a prepared word, though it appears to be spontaneous. The right Bible passages don't just pop into your mind without some prior reason. They might appear to be spontaneous, but they really arise from a heart that has prepared itself by thoughtful meditation and study. So make up your mind to build a library of carefully selected Scripture passages so that you can use them when attempting to help people with their problems. Once you grasp the principle of tying in appropriate passages of Scripture to personal problems you can then begin to build your own library of biblical texts on an ongoing basis.

REFLECTION: Counselling is not just handing out advice (even biblical advice), but it is a relationship. It is the Word becoming flesh – in you.

You may not understand

'But Jonah ran away from the LORD ...' Jonah 1:3

The Jonah story begins with the fact that he is given a task to perform which he doesn't want: Having received a prophetic call to preach in Nineveh (1:2), he plans to head in the opposite direction. Nineveh was the great capital of the ancient Assyrian Empire and was built on the banks of the Tigris River in north-eastern Mesopotamia, which we know today as Iraq. The Assyrians were enemies of Israel, and their brutality and wickedness was such that it offended the sensitive heart of God. 'Go to Nineveh,' says the Almighty to Jonah, 'and thunder in their ears that their wickedness is known to me' (v.2, Moffatt).

Why should God worry about one of Israel's fiercest enemies? Jonah is nonplussed by God's sudden interest in them and fails to understand why He should attempt to save such evil people. But shouldn't a prophet obey God's commands without question or quibble? We would think so, but Jonah is adamant. Would you be willing to follow the Lord's clear command if He asked you to do something that to you didn't seem to make sense? How many of us pull back from doing what God asks us because it appears to be against our better judgment? Those who commit themselves to serving the Lord must get to grips with this most important fact: we are not called to understand but to stand. Those who can't or won't grasp this truth make little progress along the path of discipleship.

REFLECTION: Jonah didn't object to preaching, but he wanted to choose his own pulpit!

What God delights in

'But you, O Lord, are a compassionate and gracious God, slow to anger, abounding in love and faithfulness.'
Psalm 86:15

There is a marked contrast between Jonah's attitude and the compassionate and forgiving nature of God. As the events of Jonah's story unfold, it becomes quite clear that he was more interested in pronouncing judgment than in announcing the offer of divine forgiveness. Many believers I have met are like that and fail to emphasise the fact that the thing God delights to do is to forgive.

Some time ago I gave a lecture for the Bible Society in Dublin. After I had completed my lecture, a Catholic priest commented on the statement I had made concerning the truth that God delights to forgive. He said, 'If an angel came down into this room tonight and told us that the Trinity had decided to abandon the fact of hell, many of us would be very disappointed, as we all know people we would like to see finish up there.' The audience laughed, but they identified with the point he was making. How many of us, I wonder, gain a sense of moral satisfaction from the thought that sinful people deserve judgment when we should be concentrating on their need for forgiveness? Let us be quite clear: God is against sin – all sin – and promises that the unrepentant will be punished. But what He loves to do is forgive. Listen to what God says through the prophet Micah: 'What does the LORD require of you? To act justly and to love mercy …' (Micah 6:8).

REFLECTION: Perhaps we ought to still our hearts for a moment and ask ourselves this crucial question: Am I as concerned about mercy as I am about judgment?

Saying 'no' to God

'But Jonah ran away from the LORD and headed for
Tarshish.' Jonah 1:3

I t is interesting to notice that in response to God's command
Jonah sets off, but he sets off in the wrong direction. He could
have ignored God's call and remained where he was, but
instead he sets out for Tarshish. My Bible dictionary says that in
Old Testament times Tarshish, in the popular imagination, became
a kind of distant paradise – Shangri la. I wonder, am I talking to
someone who has been called by God to do something which seems
difficult? If so, do you find yourself contemplating moving in the
opposite direction to that which you have been called? Are you just
about to buy a ticket to 'Tarshish'? For all of you lined up at the
travel agents I have this message: your attempt to escape from God's
call is just not worth it. You can run but you can't hide. The Lord
knows the end from the beginning, and though He loves you as you
are, He loves you too much to let you stay as you are. Jonah ran, but
God ran after him.

Be careful when you find yourself in circumstances that seem to
aid you in your flight from God's commands. Conducive conditions
are not necessarily indicators of the divine will. The travel ticket
which Jonah purchased from Joppa to Tarshish was, without doubt,
one of the costliest ever acquired. He moved in the opposite direction
to that stipulated by God and finished up in the deep.

REFLECTION: Had Jonah reached Tarshish he might have had
a seemingly successful life, but it would have been 'success'
that lay outside the will of God.

God is now here

'But Jonah ran away from the LORD ... and sailed to Tarshish to flee from the LORD.' Jonah 1:3

Why would anyone want to run away from the Lord? Or: Can anyone really run away from the Lord? It seems Jonah had an imperfect view of God and His presence. The prevailing opinion in many nations during Old Testament times was that each country's god was limited to its own land. Sometimes people would carry soil from one country to another in the belief that the god of that country would travel with them. The story of Naaman's quest for healing demonstrates this kind of thinking (2 Kings 5:17).

Some Israelites believed that God was confined to the Temple in Jerusalem or, at most, to the territory of Israel. So perhaps Jonah thought that when he sailed away from the shores of Israel he would be leaving God behind. Or he may have thought that when he got far away from Israel, then the impact of God's presence would be diminished in his life, in the same way that a radio signal fades the further one gets from the transmitter. Jonah would learn, as we must learn, that there is nowhere where God is not.

I once read the story of a militant atheist who wrote on a wall the words: 'God is nowhere.' But unwittingly he left a space between the letters 'w' and 'h'. As he stood back and looked at what he had written he read: 'God is now here.' It brought about his conversion.

REFLECTION: When we try to disregard something God has called us to do we cannot really escape – either from God or ourselves.

Saved by a storm

'Then the LORD sent a great wind on the sea ...' Jonah 1:4

The hurricane ruined Jonah's plans to go to Tarshish; his vacation was spoiled but his vocation was saved. None of us likes to find ourself caught up in a storm, but sometimes this is the only way God can get our attention. George Herbert, in his book *The Country Parson*, has these lines: 'Poets have wrong'd poor storms; such days are best, They purge the air without, within the breast.' A storm may bring chaos and cause great damage but it also clears the air.

I once talked to a man who told me that he had gone through a period of deep psychological depression. He described this time as like being in a storm. My curiosity was aroused when he concluded, 'Now I can thank God for my depression.' I asked him how he could thank God for depression, and he replied, 'My depression was due to wrong patterns of living. I needed those wrong patterns and ideas shaken up and challenged, for they were sending my life in the wrong direction. The depression was a message that said, "You are not thinking right, or living right. I am going to turn your life upside down and inside out. You won't like it for a while, but it will be for your ultimate good." I came out of the storm a new man.' Though it may be difficult for us to admit it, the truth is that some of us cling to things that will be loosened only by a storm.

REFLECTION: The travellers on board the ship bound for Tarshish had to encounter two storms: one was on the sea, the other was in their hearts.

Pray and act

*'All the sailors were afraid and each cried out to his
own god. And they threw the cargo into the sea to lighten
the ship.' Jonah 1:5*

The sailors were not only a praying party but a practical
group also. We must remember, of course, that these men
were praying to non-existent gods, but the point that prayer
must go hand in hand with action is still valid. There is a passive side
to prayer and an active side also. The taking from God must lead to
undertaking for God. These lines make the point most effectively:
'You must use your hands while praying, though, If an answer you
would get, For prayer-worn knees and a rusty hoe Never raised a big
crop yet.' A definition of prayer I have always liked is this: prayer is
receptivity. But if prayer were only receptivity then we would be left
leaning too much towards the passive side of life.

Frequently I reflect on the passage in the New Testament that
tells of Jesus getting up early, while it was still dark, and going off
to a solitary place to pray. Simon Peter searches for Him and when
he finds Him, says, 'Everyone is looking for you.' Jesus replies, 'Let
us go ... so that I can preach' (Mark 1:35–38). Our Lord's praying
was preaching in incubation. The praying stimulated the preaching,
the receptivity became response, the impression of the prayer hour
became the expression of the preaching hour. The most effective
Christians in the world are those who wait quietly before God in
prayer and then rise to put their hands to the practical tasks that
await them.

**REFLECTION: Perhaps the sailors believed in the old adage
that God helps those who help themselves.**

'Plenty of time for you'

'How precious to me are your thoughts, O God! How vast is the sum of them!' Psalm 139:17

God is not only powerful, but personal. The different elements of personality are affirmed of God on almost every page of the Bible. Listen to this: 'I will raise up for myself a faithful priest, who will do according to what is in my heart and mind,' said the Lord to Eli in 1 Samuel 2:35. This shows – if it needs showing – that God has a mind with which He thinks. God has emotions also. God can be angry (Psa. 2:12), jealous (Zech. 1:14–15), merciful (Psa. 78:38), and delighted (Deut. 30:9). These are just a few of the emotions which the Bible talks about.

Then again, God *chooses* and *decides*. Take this, for example: 'The LORD was grieved that he had made man on the earth … So the LORD said, "I will wipe mankind … from the face of the earth"' (Gen. 6:6–7). Many view God as being so exalted and remote that they think He cannot possibly take a personal interest in such small and insignificant creatures as ourselves. Someone once asked Dr Henry Norris Russell, a great astronomer and a Christian: 'How is it possible for such a great and infinite God to have time for me?' This was his reply: 'An infinite God can dispatch the affairs of this universe in the twinkling of an eye, thus giving Him plenty of time for you.'

REFLECTION: Read Psalm 139. If He is a personal God, as we believe He is, then God will have a concern for the people He made, and will want to involve Himself with them in *all* their affairs.

Love is ...

'Love is patient, love is kind ... it is not self-seeking,
it is not easily angered, it keeps no record of wrongs ...
It always protects, always trusts, always hopes, always
perseveres.' **1 Corinthians 13:4–7**

We Christians need the fullness of the Holy Spirit to reveal the fruit of the Spirit in our lives. Are you *filled* with the Spirit? Having the Spirit within results in a quality of life with nine characteristics, the first of which is love. This emphasis on love being foremost fits in with the apostle Paul's emphasis in 1 Corinthians 13. Love is the outcome of the Spirit within and if this is lacking everything is lacking. Make it your goal today to meditate on this priceless passage of Scripture. Do what many Christians do when meditating upon verses 4–7: substitute your name for the word *love*. If we want to become more like Jesus then we must grow in love, for without love we are nothing. You may be tempted to protest that in *your* situation it isn't easy to love. But that's the kind of environment the Holy Spirit thrives upon to make you more and more like Jesus.

A newly arrived missionary was treated roughly by the one she was responsible to. The older woman was spiritually dry, hardened through years of labour without seeing much fruit. That young lady faced the problem by daily going to 1 Corinthians 13 *on her knees* until eventually her older colleague broke down before her in tears and confessed her wrong attitudes. God's love conquers all!

REFLECTION: God's love within me breaks through the impossible. Think about Paul's life and how he displayed Christ-like love in many hostile situations – eg. 2 Corinthians 4:7–11.

How mature am I?

'Knowledge puffs up, but love builds up.' 1 Corinthians 8:1

How mature are you as a Christian? You might answer this question by saying that you have known Jesus Christ as your personal Saviour for a good number of years. But knowledge in itself does not produce spiritual maturity, as 1 Corinthians 8:1 tells us. J.B. Phillips translates this verse as: '... while knowledge may make a man look big, it is only love that can make him grow to his full stature.' Biblical meditation can help us to be more Christ-like in character – to love as He loves. The love a Christian has must be different from any other kind of love – the love of Christ. Paul the apostle was able to declare that he was controlled by this love. A lot of people are controlled by the love of success, of achievement and, most of all, money.

What kind of love controls you? Is it the love of a cause or the love of Christ? God's desire is for His Son's love to flow in and through us like water. When water moves over an incline and strikes a wheel it creates power. If it touches a plant it gives life. Does Christ's love flow into your life enough to impact the people you meet who need their lives transformed by Him?

Meditate on 1 Corinthians 8:1 and ask yourself: Am I someone who merely has a good deal of knowledge or someone who knows how to love with Christ's love?

REFLECTION: Christ's love in me is the language of God's heart. Look up 1 Corinthians 13:4–7. Ask yourself is there anything you need to do so Christ's love might flow through you to others.

Open up to the Holy Spirit

'But you will receive power when the Holy Spirit comes on you ...' Acts 1:8

No one can build a vital relationship with God unless they enter into a day-to-day dependency upon the Holy Spirit. When Paul told the Ephesian Christians to 'be filled with the Spirit' (Eph. 5:18), he was not referring to a one-off experience. The tense of the original Greek should be read: 'Be being filled with the Holy Spirit.'

We are trying to do things beyond our natural resources – hence strain. We must tap new resources. The Holy Spirit is in the world in order to provide us with all the resources we need to do God's work in God's way. When a friend of mine was prayed for to experience the fullness of the Holy Spirit in his life, he experienced an inner release and an anointing of the Spirit that set his whole being on fire. He goes around now sharing God's love with people in a way that is truly refreshing, and he says that his encounter with the Holy Spirit was as real and almost as life-changing as his conversion many years previously.

I am not concerned here about entering into a discussion of the theological implications of what is often called 'the baptism in the Holy Spirit', but let me just ask you a simple question: are you aware of the Holy Spirit's power flowing and pulsing through your life at this very moment? If you are not, then let me urge you to open your heart to God and invite Him to fill you to overflowing by the power of His Spirit.

REFLECTION: The issue is not so much do you have the Holy Spirit, but rather, does the Holy Spirit have you?

Spend time in the Bible

'... faith comes from hearing the message, and the message is heard through the word of Christ.' Romans 10:17

One of the ways we can maintain a close relationship with God is by spending time with Him in the Bible – daily, if possible. If we believe that God speaks through the Bible to His people today, then we will count any day incomplete which does not include some time given to its study and perusal.

A book so divinely inspired needs divine help in order to be understood. That is why we must come to it with a prayer on our lips, that we might not only understand it, but know how best to translate its message into our daily lives.

The eternal God lives in its pages and speaks through it with the same power and authority that He did when it was first written. How foolish we are if we fail, then, to study it daily; store precious fragments of it in our memory; learn its highways and byways and make reading it reverently a priority each day.

The better you know the Bible, the more effective you will be in leading people to Jesus Christ. We communicate to others only from out of our own understanding and our own resources. Study the Bible not only for your own personal pleasure but for the profit of others. Get to know the Bible so intimately that whatever page you open, you can find a path that leads to Jesus.

REFLECTION: Remember this – the more you acquaint yourself with the Bible, the more God can use you. I have seen this principle at work in my own life, and in the lives of countless other Christians. It never fails.

Citizens of heaven

'... our citizenship is in heaven.' Philippians 3:20

What does being a citizen of heaven involve? Examine the context of this verse with me for a moment. The apostle has just been talking about those whose minds are set on earthly things, those whom he describes as 'enemies of the cross of Christ' (v.18). True Christians, he is saying, look to the things that are eternal and set their minds on what is above.

Philippi had the distinction of being a Roman colony, with all the privileges which that brought in the ancient world. But Paul wanted his Philippian readers to understand that they had a higher allegiance – they were citizens of heaven. To be a citizen of heaven means that though during our life here on the earth we obey the laws of the state, pay our taxes and act honourably and honestly in every circumstance, our supreme loyalty and love lie elsewhere. It is heaven's commands that prevail in our lives, and it is the mind of the King in heaven that we seek to know most of all. The alien world in which we live influences us all. Its judgments affect us, its atmosphere is not conducive to our spiritual development, and its pressures bear on us in ten thousand ways. How easy it is, without us realising it, to become 'conformed to the world', as Paul warns us in Romans 12:2. We should be loyal subjects of the country in which we live, but that allegiance is secondary – first and foremost we are citizens of heaven.

REFLECTION: The secret of success in the Christian life is to realise that now you have a new nationality requiring a new allegiance.

Ambassadors of heaven

'We are therefore Christ's ambassadors ...'
2 Corinthians 5:20

Paul tells us that we are ambassadors – personal representatives of our heavenly King! Now, an ambassador's allegiance is to his own land and head of state. For instance, the American ambassador to Britain resides in London but his citizenship and love and loyalty belong to his home country. It is a high privilege to be an ambassador. But there are also dangers associated with the role. According to Lord Templewood, one of the dangers an ambassador faces is staying too long in the country to which he has been sent; that is to say, if he does not make frequent visits to his own land, breathe his own native air, reacquaint himself with his native customs and familiarise himself with all that is going on, he can quickly become 'denationalised'. He must return home frequently, absorb his own atmosphere, renew his strength by contact with his native soil so that he does not lose his orientation.

How can we who are citizens of heaven save ourselves from being not so much 'denationalised' but 'despiritualised'? We must breathe the atmosphere of heaven by talking frequently to God in prayer, meditating on the Scriptures, and setting our 'hearts on things above, where Christ is seated at the right hand of God' (Col. 3:1). There is no way that a Christian ambassador can retain his or her true citizenship in this alien world without regular (preferably daily) prayer and meditation on the Scriptures.

REFLECTION: As an ambassador of heaven you must return whenever you can to your own environment.

Becoming heaven's citizen

'Repent and be baptised ... in the name of Jesus Christ for the forgiveness of your sins.' Acts 2:38

We cannot purchase heavenly citizenship, earn it, or have it passed on to us by our parents so how do we become citizens of the heavenly kingdom? We are invited to consider heaven as a city with twelve gates (Rev. 21:21). Some think the writer is portraying heaven in allegorical terms, but whether he is or not, it is clear he is describing a picturesque and beautiful place. Notice that every gate into the New Jerusalem is made of pearl. I have often remarked that a pearl is a product of pain. When an oyster is invaded by something perhaps a grain of sand – it secretes a liquid which hardens and then becomes a pearl.

I think the reason why the gates of the New Jerusalem are made of pearl is to convey to us that the entrance into the eternal city is through the wounds of Christ on the cross, now healed of course but remaining forever the one and only way into the divine presence. Catch the symbolism of this: the only way into the city of God is through a gate made of pearl. In other words, those who enter the city do so trusting the work that Christ did for them on the cross. You can't scale those jasper walls. You must go in through a gate – a gate made of pearl. Accept in penitence the sacrifice made on your behalf by Christ on the cross and nothing will stop you claiming citizenship of the divine kingdom.

REFLECTION: Money is a passport and can buy you many things down here on earth but it has no power to gain you a place in heaven.

Continual growth

'The righteous will flourish like a palm tree, they will grow like a cedar of Lebanon ...' Psalm 92:12

I invite you now to ask yourself this important question: How well am I growing in the Christian life? Am I thriving or just surviving? Take it from me, when it comes to your spiritual development, you are meant not simply to survive but to thrive. The creative God made you for creative growth. Spiritual growth is required of us by God and is essential for our spiritual wellbeing. Violate that requirement and you violate yourself. You will be unfulfilled, frustrated and unhappy.

However much we may thrive physically, there comes a time when the body slows down and decay sets in. This process of slowing down and starting to decay may be minimised to some degree by, to use the words of one doctor, 'how well we look after our arteries and our attitudes'. Our mental state plays a vital role in keeping the body going, but eventually the body is destined to return to the dust. Not so, however, with the soul. The soul in which Christ lives is meant to go on growing and thriving until we step out of the physical realm into the eternal. But some people's sole aim is to ward off sickness and delay the moment of death – they are totally bound up with the state of their body. Thus when it decays, they decay.

REFLECTION: Spiritual growth is required of us by God and is essential for our spiritual wellbeing. How sad it is to watch a person thrive physically, yet at the same time witness the decay of their soul.

A growing Christian

'... as servants of God we commend ourselves in every way ...' 2 Corinthians 6:4

I would like to draw for you a profile of a spiritually thriving Christian. Here are what I consider to be the ten marks of someone who is growing in a balanced and not a lop-sided way.

He or she is someone who (1) understands the design of God for their being; (2) is in touch with their deepest longings; (3) knows that they can find total security, worth and significance in God; (4) has set a goal which determines all other goals – the goal of pleasing Him; (5) manages their emotions; (6) drinks deeply of the living water that Christ provides through a rich relationship with Him in prayer; (7) comprehends the importance of filling the mind with the wisdom that comes from God's Word, the Bible; (8) is free of anger and resentment, anxiety and fear, guilt and shame; (9) loves others in the way that they themselves are loved by God; (10) ensures that they are taking the necessary steps to respect their physical being.

Does this mean we can exhibit all these characteristics every moment of our lives? No, there will be times when we fail. But we can quickly get back on track again when we follow the principles I have laid down in these meditations. God has given us a clear chart and an accurate compass in the Scriptures and these provide us with all the information we need to keep on course.

REFLECTION: Don't be too discouraged if you are blown off course – seek to get back on course as quickly as possible. God has provided us with a clear chart and accurate compass in the Scriptures.

Live within your budget

'Do two walk together unless they have agreed to do so?'
Amos 3:3

A cartoon I saw some time ago depicted a newly-wed couple with a well-wisher saying, 'Have a happy marriage.' The young bride replied, 'Don't worry. We won't have any problems for we agree on most things – except money.' The Bible is full of exhortations, commands and warnings, about the subject of money. Greed is everywhere denounced in the Scriptures and generosity everywhere extolled. Someone has said that Jesus Christ had more to say about money and possessions than He did about both the subject of hell and heaven combined.

One of the major difficulties people run into in marriage is the problem of over-spending. This is usually because there is no budget or detailed spending guide. Few people would begin a journey to an unfamiliar destination without a map. Yet a survey in the twentieth century showed that only *one family in fourteen* used a simple family budget system. A budget is simply a cash forecast – a list of upcoming expenditures over a given period of time. Every good business has one, and every Christian family concerned about the right use of the Lord's money should operate one.

Remember, a budget is not necessarily a magic wand which you wave over your finances and hey presto, all your money problems disappear. It takes discipline to establish a budget and even more discipline to maintain it.

REFLECTION: Failing to plan is often referred to as planning to fail.

'The Enough'

'May God Almighty bless you ...' Genesis 28:3

The Hebrew name El Shaddai, which appears in our Bibles as 'God Almighty', can also be translated 'The Nourisher of His People'. One Bible teacher suggests that the English equivalent of El Shaddai is 'The Enough'. However we translate this name, it certainly conveys the fact that God's resources infinitely exceed our requirements. His sufficiency immeasurably surpasses every demand that we may make upon it. There is grace enough for everything – even the most heinous sin. Has it ever occurred to you that only sinners can appreciate grace? It is sin that transforms love into grace. Truly, to a believer, the message of grace is the sweetest sound.

When D.L. Moody, the American evangelist was meditating on the theme of grace, he was so captivated by the thought that, flinging aside his pen, he dashed out into the street where he accosted the first man he met and demanded: 'Do you know grace?' 'Grace who?' asked the surprised man. On the wall of an office in New York where major business deals are transacted there hangs a card which reads: 'We talk abundance here.' When Christians talk about the grace of God revealed in Jesus Christ, they should 'talk abundance'. As the old hymn so fittingly describes God's grace: 'Its streams the whole creation reach, So plenteous is its store, Enough for all, enough for each, Enough for evermore.'

REFLECTION: Consider the words of Wesley's hymn: 'Plenteous grace with Thee is found, Grace to cover all my sin.' All!

Grace for suffering

'My grace is sufficient for you …' 2 Corinthians 12:9

Not only is there sufficient grace to deal with our sin, there is grace for suffering too. 2 Corinthians 12:1–10 makes that abundantly clear. Paul talks about having a thorn in the flesh. What was it? Some think it was ophthalmia. Others believe it was recurring malaria, or epilepsy. One commentator believes it to be a troublesome evil spirit that was allowed by God to harass the apostle and so keep him humble. Chrysostom, one of the Early Church Fathers, believed the 'messenger of Satan' was 'all the adversaries of the word … for they did Satan's business'. It is impossible for anyone to be sure exactly what Paul's thorn in the flesh was. One writer has wittily observed: 'Paul had a thorn in the flesh and nobody knows what it was; if we have a thorn in the flesh everybody knows what it is!' What we do know for certain is that Paul's thorn in the flesh was sufficiently distressing for him to plead with the Lord three times for it to be taken away. Yet it remained. And at last came the comforting word: 'My grace is sufficient for you, for my power is made perfect in weakness' (2 Cor. 12:9).

I love the Living Bible paraphrase of this text that reads: 'My power shows up best in weak people.' Are you suffering at the moment? A sickness perhaps? Or harassment and persecution? God's grace was sufficient for the apostle in his suffering and it will be also for you.

REFLECTION: Take this truth to heart: there is grace not only to cover our sin but also to sustain us in times of suffering.

What we can't do without

'I became a servant of this gospel by the gift of God's grace ...' Ephesians 3:7

Grace comes in sufficient quantities from God to cover every sin, and also strengthens us to cope with every kind of suffering. But there's more – there's grace for service too. Paul, in 1 Corinthians 15:1–11, is defending himself against his critics. Referring to the other apostles, he says: 'I worked harder than all of them' (v.10). At first this sounds like an arrogant boast. But he immediately qualifies it by saying: 'yet not I, but the grace of God that was with me.' Believe me, you cannot go far in the realm of Christian service without that.

So often our labours for Christ go unnoticed by others, or unappreciated, or unrewarded (in earthly terms, I mean). They may even be apparently unfruitful. Unless we are empowered by the grace of God then it is so easy to lose heart and give up. But there is no need for that situation to arise because He has grace – grace in abundance – to give to those who need it. If you allow Him, He will give you the patience and courage to press on. Then, when at last you come to the end of life's journey and look back upon a record of faithful toil, like the apostle Paul you will disclaim any entitlement to recognition or praise and say as he did: 'Yet not I, but the grace of God that was with me.' And God has enough grace for everyone.

REFLECTION: There are many things we can do without in this world: wealth, standing, education, friends; but we cannot do without grace.

Desire more grace

'Ask and it will be given to you ...' Matthew 7:7

A characteristic I have observed in some Christians is this: they seek grace earnestly. They want it more than they want anything else. Fletcher of Madeley was a great friend of John Wesley and the man whom Wesley designated as his successor in the leadership of the Methodist people, though as it turned out he died before Wesley. Fletcher once made an important public statement on an issue that was exercising the minds of many people at that time, and by so doing rendered a great service to the government of the day. The then Lord Chancellor dispatched an official to ask Fletcher if there was anything he wanted in return for the service he had done for the country. 'How very kind,' said Fletcher to the official when he delivered his message. 'But I want nothing except more grace.' Imagine the official returning to the Lord Chancellor and reporting: 'He doesn't want anything. There is nothing we have that appeals to him. He only wants more grace.'

We must always look at the treasures of earth in the light of heaven. We should realise that the most valuable thing one can possess on this earth is grace, and want it ardently. 'Let me have that', you will say, 'and I can handle anything that comes.' So it is not enough to know that grace is there or to keep it constantly in mind; we must want it more than we want anything else. 'Ask and it will be given.'

REFLECTION: Knowing God is a God of grace is not enough; we must want the grace He gives and want it ardently.

'God's great intolerance'

'... they have rejected the law of the LORD Almighty ...
Therefore the LORD's anger burns ...' Isaiah 5:24–25

I urge you never, never to view the wrath of God as a moral blemish or a flaw in His character. Quite the reverse.

Those who think of God's wrath in terms of a grumpy tantrum or a desire for retaliation – inflicting punishment for the sake of it or in return for some injury received – do not understand it. Divine wrath is not vindictiveness; it is divine perfection, and issues forth from God because it is right. One of the things we must always be willing to face as human beings is our tendency to make God in our own image. Instead of reasoning from the divine down to the human, and recognising that sin has marred the divine image within us, we reason from our fallen condition and project our own feelings and ideas onto God. What goes on in our hearts when we are angry is generally a mixture of unpredictable petulance, retaliation, hostility and self-concern. God's anger is always predictable, always constant, and always set against sin. We must never forget that God's nature is *uncompromisingly* set against sin. Though we may tolerate it, He never does. Sin has been defined as 'God's one great intolerance', and for that we ought to be eternally grateful. No loving mother or father tolerates anything which may harm their child. As God's children, we ought to rejoice that He will not tolerate anything harmful either.

REFLECTION: Arthur W. Pink describes the wrath of God in this way: it is ' ... the holiness of God stirred into activity against sin'.

In all things

'And we know that in all things God works for the good of those who love him ...' Romans 8:28

S ome situations we face may have evil ingredients in them, but it must be clearly understood that although God sometimes uses evil, He does not purpose it or design it. The only reason God permitted evil in His universe was because He knew He could outwit it and turn it to good. Romans 8:28, in the Authorised Version – 'all things work together for good to them that love God' – may give the impression that God is responsible for everything that happens to us, but a closer examination of that text shows differently. The NIV reads, 'And we know that in all things God works for the good of those who love him'. The slight difference in the wording is crucial. To say that 'all things work together for good' is not the same as saying 'we know that in all things God works for the good of those who love him'. All things do not necessarily work together for good: they may work for evil. To say that 'in all things God works for the good' endows those 'things' with purpose – a purpose for good to those who love Him. Things by themselves have no purpose unless we and God put a purpose in them. The 'things' may not be good, and may not themselves work together for good, but 'in' those things God places His purpose and makes them contribute to His ends. He turns the evil into good if we co-operate with Him and love Him.

REFLECTION: God is not responsible for everything that happens to us, but takes responsibility to make it contribute to His purposes.

Those who love Him

'And we know that in all things God works for the good of those who love him ...' Romans 8:28

hy is our love and co-operation so necessary for God to further His purposes through the difficult events and situations that arise from time to time in our lives? The answer is found in a statement I have used hundreds of times and I make no apology for using it again. It contains a most powerful and life-changing truth: *it is not so much what happens to us, but how we view it that is important.* In other words, our inner attitudes determine the final results. God's ability to make a difficult or unpleasant situation work for good is limited by our capacity to love Him and co-operate with Him. If we love Him, we will trust Him, and if we trust Him, then we will rest assured that nothing that happens to us can successfully work against us.

To triumph in adversity means that God is doing His part and you are doing yours. First, we need to realise that, although we are Christians, we are not exempt from the ordinary problems and difficulties that afflict humanity. Unfortunately, not all Christians see it in these terms, and instead of being sweetened by life's situations, they are soured by them. If we insist that we ought to be exempt, then, when adversity strikes, we will go down like ninepins. If we say such things as, 'Why should this happen to me? I'm a Christian. God should treat me better,' then we take the first step towards depression and disillusionment.

REFLECTION: A Christian has a perspective on life that assures them that whatever happens can be used to God's glory.

Repent and turn

'... they should repent and turn to God and prove their repentance by their deeds.' Acts 26:20

The word repentance comes from the Greek word *metanoia* which means a change of mind. Several other states of mind can easily be mistaken for repentance, so before proceeding any further it may be well, as far as possible, to clear away any misunderstandings. *Repentance is not regret.* Regret is being sorry for oneself, deploring the consequences of one's actions but not necessarily making a change. *Repentance is not remorse.* Remorse is sorrow without hope at its heart; it is an emotion of disgust. It eats its heart out instead of seeking a new heart. *Repentance is not reformation.* Reformation (changing one's way of life) may follow repentance, but it can never precede it. *Repentance is not reparation.* Reparation or restitution is practical proof of the reality of repentance but it must not be mistaken for repentance.

I am afraid that what often passes for repentance in the Christian community is not real repentance at all; it is only remorse or regret. *Where there is no genuine repentance there can be no ongoing and developing relationship with God.* Where there is no struggle to face the appalling fact of inbred sin, no mourning over our stubborn commitment to independence, there will be less subsequent joy and rapture in the soul and less possibility of a great change in character.

REFLECTION: A spiritual earthquake needs to take place so we see ourselves as we really are – needy souls in need of forgiveness and a new view of reality.

Develop a prayer pattern

'Three times a day he got down on his knees and prayed
... just as he had done before.' Daniel 6:10

Decide firstly on how long your prayer time is going to be. Those who are experienced in prayer claim that they need at least half an hour to achieve effectiveness, but if this amount of time presents problems to you then begin with fifteen minutes. One can hardly get anywhere on less. Plan your time to cover the three following aspects. You will need to look at *God*. You will need to look at *yourself*. You will need to look at *others*. Divide your time into three sections so that you cover all these aspects. You can, of course, vary the timings on each aspect as God directs but no sustained prayer pattern which omits these three areas will be effective.

Looking at God means adoring Him, praising Him and thanking Him for the multiplicity of His blessings toward you. Spend some time reflecting on the fact that you, a soiled sinner, are made welcome in the presence of a holy God, and that He encourages you not only to come but to *linger* in His presence. Let your mind run over the many reasons you have to be thankful. It's surprising how they mount up as you begin to list them one by one – home, friends, family, food, health, the church, and so on. If you do not enjoy some of the blessings I have listed, then think of the things you *do* enjoy. Ponder them until your heart overflows with gratitude and thanksgiving rises, because it will.

REFLECTION: We should not rush our times with God but approach them with peace, pleasure, praise and purpose.

Carry on praying

'I urge, then, first of all, that requests, prayers,
intercession and thanksgiving be made for everyone ...'
1 Timothy 2:1

*L*ooking at yourself means praying about your own spiritual condition. At this stage of prayer, let one thought be predominant: How can I become more like Jesus? 'Christ', someone said, 'is a perfect mirror: He reflects a perfect likeness of the image which falls upon Him.' Sometimes, friends and acquaintances will overlook our faults and exaggerate our good points, but Jesus will always give us an honest appraisal of ourselves. So as you look into the mirror of Christ and measure your life alongside His, ask Him to show you any faults, imperfections or sins that need to be confessed and put right. The best place in all the world to see yourself is in Christ, because when you look at Him you not only see yourself as you really are, but He gives you the strength and the grace to do something about it. *Petition* for your own personal needs can be done in this second section of the prayer pattern.

Looking at others means praying for others. Keep lists of people you know who are in special need. Mention people by name and tell God plainly what you would like Him to do for them – to heal their sickness, save their marriage, help them to find employment, and so on. It also involves, of course, praying for such things as special events in the church, or needs in the community, nation, or the world.

REFLECTION: As I seek God for Himself and not for the things He can do for me, then He will see to it that I will get all the things I need.

The Divine Eagle

'... like an eagle that stirs up its nest and hovers over its young, that spreads its wings to catch them ...'
Deuteronomy 32:11

God is pictured as a mother Eagle pushing her offspring out of the nest in order to teach them how to fly. An eagle makes a wonderful mother. She builds her nest in the tall trees away from the prying hands of men, taking the utmost care to line it with the softest feathers she can find. When her eggs hatch and the little eaglets are born, she gives them her complete and undivided attention. Nothing is too good for her precious brood.

After several weeks of this tender, loving care, the mother eagle suddenly changes in her behaviour. She knows it is now time for her eaglets to leave the nest and learn to fly. So, reaching down into the nest, she rips out the feathers, breaks up the twigs and overturns their nice, comfortable home. The little eaglets are frightened out of their wits. Gently she nudges one of the birds towards the edge of the overturned nest and pushes it out into the air. The little bird, of course, falls like a bullet to the ground, squawking with fright, but just as it is about to hit the ground, the mother eagle swoops beneath it, catches it on her broad wings and carries it safely up into the sky. Then she tilts her wing and the bird falls once again, but this time, as it flaps its wings in fright, it discovers it can fly!

And this, my friend, is what God does with you and me.

REFLECTION: God pushes us out of our comfortable nests in order that we might expand our wings and soar towards His highest purposes.

Thrown out of the nest

'... like an eagle that stirs up its nest ... that spreads its wings to catch them and carries them on its pinions.'
Deuteronomy 32:11

The gripping truth of God pushing us forwards is a principle that is deeply embedded in Scripture. If we fail to comprehend it, we deprive ourselves of an important spiritual insight. We see it when we consider the captivity of the Children of Israel in Egypt. There can be no doubt that the Israelites were not greatly motivated to set out on the long march to the 'promised land' until God permitted Pharaoh to put such pressure upon them that they regarded any measures as better than their present distress. The oppression opened a door! Our discomforts, sorrows, disappointments and overturned nests become the starting points of progress. The deprivations we experience motivate us towards greater usefulness.

How many of us would be where we are today had not God overturned our lives, changed our circumstances, allowed us to be disappointed and deprived, permitted us to walk through the deepest darkness in order that we might find ourselves on 'the growing edge'. God had to upset us to set us up. An illustration of this is seen when Jesus announced that He was going away for good. The news must have hit the disciples like a bombshell. But at Pentecost He came back and changed His presence for His omnipresence. Not only was His presence available, but His power was available – unlimited resources at their disposal at any and all times.

REFLECTION: We are not meant to make comfortable nests but to go into all the world and make disciples.

Attitudes to trouble

'Consider it pure joy, my brothers, whenever you face trials of many kinds ...' James 1:2

Many Christians think that sudden calamity or serious trouble is an indication that God is punishing them for some sin. This attitude makes victory impossible. We must recognise, of course, that this is a world of moral consequences and that sin does bring trouble, but we are indebted to Jesus for showing us that sin and calamity are not always directly connected. In His comment on the fall of the tower at Siloam and on those who lost their lives, Jesus said the sufferers were not worse sinners than the rest. When trouble comes our attitude should be that described in James' letter. And why? Because what happens to us – sorrows, griefs, losses, disappointments – can help us to leave the nest, expand our wings and soar to new heights and new discoveries of God. Our inner attitudes determine the results.

Just in case anyone might misinterpret my meaning when I say that looking upon troubles as God's punishment for sin makes victory impossible, let me make it clear that I certainly believe some troubles are the direct result of personal sin. A lie, for example, can bring untold repercussions. Pre-marital sex can produce an unplanned pregnancy. When we violate God's laws then we have to suffer the consequences. The troubles I am talking about here, however, are those for which we have no direct responsibility but are allowed by God for our ultimate benefit.

REFLECTION: The Divine Eagle never disturbs our nest but for a good purpose and He never takes away the good without giving something much better.

Don't flap — soar!

'... those who hope in the Lord will renew their strength.
They will soar on wings like eagles ...' Isaiah 40:31

Isaiah says that an eagle 'soars', not 'flaps'. Although, of course, an eagle is well able to use its wings to propel itself across the sky, its typical pose is that of soaring. An eagle will sometimes perch on a high rock and wait for a while — testing the winds. When it feels that the right wind is blowing, it expands its broad wings and is at once lifted by the breeze into the great heights. We must understand that God does not permit trouble to come our way in order to destroy us but in order to develop us. In every trial and difficulty that God allows to come our way, there is a breeze, that if we wait for it and take advantage of it, will lift us clean beyond the clouds where we will see the face of God. You see, life is determined more by our reactions than by our actions.

When God allows things to crowd into your life, it is then that reaction counts. You can react in self-pity and in frustration or with confidence and courage and turn the trouble into a triumph. When trouble strikes and your nest is overturned — don't panic. Wait for the breeze that is springing up; it will lift you clean into the presence of God. Those who wait, who keep hoping, are those who soar. This is the eagle's secret of being able to soar so high — waiting. When troubles come, don't flap — soar!

REFLECTION: When circumstances are against us, we must be able to set the tilt of our wings and use adversity to lift us higher into the presence of God.

Wings of our spirit

'And we know that in all things God works for the good of those who love him ...' Romans 8:28

W hen the storm strikes, if an eagle's wings are set in a downwards tilt, it will be dashed to pieces on the ground; but if its wings are tilted upwards, it will rise, making the storm bear it up beyond its fury. The Christian faith, providing we interpret it correctly and apply it to our circumstances, will set the wings of our spirit in the right direction, so that when trouble or calamity strikes, we go up and not down. The same calamity strikes another, one with his wings set upwards, and he soars above it – calm and serene. Some students, discussing Romans 8:28, said to a theological professor, 'But, professor, you don't believe that all things work together for good – all the pain, suffering and misery – do you?' The professor replied: 'The things, in themselves, may not be good, but God can make them work together for good.'

That afternoon his wife was killed in a car accident. Before leaving the college, he left his students this message: 'Romans 8:28 still holds good.' When the professor died a year later, his friends and relatives inscribed Romans 8:28 on his tomb. Many a student has stood at that tomb and prayed that he might have that same spiritual insight. But it is not enough to have Romans 8:28 inscribed on our tomb, it must be inscribed in our life convictions.

REFLECTION: The wings of our spirit are tilted upwards, not on the basis of foolish optimism, but on our hope in God.

God's loving disciplines

'They knew he was running away from the LORD, because he had already told them so.' Jonah 1:10

W hen we look at God's ways from the vantage point of the whole of Scripture we see that what drives Him is not the desire to battle with the human will and win, but benevolence and love. C.S. Lewis wrote that 'When we want to be something other than the thing God wants us to be, we must be wanting what, in fact, will not make us happy'.[2] God knew that Jonah would never be fulfilled outside His will and He set about doing for him what he needed, not what he wanted. Some might consider it petulant of God to have chased Jonah when he wanted to get away, but a great tragedy would have occurred if God had allowed him to keep running.

When you know God wants you to do something, don't run. God may not stop you as He did Jonah. The fact is that God loves us too much not to discipline us. Personally, I have doubts about using the word 'punishment' in connection with a believer; a better word, I think, is 'discipline'. 'God disciplines us for our good, that we may share in his holiness' (Heb. 12:10). God was not so much punishing Jonah for the mentality that led him to run away but disciplining him so that he could still be used in the future. Sometimes God's disciplines seem harsh and unkind, but behind them is a heart that beats with love. He loves us too much to let us get away with things.

REFLECTION: The next time you feel that God is disciplining you then remember this: If He didn't love you so much He would not persist in the way He does.

Penance or repentance?

*'Pick me up and throw me into the sea ... I know that it is
my fault that this great storm has come upon you.'*
Jonah 1:12

Jonah's request can be seen as an act of penance. There was
only one way for Jonah to be restored, and that was not by
being cast into the sea but by casting himself into the arms of a
loving and merciful God. It was not penance that was needed at that
moment; it was repentance. Repentance is much more than eating
humble pie, says C.S. Lewis. 'It means unlearning all the self-conceit
and self-will that we have been training ourselves into for ... years.
It means killing a part of yourself, undergoing a kind of death.' This
'kind of death' is not something God demands of us before He will
take us back; it is simply a description of what going back to Him is
like. If we ask God to take us back without it, he says, then we are
really asking Him to take us back without going back.

When I was last in India I saw a man who had bound himself
in chains sitting outside the tent where I was due to speak.
Apparently, he was attempting to pay a penance for his sins. If he had
come into the tent he would have heard that penance is not enough.
Penance without repentance is mere self-punishment. That is what
Jonah wanted to do – he wanted to provide his own atonement.
Penance has a place in the Christian life but it always comes after
repentance – never before it. The reversal of this important issue is
'another gospel'.

REFLECTION: **An act of penance may be appropriate after one
has received forgiveness, but it must never be thought of as
earning forgiveness.**

God also loves the ungodly

'Instead, the men did their best to row back to land.'
Jonah 1:13

T he sailors who manned the ship wanted to do everything in
their power to avoid throwing Jonah overboard. Instead of
acceding to his request, they concentrate on rowing as hard
as they can towards the shore. To Jonah, the crew were heathens,
but as they showed their concern for him, he was sharing, whether
he felt it or not, a common bond with them – the bond of humanity.
I wonder, did Jonah realise as he saw them toiling in their rowing
that their concern was not only for themselves but also for him?

Jonah was fleeing from God because he did not want to carry
the message of God's loving concern to Gentiles. Yet here, before
his very eyes, a group of Gentiles were showing more concern
and compassion for him than he had for them. They were closer
in character to God and to what was right than he was. Before we
begin to feel superior to Jonah with his many failures, perhaps we
ought to take a long look at our own attitudes and ask ourselves: Do
unbelievers show more compassion and concern for us than we do
for them? God wants us to be concerned about all who live in His
world regardless of nationality or whether they are saved or lost.

R.E. White, the former principal of a Scottish Bible college, once
posed this question to his students: 'Why is it so hard for the godly to
believe that God also loves the ungodly?' Why indeed.

**REFLECTION: We need to view the ungodly as God views them
– with love and compassion.**

A whale of a tale

'But the LORD provided a great fish to swallow Jonah ...'
Jonah 1:17

Some regard the story of Jonah as an Old Testament parable but we must take into account the fact that God works miracles. First, we see a miracle of timing – God arranges for a great fish to be at the right place at the right time. Second, a miracle of sustenance – Jonah is kept alive for three days. If we look back on the story after having read the New Testament, with its accounts of such miracles as the feeding of the five thousand, the healing of the blind, the stilling of the storm and, of course, the most incredible miracle of all – Christ's resurrection – it becomes easier to accept it.

One writer says that if you believe in a personal God then you have to believe that He can act upon His creation in a way that changes things. 'The sea is his, for he made it, and his hands formed the dry land' (Psa. 95:5). He can suspend the laws of nature or speed them up at will. Every year water is turned into wine in wineries all over the world – a natural process. But one day Jesus speeded up the whole process and did it in minutes. I refer, of course, to the miracle at Cana of Galilee. If God in Christ could do that then, quite frankly, I do not find it difficult to believe that He could cause a man to be swallowed by a large fish and sustain him there for three days and three nights. With God, nothing is impossible.

REFLECTION: *The NIV Bible Commentary* **says: 'Cases are occasionally cited of men recently lost overboard being recovered by whalers, still alive inside their catch.'**

OCTOBER 1

The God of all grace

'For it is by grace you have been saved, through faith ...
it is the gift of God ...' Ephesians 2:8

The old definition of grace that almost every Christian will know is one that I believe cannot be improved upon: 'Grace is the free unmerited favour of God.' It means that at the heart of all true communion with God there lies this gripping truth: God takes the initiative. He is more inclined towards us than we are towards Him. We cannot earn His affection any more than we can earn a loving mother's affection. We have simply to receive it. When you originally came to Him you came because He drew you. The very faith by which you believe in Him is not of yourself; it is, as today's text tells us, 'the *gift* of God'. Nor is it only your salvation that is a free gift. Every step you make on your spiritual pilgrimage is possible simply because of God's grace. This teaching, I know, affronts people these days because they like to feel that they can 'work their passage to heaven', to use the words of one preacher. That is like someone in debt for a million pounds trying to get the one to whom he is indebted to accept his resources of a few pence as being sufficient to clear the debt.

Read again Paul's words to the Ephesians and let them sink deep into your soul. Grace is a gift. You do not have to achieve, but simply receive.

REFLECTION: As one writer puts it, 'Grace is bound to be sovereign since it cannot by its very nature be subject to compulsion'. That is why we often refer to grace in hymns and prayers as *free* grace.

Honesty is the best policy

'Search me, O God, and know my heart; test me and know my anxious thoughts. See if there is any offensive way in me, and lead me in the way everlasting.' Psalm 139:23–24

I t is a mistake to overlook the fact that honesty can be challenging, but it is equally wrong to assume that being honest is a miserable and terrifying experience. On the contrary, when the issues that go on in the soul are faced, really faced, then real healing begins. Reality is hardly ever as bad as the fear of it ...

The soul can never function as it was designed to function unless there is complete honesty. But self-honesty does not come painlessly. Those who study the function of behaviour tell us that the reason we lie to others or ourselves is to avoid the pain that honesty might cause us. President Nixon's lying about Watergate was no more sophisticated or different in kind than that of a four-year-old boy who lies to his mother about how the lamp fell off the table. Both are an attempt to circumnavigate legitimate suffering. The healing of the soul is such a major issue that we must not let anything stand in its way. There must be no evasions, subterfuges, or prevarications. Honesty really is the best policy.

I urge you to fight with every fibre of your being the temptation to avoid facing the demands that rise up from within your inner being. Be alert to the tendency we all have to deny reality. Being open to challenge is disturbing, but life, real life, cannot be found without experiencing some upheavals in the soul.

REFLECTION: Ask God to help you search and see if there is any denial in you.

What is the answer?

'... let us draw near to God with a sincere heart in full assurance of faith ...' Hebrews 10:22

We need God if the ache in our souls is to be satisfied – that's the truth of it. The emptiness of our hearts will never be filled until they are filled with God. But how do we find God? How do we get to know him?

Getting into a relationship with God is not essentially different from getting into a relationship with a human being. First there is the stage of drawing near. This is the tentative, explorative stage. Then there is the second stage – when there is a desire to give yourself to the other person – the stage of decision. The third stage is when you actually give yourself to the other person and there is a mutual exchange of the selves. The stage of commitment. You belong to the other person and the other person belongs to you. From then on there is a continuous mutual adjustment of mind to mind, will to will and being to being, down through the years.

There are those, of course, who say they will not believe in God or give themselves to Him until He proves Himself to them. What they reveal by that statement is their lack of awareness of the elements of relationship. 'Prove Him to me', someone said to me on one occasion, 'and I will believe in Him'. The only way to *know* another person is not by logic, mathematical systems or laboratory experiments, but by venturing upon a relationship.

REFLECTION: God has invited you to know Him and to enter into a deep personal relationship with Him.

Why am I so thirsty?

'Let them give thanks to the Lord for his unfailing love ...
for he satisfies the thirsty and fills the hungry with good
things.' Psalm 107:8–9

When the Creator made us in the beginning, He put within us a thirst for Himself which is too strong and powerful to be satisfied by anything less than Himself. A legend which comes from the Western Isles of Scotland illustrates this point most graphically. It concerns a sea king who greatly desired the company of a human being.

One day he heard in his cavern under the sea a cry – a human cry – and rising to the surface he saw in the distance a little child in a derelict boat. Just as he was about to make for the vessel and take the child, a rescue party intervened and he missed his prize. As the rescue party hitched a line to the boat and drew it away, the sea king cupped his hand and threw into the heart of the child a little salt wave and said as he submerged: 'The child is mine. When it grows the salt sea will call him and he will come home to me at last.'

The legend ends with the account of how when the child grew up he felt the call of the ocean in his blood and spent his life sailing the high seas. It is only a story of course, but it enshrines the timeless truth that God has put into every human heart a desire for Himself which though it may be hidden, ignored, overlaid or even denied ... it cannot be removed.

REFLECTION: We were made with a thirst no water on earth can satisfy – an ache only God can assuage. Do you tend still to look to other things to satisfy? Why?

Wrong thoughts

'... whatever is true, whatever is noble ... right ... pure ... lovely ... admirable ... excellent or praiseworthy – think about such things.' Philippians 4:8

Wrong thoughts in themselves are not sin. 'We can't stop the birds flying over our heads,' said one theologian, 'but we can stop them building nests.' Evil thoughts only become sin when the mind fondles them, nurtures them and continues to hold on to them. Encourage people not to repress the thoughts, but to lift them up to God in *praise*. Though at first this might sound like a very unspiritual technique, it does in fact work. For if we push wrong thoughts into our subconscious mind and try to bury them there – they are buried *alive*. They continue to work in the subconscious in different ways. So we lift them to God. But why praise God for evil thoughts? Isn't that going too far?

See how this principle works in the life of a Christian familiar with the technique. One day he is going down the road thinking of nothing in particular when a wrong thought enters his mind. Instantly he brings that wrong thought to God in an attitude of praise. He says, 'Thank You, Lord, for this wrong thought, because through it my attention is being drawn to You; it has become a stepping-stone which is making me more aware of Your presence and Your love in my life.' You can be sure that if Satan is responsible for sending the wrong thoughts, he will soon give up, because the last thing he wants to do is divert a believer's attention to his heavenly Father.

REFLECTION: Next time you have a wrong thought try immediately focusing on God and praising Him. And encourage others to do the same.

Not growing spiritually

'Do your best to present yourself to God as one approved, a workman ...' 2 Timothy 2:15

There are four major reasons why Christians fail to grow: (1) *Failure to maintain a clear conscience.* If any sin, or violation of God's Word, is not dealt with immediately, then it lies in the heart and festers. Probe gently to see if the person can remember violating God's Word in any way, and once something is discovered begin to put it right. (2) *Neglect of personal prayer.* Every Christian needs to spend some time alone with God every day. If this is not done or the 'quiet time' is skimped, then it will not be long before spiritual dryness sets in.

(3) *Lack of daily Bible reading.* In order to grow, a Christian must have a daily intake from the Word of God, the Bible. The Word of God is a Christian's nourishment. Failure to feed one's spirit with the truths that flow out of Scripture will result in spiritual apathy and indifference. (4) *No clear understanding of one's place in the Body of Christ.* Many Christians become frustrated and fail to grow because they have never discovered their place in the Body of Christ. Every Christian is designed by God to fit into a special place in His Body, the Church.

Examine Romans 12:6–8 to see the seven basic gifts that contribute to the growth and health of Christ's Body. *Every* Christian has at least one of these gifts. Help the person discover and develop it.

REFLECTION: Do you know someone who needs to hear these four reasons why they may not be growing? And what about you?

Finding it hard to pray

'... pray continually, give thanks in all circumstances ...'
1 Thessalonians 5:17–18

Offer the following suggestions to someone who is finding it hard to pray, and encourage the person to put them into operation immediately:

(1) *Make a daily prayer appointment with God and keep it.* In earthly affairs when we make an appointment with someone, we keep that appointment whether we feel like it or not. Making a daily appointment with God means that courtesy will carry us into His presence even if feeling doesn't.

(2) *Begin your prayer time by meditating in the Scriptures.* Experience has shown that the best way to begin one's daily prayer is by meditating on a passage from the Bible. This devotional meditation prepares the soul in a wonderful way for fellowship and communion with the Lord.

(3) *Use a prayer list.* Put down on a piece of paper items about which you want to pray, and talk to God about them.

(4) *Pray out loud, if possible.* Hearing ourselves pray often gives a deeper intensity to prayer.

(5) *Don't fight wandering thoughts – use them.* Encourage the person to pray for the thing to which his mind wanders. In this way he can weave even wandering thoughts into the pattern of his prayers.

(6) *Thank God for what He has done for you.* God wants us to be thankful. Think on all He has done, and the heart will soon begin to swell with gratitude.

REFLECTION: God loves to hear us and He does listen.

What splashes out?

'Whoever believes in me ... streams of living water will flow from within him.' John 7:38

When we pursue the reasons why God overturns the nest of our calm and comfortable experiences and tips us out into the midst of seemingly endless difficulties and problems, the clear conclusion is that He does it not in order to destroy us but to develop us. Hudson Taylor was seated in a room with a new missionary to China. He filled a glass with water, placed it on a table, and then struck the table with his fist. As the water splashed out, he said to the young missionary: 'You will be struck by the blows of many sorrows and troubles in China, but remember, they will only splash out of you what is in you.' Out of some splash the emotions of bitterness, resentment and despair. Out of others splash joy, forgiveness and victory.

Says Edwin Markham: 'Defeat may serve as well as victory To shake the soul and let the glory out. When the great oak is straining in the wind The boughs drink in new beauty, and the trunk Sends down a deeper root on the windward side.' An elderly Christian stood in the corridor of a train as it was coming into a station. The train lurched several times, before it stopped, throwing him from one side of the corridor to the other. When he hit one side, those near him heard him say, 'Hallelujah!' The jolting brought out what was in him. What does trouble do to you? Does it shake the glory out? If so, then you have victory!

REFLECTION: What is in us will come out of us.

Counsellor and Comforter

'... he will give you another Counsellor to be with you for ever ...' John 14:16

Our divine Counsellor will be there for us – empowering us with His comforting presence, sharing our pain and entering into all our sorrows. The Greek term for the Holy Spirit is *parakletos*, derived from *para* (beside) and *kaleo* (call), and means 'one who comes alongside to help'. I wish the word could be translated 'Counsellor and Comforter' – a phrase which would convey the fuller idea that the Holy Spirit is not just someone who gives us advice but someone who feels *for* us and *with* us also. The word Comforter – *con* (with) and *fortis* (strength) – means one who strengthens you by being with you. It's astonishing what strength we draw from someone just being with us when we are going through a painful experience.

Prior to her death my wife spent many hours sleeping. At first I would steal away to my study and work after she had gone to sleep, but she told me on one occasion that even in her sleep she could sense whether or not I was there. 'Just being there,' she said, 'just sensing you are at my side is more of a comfort to me than I can ever explain.' I have had the same impression of the Holy Spirit, haven't you? Simply sensing He is at our side is a comfort that we can never explain. He enters into our hurts, empathises with our pain, and is there for us in every difficult situation of life.

REFLECTION: The Holy Spirit is a Counsellor who does more than give us advice from a distance; He comes alongside to help and comfort us.

The Spirit's first work

'... he will give you another Counsellor to be with you for ever ...' John 14:16

There are those who claim that the *first* task of the Holy Spirit is to be with us. What He does in us and through us is important, but His primary service is *to be there for us*. If this is so then we must see that our preoccupation with gifts rather than the Giver is entirely out of place. Many Christians seem to be more taken up with possessing the gifts of the Spirit than possessing the Holy Spirit Himself. He is the gift, and although we are instructed by Paul in 1 Corinthians 14:1 to 'eagerly desire spiritual gifts', this does not mean that we are to think more highly of the gifts than the Giver. Peter talks about the Holy Spirit being *the* gift (Acts 2:38).He is the gift of gifts, and when He is with us and in us then He supplies us with the gifts that enhance our spiritual effectiveness.

Early in my Christian experience I made the mistake many make today. I was in a church where a great emphasis was placed on the gifts of the Spirit but little on the Giver. I laid out my shopping list before the Lord and said, 'Father, these are the gifts I want from You.' The Spirit whispered to my heart, 'Are the gifts more important than the Giver?' This gentle rebuke helped me to see that I was more interested in the gifts of the Spirit than the Spirit who gave the gifts. This is a danger we must all avoid.

REFLECTION: Seek the gift of the Holy Spirit Himself and He will supply the gifts we need for effective service.

'Trust my love'

'... I will be with you always ...' Matthew 28:20

There are occasions in life when problems don't go away despite our most ardent praying. At such times the divine Counsellor ministers to us His comfort and supernatural strength. I recall a vivid memory of when I was a little boy being taken to hospital to have my tonsils removed. When I entered the place, smelt the distinctive smell that hospitals had in those days, saw the white-coated nurses and doctors, I became very frightened. Looking up into my mother's face I said, 'Do I have to go through with this? Will it hurt? What is it all for? Will I die under the anaesthetic?' Well, what can you say to a small boy about to have such an operation? My mother could have given me all the medical reasons why the operation should be performed, but I would not have understood. So she simply said, 'I can't save you from it, my dear. For your own good this has to be done, but some day you will understand. You must trust my love. I shan't leave you and I will be here waiting for you when you come out of the anaesthetic.'

That boyhood experience has been a parable to me. There have been many times in my life (and I am sure in ours also) when the Holy Spirit has whispered in my soul, 'I cannot shield you from this. You will have to go through it, and you may feel some pain. But I will be with you all the way.'

REFLECTION: When God does not provide a way to avoid painful situations, His presence will always be there to help us through them.

The world has gone grey

'And I will pray the Father, and he shall give you another Comforter ...' John 14:16, AV

The comforting ministry of the Holy Spirit is not simply a theory; it is a glorious fact. Sooner or later every one of us needs comfort. It does not matter how strong we may be, how composed and free from sentimentality, the time will come when we need to feel God's solace. The Holy Spirit is the minister of comfort and grace. He is the One who brings into our hearts the resources of the Godhead. Let us never forget that. Some, when needing comfort, turn to drink. But there is no real comfort to be found in the cup. Drink can no more cure our sorrows than an anaesthetic can cure a cancer.

Others turn to literature. 'The anodyne you need', they say, 'is reading. Relief can be found in a library. Turn for consolation to the infinite resources of literature.' I love literature and have made it a habit to read several books a week. But in the time of real sorrow there is no adequate comfort in books. Some comfort perhaps, but not enough to heal a heart that is torn. What about nature, or music, or art? They can be helpful supplements but they can never be substitutes. They are not a fount of comfort in themselves. I can tell you from a lifetime of facing trials, including bereavement, that the only sure comfort when all the world has gone grey is the Comforter of God – the Holy Spirit.

REFLECTION: How reassuring it is to know that when we need comfort and consolation the Holy Spirit is more than equal to the task. Others can *bring* us comfort but He *is* comfort.

The work of the Holy Spirit

'I will ask the Father, and he will give you another Counsellor ...' John 14:16

As we make our way towards heaven life may be hard and perplexing, but God has given us His Holy Spirit to be our Counsellor along the way.

(1) He seeks to draw out of us all the potential which God has built into us, and is continually at work developing us into the kind of persons God sees us to be. (2) He prods us to prayer, and on those occasions when we don't know how to pray as we ought He prays in us and through us. (3) He brings hidden things to light in our souls and seeks to rid us of all sin.

(4) He shines the laser beam of knowledge and wisdom through the fog that sometimes surrounds us, and guides us in ways of which we are both conscious and unconscious along the path He wants us to take. (5) He teaches us as no other could teach us, and leads us into the thing our hearts were built for – truth. (6) He comforts us whenever we are in need of solace, and strengthens our hearts to go on even though we have no clear answers to our predicament.

When we refuse to open up to Him, to depend on Him and consult Him, we deprive ourselves of the love, wisdom, and spiritual sustenance we need to live effectively and dynamically. He will open up to you, but only if you will open up to Him (James 4:8).

REFLECTION: Believe me, take one step towards the Holy Spirit and He will take two towards you.

Spiritual complacency

'... I have come that they may have life, and have it to the full.' John 10:10

Many Christians have become spiritually complacent because they are content to snuggle down in their spiritual nest and live out their Christian lives at a level far below the best. It might be warm and comfortable in the nest, but it is better by far to expand one's wings, launch out into the clear, blue sky and live life to its fullest potential. Mark this and mark it well – God's desire is to get you out of the nest and up into the air. I am thinking particularly at this moment of those Christians who, although soundly saved and fully committed to Jesus Christ, have never experienced all the fullness of the Holy Spirit. They are like the little girl who, when asked how she came to fall out of bed, replied, 'I slept too close to the place where I got in.' You see, although every Christian has the Holy Spirit, the Holy Spirit does not have every Christian.

When you surrendered your life to Jesus Christ, the Holy Spirit came in to regenerate you, give you a new birth, but now you need to experience another encounter with the Spirit that lifts you out of the nest to soar in the heavenlies. The Good Shepherd came not merely to give us life but to give it – abundantly. One writer says of this verse: 'At conversion, Christ gives us life, but when we experience the fullness of the Spirit, we encounter not merely life, but life that is abundant.'

REFLECTION: 'In conversion, God's life is imparted to us. In the fullness of the Spirit, God's life inundates us.'

An adventurous life

'It is the glory of God to conceal a matter; to search out a matter is the glory of kings.' Proverbs 25:2

I am convinced that the vast majority of us are content to settle for the accustomed rather than the adventurous. God has designed us for creative living, creative thinking and creative venture. We are only truly fulfilled when we live, think and act creatively. How does God go about doing this? He does it first by dropping a powerful thought or idea into our minds. Today as you go about your daily tasks, hundreds of thoughts will flow through your mind. Many of them will arise from your subconscious. Some will come from Satan. Others will come from God. The thoughts that come from God are sometimes so challenging that we ignore them and push them right out of our minds.

Proverbs 25:2 says, 'It is the glory of God to conceal a matter; to search out a matter is the glory of kings.' God carefully, quietly hides His most precious gifts so that we may become joyous 'kings' by discovering them. It is a universal truth that the most valuable treasures are hidden from clear view. The pearl is hidden within the oyster. The diamond is buried deep within the earth. The gold nugget is concealed in the heart of a great mountain. God plans life in such a way that the greatest treasures are concealed waiting for you to discover them. And there is no thrill like the thrill of making a great discovery. You will feel like a king.

REFLECTION: Some thoughts that lead to great adventures in God can seem humdrum and be easily dismissed; phone a friend, give a present, comfort the broken hearted.

The adventure of living

'... *I have come that they may have life, and have it to the full.' John 10:10*

One of the greatest mistakes we can make in life is to block the efforts of the Divine Eagle when He attempts to push us out of the nest of the accustomed into the world of the adventurous. Asher did this – the Moffatt translation of Judges 5:17 reads: 'Asher sat still by the sea board clinging to his creeks.' There was Asher sitting by the sea board, clinging to his creeks, when he could have launched out into the ocean and experienced the joy of a great adventure. In the face of the big, he settled for the little. They were 'his' creeks and he wasn't going to let the accustomed go in order to venture into the unaccustomed no matter how great the possibilities. Asher is a type of the Christian who wants to stay by the safe and secure, and finishes up by doing nothing and getting nowhere.

I am not advocating spiritual recklessness, nor am I arguing for an unmindful approach to the Christian life, I am simply saying that we ought to be ocean-minded and not creek-minded Christians. The people who try to find poise and inner security by clinging to the creeks are invariably unfulfilled for we are inwardly made for growth and creativity. For many Christians, life has settled into ruts – mental, physical and spiritual ruts. 'And a rut', said someone, 'is a grave with both ends knocked out.' Allow God to push you out into a more creative way of thinking, acting and living.

REFLECTION: Life for those in a rut is not an adventure. It holds no surprises, offers no excitement and is uncreative.

Accepting ourselves

'Love your neighbour as yourself.' Matthew 22:39

I know that for many the reality of facing themselves as they are, and accepting themselves as they are, is a challenge from which they would shrink, but if you let God have His way in your heart and life, a new dimension of living can open up for you. The mask that so many of us wear says, 'I am not sure you would like me as I am, so I will present myself the way I would like you to see me.' And that, deep down, is dishonesty.

Someone might say, 'But how can we accept ourselves, our faults, our failures, our mistakes, our blunders and our inadequacies, until we have reached spiritual maturity?' Accepting ourselves as we are does not mean that we will not dislike our failures, our mistakes and our inadequacies. It means that we will not be bowled over by them or intimidated by them to the extent that we lose our spiritual balance. Whenever we make a mistake, commit a sin or make a foolish blunder, God begins to work in our lives to correct the situation. But His corrections and His disciplines are always motivated by love and compassion. He is never punitive, judgmental or authoritarian. And the way God deals with us is the way we must deal with ourselves. His discipline is never given in anger but always in love. He corrects us not because He delights to punish us, but because He loves us too much to let us remain immature.

**REFLECTION: I am learning to love myself as God loves me –
warts and all.**

Self-deceit

'The heart is deceitful above all things ... Who can understand it?' Jeremiah 17:9

L ying of any kind is to be strongly condemned and must inevitably result in spiritual loss (see Jer. 9:5). But if I had to decide which kind of lying is worst, I would say that it is lying to oneself. This leads by scarcely perceptible degrees to the worst state into which a man or woman may fall. At first it might sound absurd to speak of lying to oneself. Men and women lie to deceive somebody who is unacquainted with the facts. It is usually a cowardly device for concealing the unpleasant truth from a person at present in ignorance, and hence it seems possible only to lie to somebody who has less information upon the point than you have yourself. If they knew the truth as you knew it, you couldn't deceive them.

How, then, can a man or woman lie to themselves? Such arguments will be used only by those who are ignorant of the cunning of the human heart. The truth is that we can and do lie to ourselves, and I suspect we all know something of the danger from personal experience. I can think of nothing more injurious to the spiritual life than having a conscience that does not operate in the way it was designed. King David deceived himself to such an extent that his conscience failed to function correctly until God brought Nathan to him with a barbed parable that penetrated his defences and helped him see himself as he really was (2 Sam. 12:1–14).

REFLECTION: 'Do not merely listen to the word, and so deceive yourselves. Do what it says.' James 1:22

Let me tell you a story

'Search me, O God ... test me ... See if there is any offensive way in me ...' Psalm 139:23

When will we learn that there is just no way we can outmanoeuvre God? There are many degrees between a life lived with God and the complete moral collapse of a man or woman. Are you lying to yourself? Let me warn you against doing so. Permit me to do as Nathan did with David and tell you a story.

There was once a man who was brought up in a good home, received training in the way of righteousness and had the reputation of being a fine Christian. But gradually things began to change and he found himself becoming more concerned about his work than what pleased God; spiritual matters began to take second place. He kept up the duties of the Christian life, said a prayer at the end of the day, faithfully read his Bible, but never admitted that what was being said applied to him. *Are you that man?*

There was once a young woman who was a bright and shining light for Jesus. Then she got married and had children. Gradually she began to lose her interest in spiritual matters, the fire in her life burned low, and she settled for spiritual mediocrity. She, too, read the Bible, but neatly deflected the truth onto other people. She thought of others who needed spiritual renewal; never herself. *Are you that woman?*

If so, then I commend you to God who forgives, cleanses, restores and redeems.

REFLECTION: Have your feet strayed from God's path?

Authorities

'The authorities that exist have been established by God.'
Romans 13:1

I 'm amazed at the number of Christians who fail to see that the principle of authority is not something thought up by autocratically minded individuals, who delight in lording it over others, but is something which the Creator established when He designed the universe: 'To oppose authority then is to oppose God, and such opposition is bound to be punished' (Rom. 13:2, Phillips). The wave of anti-authority sweeping the world at the moment is yet another evidence of mankind's stubborn refusal to bring their lives in line with the design which God has set for them. This general attitude is in danger of infiltrating the ranks of those who are followers of the Lord Jesus Christ.

Some time ago I had occasion to speak to a Christian who told me that he was thinking of changing his job because he couldn't stand the personality of the man who was over him. I said, 'Have you considered that God may want to use the irritating characteristics of your boss as a kind of hammer and chisel to chip away at the rough spots in your personality?' He admitted that he had never considered it in that way. He wrote to me later to say that the concept of seeing his boss as God's hammer and chisel transformed his attitudes towards God, towards his work and towards himself. God prunes through many things, not the least the authority He places over us.

REFLECTION: Satan's very spirit of rebellion was the cause of his own downfall and he seeks to bring about deception in the area of authority more than in any other.

The principle of authority

'The authorities that exist have been established by God.'
Romans 13:1

A careful examination of Scripture shows that the principle of authority comes into operation at all stages of our development. We first begin to understand authority through the disciplines of home and family life (Eph. 6:1–4). Later, we come in contact with it when we start school, and later still when we take up employment (Col. 3:22–25). God has established in society a structure of authority by which men and women can live peaceably and in harmony with one another (Rom. 13:1–2). Once we become Christians, we become members of the Christian Church, where there is also a clear line of authority (Eph. 4:11–12).

Almost every day of our lives we find ourselves in situations and circumstances which bring us directly under someone's authority, and unless we see that God wants to use this authority to bring His purposes to pass in our lives, then we will miss out on one of life's greatest character-building processes. One of the most freeing insights of Scripture is the fact that God is the highest authority in the universe, and that He works through all lesser authorities to prune our lives and develop our effectiveness. It is 'freeing' because, once we discover it and grasp it, we have the insight we need to cope with any pressure that is put on us by those who are in authority over us. We know, as Jesus said to Pilate, 'You would have no power over me if it were not given to you from above' (John 19:11).

REFLECTION: God is the highest authority in the universe, and He works through all lesser authorities to prune our lives and develop our effectiveness.

The highest authority of all

'The authorities that exist have been established by God.'
Romans 13:1

I n the home, in the Church and in society, we must recognise that all legitimate authority is derived from God's authority. Are you under pressure at the moment from the authority over you at work, at school, at home or at church? Is it hard to take? Then lift your gaze higher to the highest authority of all – God. Ask yourself: is God allowing this pressure because He sees in me a character deficiency which He wants to correct? Is He permitting, or even influencing, the person who is over me to come down upon me more heavily than usual because He wants to bring about important changes in me?

Once we see that the hand of God may be at work, and expressed through the attitudes and actions of those in authority over us, we begin to learn something of how such pressure can, in the Almighty's purposes, work for good in our lives. Any failure on our part to observe how God works through the authority over us can hinder His purposes for us and prevent us from entering into all that He plans for us. The most important thing we can discover, when under pressure from authority, is not how to get away from it, but to ask God what lesson He may be trying to teach us in the circumstances. Once that lesson is learned, then God will see that the pressure is released.

REFLECTION: Once we see that all legitimate authority is derived from God's authority, and live by it, then we bring our lives in line with the fundamental structure of the universe.

OCTOBER 23

Respect the *position*

'Then he [Jesus] went down to Nazareth with them and was obedient to them.' Luke 2:51

Whenever I mention the subject of a right Christian attitude to authority someone usually asks: 'The person over me is unfair, inconsistent and undeserving of respect. How can I obey someone I cannot respect?' My answer is this: a person in authority over us may have many character deficiencies but these deficiencies must not stop us from adopting an attitude of respect for the person's *position*, even if we find it difficult to respect that individual's personality. You see, when you respect a person's *position* of authority, you are respecting God, for it was He who ordained authority in this universe.

It is more important for you to recognise that God is working through even the deficiencies of the one above you, to bring about improvements in your character, than it is for that person to act more kindly and considerately towards you. Our Christian growth is often hindered by wrong attitudes and suffers more from a wrong attitude towards authority than any other thing. One of the first lessons we must learn, therefore, is to respond as God wants us to respond, irrespective of whether the authority over us improves or not. Everyone is under authority (or should be), and the person who is a law unto himself is in an extremely dangerous position – morally and spiritually.

REFLECTION: He may have a bad temper, use obscene language, be subject to moodiness, shout, rave or become abusive, but he may be God's instrument to make you more like Christ.

Triumphant faith

'By faith we understand that the universe was formed at God's command ...' Hebrews 11:3

There are a great many who have a faith in God, but it isn't an adequate, working faith. It doesn't function at the place of poise and power. The headmaster of a school in India was invited to attend a Christian gathering where it was announced that a famous missionary would answer questions on matters relating to the Christian faith. The headmaster declined to attend, giving this as his reason: 'At the moment I have a satisfactory faith, but if I come to that meeting a non-Christian might ask a question which will upset my faith.' His faith was a troubled one – not a triumphant one.

How does God go about the task of helping us attain a serene, assured faith rather than one that is uncertain and inadequate? Does He keep dark and desolating doubts from us? Does He protect us from the incisive questions of non-believers? No. He gently nudges us out of the nest, forces us to face the reality of a world where our faith is put to the test, makes sure that we come face to face with issues that have to be grappled with, for He knows that it is by grappling that we grow. We must not be afraid of the twenty-first century with its great scientific advances, its space exploration, its nuclear energy and its amazing discoveries. Neither must we shrink from facing fearlessly the challenge this age brings us in terms of our faith.

REFLECTION: The God of nature and the God of the Bible are not two different gods – they are one God and so our faith is unassailable.

Sharing what we have

'... what I have I give you.' Acts 3:6

Every scientist, when once he has verified the results of an experiment, proceeds to share those results with everyone who cares to listen. When once a Christian experiences the reality of Christ's transforming power at work in his heart, he then sets about the task of sharing it with as many as will listen. How could it be otherwise?

A boy of 23, dying in a hospital, said to his pastor, 'Everybody has been so good to me. I haven't a thing in the world to leave anybody. Couldn't I leave my eyes to somebody?' He offered to share what he had – and he was happy in the offering. Each one of us propagates something – whether we realise it or not. When we meet men and women, they give us a dominant impression – an impression of inner conflict or an impression of serenity and poise. The dominant impression we must leave with people is one of faith – not faith in our own faith but faith in His faith. We have seen that in today's scientific climate, many are concerned that their faith will not develop. But this is simply not true. When we allow the Divine Eagle to nudge us out of the nest, we may feel, when faced with the biting challenge of today's society, that our faith will fail us. But such will not be the case. Confronted with a challenge, a troubled faith has the very opportunity it needs to become a triumphant faith.

REFLECTION: We can develop a serene, joyous and triumphant faith to share in the midst of a world beset by so many difficulties.

Endless creativity

'My Father is always at his work ...' John 5:17

I s our time in heaven to be entirely filled with praise? Not according to Scripture. Humourists have had much fun depicting heaven as an interminable church service where mortals grow wings and are given a permanent place in the eternal choir. Lloyd George, one-time British prime minister, used to say that when he was a boy the idea of heaven used to terrify him more than hell because he thought of it as a perpetual Sunday. To understand his horror one must remember that in his day Sunday was quiet and solemn, and children were often required to stay indoors after they had attended church and do nothing but read. He claimed that his concept of heaven resulted in him turning to atheism, although in later years he came at least to accept the idea of God and of heaven.

In contrast, we are told that in heaven the redeemed serve Him day and night (Rev. 7:15). So heaven is not just a place of praise; it is a place of endless service also. One of the sweet things we experience down here on earth is the knowledge that we are working with God. It will be no less sweet, I believe, in heaven. There is nothing stagnant or static about the bliss of heaven. We serve a God whose creative ability is endless. I see Him as a Worker who will involve His children in working with Him in the kind of work that is purposeful and satisfying.

REFLECTION: F.M. Knollis wrote these lyrical lines: 'In that blessed world above Work will not bring weariness For work itself is love.'

On talking terms with God

'From inside the fish Jonah prayed to the Lord *his God.'*
Jonah 2:1

The very first thing the prayerless prophet does inside the fish is to pray. But when you think of it, there is very little else he could do there. Do not let this thought, however, detract from the fact that he opened up his heart once again to God. Jonah's prayer is not a prayer for deliverance, but one of thanksgiving. The prophet's heart overflows with gratitude for the spectacular way in which he has been saved from certain death. Some might consider Jonah contemptible for crying out in prayer only when he was in trouble, but such is the mercy and goodness of God that He listens to prayers made in such circumstances nevertheless.

Isaac Bashevis Singer, quoted by William Barrett in *The Illusion of Technique*, says, 'Whenever I am in trouble I pray. And since I'm always in trouble, I pray a lot. Even when you see me eat and drink, while I do this, I pray.' It's sad, however, if prayer is limited only to times of trouble. A little boy was asked by his vicar if he prayed every day. 'No,' responded the boy, 'as there are some days when I don't need anything.' The highest form of prayer is not petition but communion; just talking to God and deepening our relationship with Him. Jonah had not been doing this kind of praying for some time, but now things have changed. He communes with God from inside the fish and is once again on talking terms with the Almighty.

REFLECTION: Do you pray only when in trouble or when you want something?

Your waves

'... all your waves and breakers swept over me.'
Jonah 2:3; Psalm 42:7

J onah reflects on the fact that he had been hurled into the deep and was in a desperate situation. But as he muses further he says something quite remarkable: '... all your waves and breakers swept over me'. Notice the words again: '... all *your* waves and breakers swept over me' (my italics). When we find ourselves in the midst of a storm or buffeted by waves of trouble we are in danger of misunderstanding the meaning of our circumstances. We can view the situation as the refutation rather than the confirmation of God's faithfulness. It behoves us to be careful in seasons of inexplicable trial not to regard the billows as an expression of divine displeasure but as the proof of His concern – concern that we should become the people He wants us to be.

When plunged into adversity's icy waters we are apt to forget that it is His waves and His breakers that are sweeping over us. And because of this they cannot harm or hinder, but contribute to the purposes God has for our lives. We must be careful not to foolishly charge God with neglect or imagine that we have been removed from His keeping when the waves wash over us. Though we might think the billows have been sent to bring us down to death, they are, in fact, meant to bring us into life. The billows God sends will not carry us off course, but sweep us into His arms.

REFLECTION: God is in control of the waves.

Need a new start?

'I said, "I have been banished from your sight ..."'
Jonah 2:4

T he words 'banished from your sight' are an indication
that Jonah has actually repented, and is now experiencing
once again a close relationship with God. Jonah tells
us that his eye is turned towards the light which he had spurned:
'yet I will look again towards your holy temple' (2:4). One of the
effects of disobedience is that the soul is filled with a sense of shame.
And when we feel shame two things happen. First, we find it difficult
to look into the face of the one we have wronged, and second, we find
it equally difficult to be looked upon by the one we have wronged.

Shame has been described as the 'haemorrhaging of the soul'.
Our soul bleeds when it is filled with shame and stains every other
emotion. But for the first time in a long while Jonah admits he is
able to look towards God's holy Temple – which implies he is again
looking to God for His strength and support. His heart is filled
with hope and expectancy; it is a new day and a new beginning.
Is there someone reading these words right now who needs a new
start spiritually? You feel alienated from God because of some sin
and your heart is filled with shame. Turn from that sin now, ask God
to forgive you, and I promise that through divine forgiveness the
shame will be dispelled from your soul and you will look once again
into His eyes with joy.

**REFLECTION: Just as entering a relationship with God isn't
possible without repentance, so restoring a broken relationship
with Him isn't possible without repentance either.**

The blessing of confinement

'From inside the fish Jonah prayed to the LORD his God.'
Jonah 2:1

C onfined in the fish's stomach, Jonah became a different man.
In confinement, I believe, God does some of His greatest
work. Have you ever found yourself in a situation you know
has been engineered by God in which you can't move one way or
the other – where you are hemmed in by Him? 'You have taken
me from my closest friends ... I am confined and cannot escape ...'
(Psa. 88:8). Why does God put us in such a situation? It is because
only then will we stop trying to work things out for ourselves and
begin to listen to Him.

All of us are tainted with the terrible tendency to insist on getting
our own way. We prefer to act as a god rather than worship the true
God. The story that was enacted in the Garden of Eden is re-enacted
every day in our homes, offices, factories, shops, boardrooms, schools
and colleges. The tempter is at work telling us what he told our first
parents in Eden, 'You will be like God' (Gen. 3:5). Confinement is
a calculated and deliberate interference with the god-lust that is in
us. As a pastor I would discover that in the confinement caused by
illness or accident my parishioners suddenly woke up to the fact that
they had lost touch with God and eternal things. Some of the most
profound passages in the New Testament were written by Paul from
a prison cell. He was shut up to write immortally.

**REFLECTION: Our lives are not diminished by confinement,
but deepened by it.**

The school of prayer

'In my distress I called to the Lord ...'
Jonah 2:2; Psalm 18:6

Jonah's prayer is modelled on the prayers of the psalmists. Almost every verse has words that are borrowed from the vocabulary of the psalms. The book of Psalms has two dominant themes: lament and thanksgiving. The writers either cry out in pain or burst forth in praise, and Jonah echoes their thoughts. He had apparently been nourished by the book of Psalms, and in the midst of a crisis he prayed in the way that others before him had prayed. Jonah's prayer was not so much spontaneous as set, clearly furnished with the stock vocabulary of the psalms.

One Bible scholar who has studied the phrases used by Jonah in his prayer shows them to be exact quotes from more than a dozen different psalms. He said: 'Jonah got every word – lock, stock and barrel – out of the book of Psalms.' What does this say to us? If we want to pray effectively then we need to consider undertaking some apprenticeship in prayer. I thank God for my pastor who told me over and over again in my youth: 'If you want to learn to pray then you need to soak yourself in the book of Psalms. It is the best school of prayer you will ever attend.' And I pass on to you the advice I was given: saturate yourself in the psalms, and when you find yourself in a crisis and don't know how to pray, or what to pray, the words of the psalmists will provide a framework for you.

REFLECTION: When I am asked what is the best advice I have ever been given, this is what I say: to soak myself in the book of Psalms.

God knows all

'... I know what is going through your mind.' Ezekiel 11:5

An aspect of God's nature that we will examine together is His knowledge and wisdom. I link these two characteristics together because really it is almost impossible to consider one without the other. The difference between knowledge and wisdom has been described like this: 'Knowledge is what we know; wisdom is the right application of what we know.' God, of course, knows everything – everything possible, everything actual. Nothing escapes His notice, nothing can be hidden from Him, and nothing can be forgotten by Him.

I am aware that many Christians, when referring to their conversion, say that God has forgotten their sins, but strictly speaking that is not so. God never forgets anything. What He promises to do with our sins is to 'remember [them] no more' (Jer. 31:34). There is a great difference between forgetting something and deciding not to remember it. Those who are rebelling against God hate this aspect of His Being. They wish there might be no Witness to their sin, no Searcher of their hearts, no Judge of their deeds. How solemn are the words of the psalmist recorded in Psalm 90:8: 'You have set our iniquities before you, our *secret* sins in the light of your presence' (my italics). To the believer, however, the truth of God's omniscience (His infinite knowledge) ought to bring us tremendous comfort and security.

REFLECTION: In times of perplexity we ought to be like Job and say, '... he knows the way that I take; when he has tested me, I shall come forth as gold' (Job 23:10).

No puppets

'You, my brothers, were called to be free. But do not use your freedom to indulge the sinful nature; rather, serve one another in love.' Galatians 5:13

If God is love, why does He allow tragedies to happen? Why does He not intervene to prevent them? If we think about life's evils we realise they are the product of human ignorance, stupidity, carelessness and sin thwarting the good desires of God for this world. They are a consequence of God's gift of free will, without which we would be puppets not people.

So, to my mind, the deeper question is: Why did God create human beings but not subject them to His control? In our world, power and control are merged: in God's world they are separate. His power is not control. He created us free agents, made to love, serve, influence and help one another. By the same token we have the ability to hurt one another. We could not have the blessing without the risk, and God took the risk. Sin entered the world bringing with it sorrow and suffering, vulnerability to the folly and crimes of others. But would we rather live in a world in which this could not happen? Rather than make us puppets, God in creation gave a divine salute to freedom. God gave us freedom and we misuse it, but God allows only what He can use because He is committed to bringing good out of evil. Now we see the wrong side of the tapestry with all its roughness and tangled threads, its seeming confusion, but one day we will see the eternal tapestry from the right side, in all its beauty.

REFLECTION: God is with us in these tragedies, hurting, seeking to turn tragedy to triumph, loss to gain. He does not cause them but works creatively through them.

Yes ... but

'But Moses said to God, "Who am I ..."' Exodus 3:11

G od wants us to grow up and deal with life realistically rather than defensively. Many of us, although we are adults, still behave like children. Our outward behaviour, of course, is more sophisticated, but inwardly we carry the same attitudes to life that we had when we were growing up. One writer, Eric Berne, has written a book entitled, *Games People Play*, in which he shows that many of us go through life playing childish games with each other. The word 'game' here is not to be understood as similar to 'Monopoly' or 'Snakes and Ladders', but as an attitude we adopt when relating to other people, in which we become defensive rather than honest. Paul wrote to the Corinthian church about putting away childish things (1 Cor. 13:11). The Greek word used here is a very forceful one – *katargeo* – which means to cut off, render inoperative, disassociate from.

Paul came to a place in his life where he realised he was acting childishly and needed to decide to stop acting that way – and grow up. He did – and so must you. A game is a device we use in our relationships with God or others to stay at a childish level and thus opt out of the responsibility of growing up. When God approached Moses at the burning bush, announced to him that He had confidence in him and would give him His support, Moses began to play one of the most repeated games in history. It is called, 'Yes ... but'.

REFLECTION: If we do not put away childish ways of behaving and relaying we will forever remain immature.

Adam's game

'... I was afraid ...' Genesis 3:10

The game Adam played is the first game of its type ever recorded in history. After eating the forbidden fruit, he would doubtless have felt the immediate effect of his sin in every part of his personality. One writer says, 'Adam's body would have reeled ... His brain would burn with fear and disbelief ... He found himself crying out like a man drowning in a stormy sea: 'The woman You gave me – she gave me from the tree and I ate.' Here Adam laid down the foundations of a game that people have played ever since. The game is: 'If it weren't for you ...' Adam blamed God because he reasoned that if Eve had not been created for him, there would have been no temptation to eat of the forbidden fruit.

Was it God's fault? Apparently Adam thought that it was. How many times have you done the same thing? Something happens to you and you immediately blame someone else, perhaps even God. Many of us excuse ourselves with such statements as, 'If God had given me a different wife ... If only I had been born into a different family ... If circumstances had been different then things would have been much better.' If ... If ... If. If this is a game you play then let me make one thing clear – no one ever grows in the Christian life until they accept the responsibility for the decisions they make, stop blaming others for their predicament and face the present realistically – and not defensively.

REFLECTION: When we try to blame others for our mistakes we fail to take responsibility and walk the path of deceit and fear rather than honesty before God.

Cain's game

'I don't know', he replied. 'Am I my brother's keeper?'
Genesis 4:9

Although Cain undoubtedly knew that God must be approached by an offering taken from the animal kingdom, he decided to offer instead an offering selected from the vegetable kingdom. It was an incorrect offering and he knew his gift would be unacceptable. Cain discounted God's commands and also the offering of his brother. Here we see Cain initiate a game called 'Uproar' – a game where conflict is purposefully started to avoid intimacy. It happens when a non-Christian, feeling drawn towards God and His kingdom, sets up some argument or point of conflict in an attempt to prevent himself reaching the place where he has to surrender to God.

In the early days of my Christian life, I could never understand why it was that a person, when close to the kingdom of God, would say something like this, 'Why does God allow suffering?' Or, 'Why did God create the devil?' I came to see that such questions (not all) were really an unconscious attempt to keep God out of their hearts. You see, when God comes close to a person, their inner life is greatly disturbed. It must inevitably be so for inbred sin must be repented of, confessed and put away. But this game is not only played by unbelievers, it is played by some Christians also. When God draws near to your heart, you can choose to open yourself or create an issue which avoids spiritual intimacy. Is this a game you sometimes play?

REFLECTION: Arguments and debates are sometimes not a genuine search for questions but a technique people use to avoid intimacy.

Playing games

'His mother said to the servants, "Do whatever he tells you."' John 2:5

Although everyone plays games in life – both Christians and non-Christians – the favourite game we Christians play is this: 'Let God do it.' Some time ago a lady asked me if I would pray with her about the difficulty she was having in her relationships with people. She said she felt rejected, no one seemed interested in her, and the people in her church just ignored her. I asked, 'What are you doing about your problems?' She said, 'Well, I pray every morning and evening about them.' I said, 'That's fine – but what else are you doing?' She looked at me in amazement and said, 'What else can I do? If I pray about it, and get others to pray along with me, then won't God make the people who reject me a little more friendly towards me?' There was nothing wrong with her praying, but really she was playing a game. It was this: 'Let God do it.' She wanted God to do what He had already done – give her the ability to relate, share and have fellowship with others. What she needed to work on was her own attitudes.

Someone said, 'To have friends – be friendly.' Fortunately she took the advice I gave her, worked on it and began to see some success. If we are to enjoy the freedom of being mature then we must be able to differentiate between what we should be doing ourselves and what God alone can do in our lives and circumstances.

REFLECTION: Sometimes we pray for God to do things He has already given us the responsibility and ability to do.

Departure

'We ... would prefer to be away from the body and at home with the Lord.' 2 Corinthians 5:8

What is the mode of our departure to the heavenly city? It is through death. When I was newly converted I used to think: Wouldn't it be wonderful if, when the time came for us to leave this world, God would just whisk us away and put us down in heaven without the necessity of having to experience death. Alas, sin has affected human life to such a degree that our bodies have become corruptible and thus have to be left behind at the door of death. '... flesh and blood cannot inherit the kingdom of God' (1 Cor. 15:50).

Death has been described as a toll-bar. At a toll-bar or gate one has to pay 'dues' in order to continue the journey. The body in which you and I live is one of the 'dues' which has to be paid. It belongs to this earth. We live here in a material world, and the only way we can correspond with our environment is through a material form. But heaven is a spiritual plane and thus this 'form' must be left behind.

William James was once asked, 'Do you believe in personal immortality?' 'Yes of course I do,' he retorted, 'and ever more strongly as I get older.' 'Why?' questioned the enquirer. 'Because,' he replied, 'I am just getting fit to live.' The life inside him was bursting at the seams. For that reason he had no qualms about having to pay his toll-bar 'dues'. They put him on the road to life – real life.

REFLECTION: How can a Christian view death as a terror when all it does is usher him or her into the Father's presence?

Fallen asleep

'... Our friend Lazarus has fallen asleep ...' John 11:11

There can be absolutely no doubt that Lazarus was, by our definition, dead. Why did Jesus use the word 'sleep' when talking about death? Because He saw it in its true perspective – as falling asleep in one world to awaken in another. Of course the world in which one awakens depends on one's relationship to Jesus Christ. Those who do not know Christ and have not had their sins forgiven will see death as far more sinister than just falling asleep. And rightly so. Nothing can be more disastrous than to fall asleep in this world and wake up in a world where Christ is not.

The early Christians carved on the walls of their prisons the words 'Vita! Vita! Vita!' which means 'Life! Life! Life!' Prison walls could not stifle the life that was in them because it was *eternal* life. Eternal life is a life that death cannot extinguish. By its very nature it is bound to extend beyond the limits of this life. Can the shell confine the growing seed? Of course not, and neither can earth's circumstances quench the life of God that is in the soul of the man or woman who has entered into a personal relationship with Jesus Christ. Jesus never used the word 'immortality' when speaking of the future life. He preferred the phrase 'eternal life' because that conveyed not merely duration but a quality of life so rich, so abundant, so inexhaustible, that it could not be confined to this present existence.

REFLECTION: We fall asleep in one world to awaken in another.

Hope beyond the grave

'... we do not want you to ... grieve like the rest of men, who have no hope.' 1 Thessalonians 4:13

A funeral director once told me he had observed that Christians handle death in a much better way than those who are not Christians. I asked him why he thought that was. After pausing for a few moments he said, 'I suppose it's because Christians have a hope beyond the grave.' Simple, but profound. The word 'hope' is a word that has to be clarified, however, for it has come to mean different things to different people. Some think of hope as a poor precarious thing, an illusion or unfounded optimism. But hope is not so thought of in the New Testament. The hope the Bible talks about – the hope of life beyond the grave – is more than optimism. It is based on an incontrovertible fact – the resurrection of Jesus from the dead. Jesus not only proclaimed life after death; He demonstrated it. Without that demonstration belief in immortality would not have much going for it. Now it has everything going for it.

The hope we Christians have for a better life beyond death is based on the resurrection of Christ. Because He lives we also will live (John 14:19). Whatever the circumstances of our dying, we must never forget that Christ will be with us to the end. But what we must remember above all is this: death has but one mission, and that is to conduct us into the presence of our heavenly Father and to give us a permanent place in the great company of the redeemed.

REFLECTION: Jesus not only proclaimed life after death – He demonstrated life after death.

How do you see God?

'... worship God acceptably with reverence and awe,
for our "God is a consuming fire.'" Hebrews 12:28–29

'The idea of "cheap grace"', says Dr Larry Crabb, 'develops when we talk about grace before we tremble at God's holiness.' Ask yourself this question: How do I see God? As an indulgent old grandfather who smiles at wrongdoing or as a God who is awe-ful in His holiness?

The way we view God will be the way we approach Him. If we see Him as indulgent then we will approach Him with the kind of prayer I once came across in a liberal American church: 'We have done the best under difficult circumstances ... we have been badly influenced by our homes and environment ... so deal lightly with our lapses ... and grant us the power to live harmless lives full of self-respect. Amen.'

Can it be, as Larry Crabb suggests, that our Christian culture has weakened our understanding of the holiness of God by introducing too soon the idea of grace? When I first considered that comment I winced. It seemed a devastating indictment, too painful to consider. But the more I thought about it the more I came to see that it is true. If we talk about grace in a way that makes God an indulgent figure who cares little or nothing about us measuring up to His standards then we have missed our way.

REFLECTION: We are in serious trouble spiritually if we speak of grace in a way that changes the view of God from One who is the holy and righteous Judge to someone who wants us to come up to His standards but is indulgent when we don't.

God's hatred of sin

'The wrath of God is being revealed ... against all the godlessness and wickedness of men ...' Romans 1:18

A recovery of the sense of God's holiness is, I believe, essential for the contemporary Christian Church. The fact with which we must come to grips is that God is not 'a senile benevolence' – someone who wants us to come up to His standards but is indulgent when we don't. In my experience very few Christians today believe God hates sin. The picture many believers have of God nowadays is of someone who is so kind and considerate that He overlooks our moral lapses and encourages us to try harder next time so as not to fail. Personally, I blame many of today's preachers and evangelists for this state of affairs. Instead of starting (as does Billy Graham) with the bad news – that 'all have sinned and fall short of the glory of God' (Rom. 3:23) – they start with the good news – that God forgives all sin and is willing to receive us into heaven providing we submit to Jesus, His Son. But the presentation of the good news must be preceded by the bad news.

This was how John Wesley preached. 'First,' he said, 'I present the law, then I sprinkle it with grace.' Notice how Paul writes to the Romans: he presents God not as a loving Father who indulges all the people in His universe and wants them to have a good time. The Almighty, he says, is furious at everything that is sinful. The gospel begins with bad news before it goes on to give us the good news.

REFLECTION: It is my conviction that the Church needs nothing greater at this time than a fresh vision of God's holiness.

'The scandal of grace'

'For Christ died for sins ... the righteous for the unrighteous, to bring you to God.' 1 Peter 3:18

The point cannot be overemphasised: a person who sees grace as permission to sin has missed the meaning of grace entirely. Someone said: 'Mercy understood is holiness desired.' How can we balance God's desire for us to live holy lives with the fact that grace is available to cover every sin? One man said: 'I treat grace as an undeserved privilege, not as an exclusive right.' This will help you, too, to keep your balance. Live gratefully, not arrogantly. One writer, a secularist, wrote about what he called 'the scandal of grace'. This is what he said: 'God wants people to live righteous lives but then He does the strange thing of offering forgiveness in advance. He also says that the more sin increases the more grace increases. It's a scandalous doctrine and doesn't make any sense. Why be good if you know in advance you are going to be forgiven? Why not be like the pagans – eat, drink, and be merry for tomorrow we die?'

Well, grace may seem scandalous to the uninitiated, but to those of us who have tasted of it, it is the most wonderful gift in the universe. How can God both punish and love the sinner? 1 Peter 3:18 gives the answer. The perfect record that belongs to Christ has been given to us, and our imperfect record has been given to Him. When first heard and understood this seems too good to be true. But in reality it is too good not to be true!

REFLECTION: Holiness demands that sin needs to be punished. Grace compels that the sinner be loved.

A revived church

'All the believers were one in heart and mind.' Acts 4:32

What can we expect a revived Church to look like? The Church of Jesus Christ will shine with a new light when revival comes. Denominationalism – already beginning to be broken down – will in the flow of revival power be broken down completely. In revival people are not inclined to say 'I am an Anglican', 'I am a Baptist', 'I am a Methodist' or 'I am a Pentecostal'. Those attitudes dissolve in the river of God's Spirit. In revival times God acts quickly; His work accelerates. The Early Church operating in the power of the Holy Spirit saw 8,000 converted within a few weeks (Acts 4:4; 5:14). The truth of the gospel makes rapid strides in times of revival. People are born again and grow quickly at such times.

Holiness, another characteristic of revival, will add a sharper edge to Christian living bringing a clearer line of demarcation between the Church and the world. Love flowing between believers will show itself in ways that defy human analysis and cause unbelievers to say, 'How much they love one another.' Yet another characteristic of a Church in revival is a responsiveness to God's Word. A powerful sense of God's presence imparts new authority to the truth of His Word. Whereas before, the Word of God made only a superficial impact, now it searches the hearts of the hearers to the depth of their being.

REFLECTION: At Pentecost, and for several decades afterwards, the Word of God touched the hearts of people in a dynamic way.

The needs of our nation

'Righteousness exalts a nation ...' Proverbs 14:34

Our nation needs God, that is for sure. The answer to the needs of our nation does not lie entirely in the Houses of Parliament but in the house of God. How would revival influence our nation? One of the best answers to that question I know, was given by Dr W.E. Sangster. One Monday morning in the mid-1950s, the nation woke up to read in a number of national papers the substance of a sermon preached by him the previous day. Some newspapers printed the main points of his sermon on their front pages. His theme was: 'Revival: The Need and the Way'. Sangster raised the question: What would a revival of religion do for Britain?

He gave the following ten answers: 1. People would pay old debts. 2. It would reduce sexual immorality. 3. It would disinfect the theatre and the press. 4. It would cut the divorce rate. 5. It would reduce juvenile crime. 6. It would lessen the prison population. 7. It would improve the quality and increase the output of work. 8. It would restore to the nation a sense of high destiny. 9. It would make us invincible in the war of ideas. 10. It would give happiness and peace to the people.

Britain, said Sangster, speaking in the 1950s, has many needs, but her greatest is revival. Today, close on six decades later, the needs of the nation are much greater and our greatest need is still revival.

REFLECTION: The answer to the needs of our nation does not lie entirely in the Houses of Parliament but in the house of God.

A 21st-century revival?

'Return to me, and I will return to you ...' Malachi 3:7

God longs for revival more than we do. 'Return to me and I will return to you,' He said in Malachi 3:7. So let's not settle for the spiritual status quo, a mediocre, weak and anaemic brand of Christianity, when God wants to make available to us the same kind of power that energised the Early Church. Dr Martyn Lloyd-Jones said on one occasion that the Christian Church is like a sleeping giant. If that is so then it is time for it to awake.

There have been two great spiritual awakenings which have affected Britain in the last 500 years. One was the Reformation in the middle of the sixteenth century, triggered by that great reformer, Martin Luther. The second was the Evangelical Awakening in the eighteenth century under such men as John Wesley, George Whitfield and others. Now in the twenty-first century we are ready for a third awakening, one which will turn the tide and make the Church once again the power God intends it to be. To absorb ideas about revival costs nothing, but to enter into revival costs everything – our time, changes in our behaviour. Let us report for duty in the battle for our nation's soul. Let the prayer of Isaiah become our prayer. 'Oh, that you would rend the heavens and come down, that the mountains would tremble before you! ... come down to make your name known to your enemies and cause the nations to quake before you!' (Isa. 64:1–2).

REFLECTION: Whatever the needs of the Church and the nation, our greatest need is revival.

Grace and freedom

'The servant's master took pity on him, cancelled the debt and let him go.' Matthew 18:27

We must learn how to enter into the freedom that grace provides and understand that the Master has forgiven us an insurmountable debt and that He doesn't demand reimbursement. After years of listening to people talking about their problems I have come to the conclusion that by far the biggest single difficulty evangelical Christians struggle with is the failure to live a 'debt-free' existence. Let me explain. The servant had a serious problem. Somehow he had run up a massive debt; the Amplified Bible tells us it was 'probably about 10 million dollars'. Now it is important to realise that Jesus is deliberately using an exaggerated amount here to make it clear that the servant's debt was far greater than his ability to pay.

That's the main point Jesus is making here. The king to whom he owed the debt decided to call it in and ordered the servant to take immediate steps for its repayment. Falling to his knees, the servant begs for time to pay, whereupon the king decides to cancel the debt and set him free. The servant then goes out and comes across a man who owes him a mere pittance (about 20 dollars, says the Amplified Bible) and, because he is unable to repay the money, has him put in prison. Why did he act in this way? There is only one explanation: he still felt in debt. The good news he had been given was still in his head and had never reached his heart.

REFLECTION: Bible truths do not become truth in our lives if they only remain in our heads.

Unrealised forgiveness

'If the forgiveness is minimal, the gratitude is minimal.'
Luke 7:47, The Message

If we really understood how much we have been forgiven then we would have little difficulty in forgiving others. The sins others have committed against you (though they may be vile) cannot compare with the massive debt you built up by your denial of God's right to rule in your heart. I realise that those of you reading these lines who have been the victim of such evils as sexual abuse or brutality may find that difficult to accept. I would not judge you or condemn you if you said: 'I can never forgive that person for what he (or she) did to me.' But what I would say to you is this: the more you reflect on the wonder of how much you have been forgiven the easier it will be to forgive even the worst sins that have been committed against you.

There are many principles to consider in relation to forgiveness, but this without any doubt is the first principle: the more we realise how much we have been forgiven the more forgiving we will be. I was interested to read this in Dr David Seamand's book *Healing Grace*: 'I am convinced that the basic cause of some of the most disturbing emotional and spiritual problems which trouble evangelical Christians is the failure to receive and live out God's unconditional grace, and the corresponding failure to offer that grace to others.'

REFLECTION: Realise the enormity of the debt you owed to God and the grace He showed you in cancelling it until your heart awakens fully to the news of total forgiveness.

The performance trap

'... God, who has saved us ... not because of anything we have done but because of his own purpose and grace.'
2 Timothy 1:8–9

We must learn to avoid the performance trap. The performance trap is living out our lives with the idea that we must always do something in order to be accepted by God. Philip Yancey says this: 'Grace sounds a startling note of contradiction ... and every day I must pray anew for the ability to hear its message.' If you are anything like me then you will need to remind yourself every day that we are precious to God not because of what we do but because of who we are. That does not mean our service for God is unimportant or that God does not appreciate it. However, the ground of our acceptance is not what we do for Him but what He does for us.

In the fourth and fifth centuries there were two notable Bible teachers. One was named Augustine and the other Pelagius. Augustine believed that salvation was a matter of grace, and that had God not taken the initiative in saving us then we would not be saved. Pelagius took the opposite view and believed that people can take the initial steps towards salvation using their own effort and do not require grace to do so. Augustine, of course, held the right view. Eugene Peterson claims that many Christians are Augustinian in theory but Pelagian in practice. In other words, they work to please God rather than rejoicing in the fact that because they are in Christ He is already pleased with them.

REFLECTION: Pelagius methodically worked to please God, Augustine rejoiced in the fact that he was 'chosen by grace'.

Pruning through the Church

'Instead, speaking the truth in love, we will in all things grow up into him ...' Ephesians 4:15

Looking back over my life, I am filled with gratitude to God for the way He has prodded me into usefulness, not only through His Word or directly by His Spirit, but also through the ministries which He has placed in His Body, the Church. Take first the ministry of teaching and preaching. How many times have you listened to a preacher or Christian teacher and realised that what he was saying was a direct word from God to yourself?

He also prunes through the small fellowship group. For many years I lived without a disciplined group correction. My life was overgrown with a lot of useless things. However, when I joined a disciplined group, the pruning process began. I have said before that every Christian needs to be involved in a small group of loving, caring believers, where the true *koinonia* can be developed. *Koinonia* is the Greek word for fellowship: the kind of fellowship which functions under the constraint of love *and* truth. Notice I say love and truth. Some Christians are good at speaking the truth, but bad at loving. Others are good at loving, but hesitate to speak the truth, or the whole truth. How impoverished we are in if we do not cultivate such groups. The small fellowship group, if properly constructed and supervised, is one of the most effective pruning processes in the world.

REFLECTION: There is a world of difference between destructive and constructive criticism. Christian criticism is always constructive – or else it isn't Christian.

Holy Communion

'We love because he first loved us.' 1 John 4:19

'A man ought to examine himself before he eats of the bread and drinks of the cup' (1 Cor. 11:28). Why does God command us to examine ourselves before we take the bread and wine? Where better? It is at the foot of the cross that we discover the mainspring of all Christian action. Some press on to perfection and self-improvement out of a desire to earn God's approval. They long to hear the words, 'Well done, good and faithful servant.' But sometimes there is a tinge of self-centredness in such a desire. We like to feel that we have done something to *deserve* His love. The mainspring of any Christian action, be it caring, evangelism or self-discipline, should not be on the basis of attempting to earn His love, but on the basis that we are already loved.

In bidding us come to the Communion Table to examine ourselves, God wants us to see how much He loves us so that love, not fear, can be the challenge that brings about change. You see, if you try to love God without first realising how much He loves you, then all attempts at self-improvement and self-discipline will be mechanical. In the light of His love for us at Calvary, as vividly dramatised through the bread and the wine, we are fortified to let go of all that is unlike Him, and to let Him love us into greater Christlikeness.

REFLECTION: The mainspring of any Christian action, be it caring, evangelism or self-discipline, should not be on the basis of attempting to earn His love, but on the basis that we are already loved.

Church discipline

'Those whom I love I rebuke and discipline.'
Revelation 3:19

The problem of church discipline is a thorny one, but it is one the Church must take up, nevertheless. God is eager and ready to forgive anyone who is repentant and willing to give up their sin, but when sinful behaviour continues in the life of a Christian, then the Church must obey the Word of Christ and institute disciplinary action. People fear that discipline will divide and destroy the Church. Actually the opposite is true. Wise biblical discipline will unite the Church, revive its spirit and produce solid growth. My words might sound strong and, in some quarters, may be resisted, but those churches who refuse to institute proper disciplinary measures are in danger of having Christ withdraw His presence from them.

Can Christ leave a local church? He left the Laodicean church. Outwardly they got along so well without Him, they never even missed Him. They had forgotten their dependence and their loyalty to Him. Exactly what sins call for discipline? Do we discipline people who, as we say, *have* to get married? Or what about people who get caught exceeding the speed limit? Or someone who has been convicted of crime? The issue is not what sin a Christian has committed, but whether he has repented. Is he walking with God now? Discipline aims to produce repentance and restore fellowship. Under the guidance of the Holy Spirit, the Church must give whatever discipline is required to accomplish these objectives.

REFLECTION: When a church fails to discipline, it loses its soul.

Come and drink

'... Jesus stood and said in a loud voice, "If anyone is thirsty, let him come to me and drink."' John 7:37

O n the last day of the feast, the priest would go down to the pool of Siloam, draw water from it, then return to the Temple precincts and pour it into the dry earth, once again commemorating God's provision of water for His ancient people when they travelled through the wilderness. Now against that background consider once again the words of John: 'If anyone is thirsty, let him come to me and drink' (John 7:37). Note that when Jesus uttered those words, they were said not in measured tones but in a 'loud voice'. I imagine that more often than not He spoke in calm, measured tones. But on this occasion something moved His soul so deeply that He stood (in those days teachers usually sat) and shouted.

What was it that stirred our Lord so much that made Him stand up and cry out? Perhaps this: As the Saviour witnessed the pageantry and ceremony going on around Him and sensing that both people and priests were depending on the religious ritual rather than a personal relationship with the living God to satisfy their spiritual thirst, He was moved to shout out in their midst, 'Come to Me and drink.' His voice still rings out across the centuries with the same message: Come to Me, he says, not to your wife, husband, friend or any other thing. I am the only One who can slake your thirst. Come to Me and drink.

REFLECTION: If we do not acknowledge our deep longings for God, we will remain satisfied with duty rather than devotion, with the things of Christ rather than with Christ Himself.

Paul's priorities

'... we ... put no confidence in the flesh ...' Philippians 3:3

O ne of the reasons why Paul was so open to God's grace was because, as he tells us in Philippians 3, he put no confidence in the flesh. What was his flesh like? What was it like to be in Paul's skin before he became a Christian? He was 'circumcised on the eighth day, of the people of Israel, of the tribe of Benjamin, a Hebrew of Hebrews; in regard to the law, a Pharisee; as for zeal, persecuting the church; as for legalistic righteousness, faultless' (Phil. 3:5–6). 'That's my record,' Paul is saying. 'It may look impressive in the sight of the world but in the eyes of God I was lost and in great need.' Notice how he states that fact: 'But whatever was to my profit I now consider loss for the sake of Christ' (v.7). He goes on to say: 'What is more, I consider everything a loss compared to the surpassing greatness of knowing Christ Jesus my Lord, for whose sake I have lost all things. I consider them rubbish, that I may gain Christ and be found in him ...' (vv.8–9).

Paul had a great track record but he did not rely on it. Those who master the inner struggle and put no confidence in the flesh become wonderful recipients of God's grace. They move along the path of Christian discipleship at a rapid rate. Though problems still arise they are able to handle them with God's help.

REFLECTION: Once Paul had no confidence in the flesh he became more open to receiving God's grace.

Wandering thoughts

'You will keep him in perfect peace, Whose mind is stayed on you ...' Isaiah 26:3, NKJV

One of the biggest hindrances to an effective prayer life is the problem of mind wandering. Time and time again I have come across this problem when counselling Christians on the subject of effective praying. They say, 'I know the value of prayer but I just can't beat this problem of mind wandering.' How do we cope with this vexing problem?

A lady once said to me in a counselling session: 'But I am distracted by *anything*. The slightest noise in the house, the sound of barking dogs, an ambulance or police siren in the distance ...' At the moment she was speaking a police car went by with its siren sounding and I said, 'Now that your mind is focused on the siren how will you use it to aid rather than defeat your prayer life?' She thought for a moment and bowed her head in the counselling room and prayed this prayer. 'O Lord, this siren is distracting me but I realise it is just a warning for people to move out of the way so that the police, or ambulance, might get to the emergency faster. Father, I am so deadened to the plight of those who are lost and going to hell that I, too, need to be alerted by an even louder siren than this. Make me aware of the danger by which men and women are threatened without Christ.' Tears ran down her face as she prayed that prayer. The distraction has become a direction – to God.

REFLECTION: When your mind is distracted and wanders let it wander to God so the distraction itself becomes a point of prayer.

Capturing thoughts

'... we take captive every thought to make it obedient to Christ.' 2 Corinthians 10:5

I advised one man beset by lustful thoughts to ask the Lord to fill his imagination with such a picture of Himself that it would take up the whole perspective of his thoughts. Christ is the centre of all things pure. Lustful images steadily dissolve on the steady gaze of His searching eyes. The thing that looked so seductive a moment before looks loathsome with Jesus consciously present. Coolness in the place of heat and serenity instead of desire, are the reward of those who are swift to bring Jesus alongside the pictures that enter the mind. The man told me some months later that practising this method of overcoming mind wandering made Jesus more real to his heart than He had ever been before. 'I have such a clear picture of Christ in my mind and I have developed the art of conversational prayer to such a great degree,' he said, 'that, although I hesitate to say it, I feel almost thankful that I was plagued with these evil thoughts, as they have become the stepping-stones to a more personal and dependent relationship with the Lord.'

Any Christian, bent on winning the battle over evil thoughts, can, by using the method I have described above, outmanoeuvre the problem in a few weeks, or at the most a few months. After a while, and with practice, you will be able to bring every thought into captivity to the obedience of Christ.

REFLECTION: If you are beset by wandering thoughts, perhaps even *evil* thoughts then, instead of wrestling with them, use them as a prayer focus.

Respect your body

'Do you not know that your body is a temple of the Holy Spirit, who is in you, whom you have received from God?'
1 Corinthians 6:19

S ome years ago, when reading a book on theology by Dr Cynddylan Jones, a famous Welsh preacher, I came across this statement: 'The end of all God's purposes for mankind is embodiment.' For some reason only faintly seen by us but of course clear to Him, God's purpose for human beings, both now and in the future, is that our capacities of thinking, feeling, longing and choosing should function within a physical frame. This means that with the exception of the time after death and before the resurrection we will not be without a body. The body we now have will return to dust when we die, but at the resurrection we will be given a new body – a body 'like his glorious body' (Phil. 3:21).

While in this present body, however, even though it is affected by sin, we are expected to treat it with respect for, as the apostle Paul tells us, our body is 'a temple of the Holy Spirit'. In Romans 12:1–2 he encourages us to offer our bodies 'as living sacrifices, holy and pleasing to God'. This offering of our bodies, he says, is to be a 'spiritual act of worship'. Anyone who ignores or minimises the importance of the physical is going against the teaching of Scripture, and thus will never reach the degree of maturity and development that God longs for them to have. If you thought that you could thrive spiritually without considering the importance of the physical then think again.

REFLECTION: Our soul is housed in a body, and we have a responsibility to take good care of it.

Remember

'When my life was ebbing away,' confessed Jonah,
'I remembered you, Lord.' (Jonah 2:7)

Frequently this God-given sense of memory is what redeems the soul from discouragement and despair. Many a sorely tried person has been brought back to confidence in God by recalling some spiritual experience or memory of the past. Often it is because we forget that we faint. Jonah had been running away from God, and no doubt had attempted to push God out of his thoughts. But as he sinks into the turbulent ocean, the temple of his memory is illuminated by his knowledge of God in the past.

This verse made a particular impact on me shortly before I wrote these thoughts on Jonah: 'After he was raised from the dead, his disciples recalled what he had said. Then they believed the Scripture and the words that Jesus had spoken' (John 2:22). It was when the disciples *recalled* what Jesus had said that they *believed*. Here are two kindred forces that form a powerful and fruitful partnership which can be responsible for incalculable good in the life of every believer. Quickened memory often propels the soul to the place of faith in God. This is what happened to Jonah. He remembers the Lord, turns his thoughts once again to Him, reflects on his relationship with Him and the prayer that had previously dried up begins to flow again. An anonymous poet wrote: 'How oft in hours of threatened loss, When heart was numb with many fears, Has come a flash of light and truth, Across the interspace of years.'

REFLECTION: 'Recollection', it has been said, 'is often the first step towards realisation.'

The truth about idolatry

'Those who cling to worthless idols forfeit the grace that could be theirs.' Jonah 2:8

Jonah identifies the biggest single hindrance to knowing God – idols. Jonah was obviously thinking of the idols used by the heathen – idols of wood and stone. But idols can take many other forms too. *Self* can be an idol. *Possessions* can be an idol. *People* can be an idol. Anything that becomes a centre of love and attention – love and attention greater than that which we give to God – is an idol. Idolatry has been described as 'substitution' – substitution of the marginal for the important, the unreal for the Real. Anything or anyone we treat as the object of our absolute loyalty and love takes the place of God.

In this sense Jonah, too, was an idolater, for he put his own interests before God, and, as we shall see later, continued to do so, despite the seemingly sincere utterances in his prayer. One of the devil's tricks is to get us to believe that because we do not bow down, as some pagans do, to idols of wood and stone, we are free from idolatry. Many can offer a prayer similar to Jonah's and thank God they don't worship idols, and then depend on something other than God. When we do this we are just as guilty of idolatry as the heathen. John Calvin saw the human heart as a relentlessly efficient factory for producing idols. Most of us, as we acknowledged earlier, want to be our own god. Any idols in your life I wonder? I found one lurking in mine.

REFLECTION: '... greed, which is idolatry' (Col. 3:5).

The message of salvation

'... Salvation comes from the LORD.' Jonah 2:9

T he climax of Jonah's prayer, when he cries 'Salvation comes from the LORD', is one of Scripture's most wonderful statements. This was one of the great texts used during the Evangelical Revival of the eighteenth century, and is the cornerstone of evangelical truth. I imagine thousands, if not millions, have been converted through hearing this text. It was one of Martin Luther's favourite verses. And it was said that if the great preacher C.H. Spurgeon was ever called upon to preach unexpectedly, he would base his sermon on it. The words have been described as the marrow of the gospel because through them we learn that God is the One who saves us. We can do absolutely nothing to save ourselves. Always the initiative is with God. The very faith by which you take hold of Him is not yours; it is the gift of God. Jonah's life was ebbing, *but* salvation was at hand.

'Where would we be,' said Dr Martyn Lloyd-Jones on one occasion, 'were it not for the "buts" of the Bible.' He was preaching on Romans 5:8 at the time: 'But God demonstrates his own love for us in this: While we were still sinners, Christ died for us.' If you have never accepted the salvation which is offered then I plead with you to do so now. This is the good news Jonah sounded out from inside the whale. This is the heart of God's mercy. I sound it again with jubilation: *Salvation comes from the Lord.*

REFLECTION: Jesus Christ is our Saviour, the Lord.

The patience of God

*'And the LORD commanded the fish and it vomited Jonah
onto dry land.' Jonah 2:10*

Jonah emerged from the fish's stomach a better man than
when he went in. But was Jonah a completely changed man?
Clearly, the confinement had produced some positive results.
It had rid him of the delusion that he could disobey God's commands
without suffering the consequences. It had brought him to a place of
repentance and restored his relationship with God. But deep down
some characteristics remained unaltered: he was still self-concerned
and self-justifying. It is a fallacy to think that one event, albeit a
significant or traumatic one, can bring about significant changes
in our hearts. Sanctification is an ongoing process. There are many
things God can do in a moment but, as George Macdonald put it,
'It takes time to make a saint.' Jesus could give sight to the blind –
instantly. He could turn water into wine – instantly. But it took time
to turn His disciples from weak, vacillating personalities into men
who were invincible.

What we should be glad about, however, is that God does not
wait until we are perfect before He uses us. If He did, then many
of us would have been disqualified years ago. Embedded like
splintered glass in Jonah's heart (and also in ours) is a stubborn
commitment to independence. God finds some further resistance in
His prophet and He sets about removing that. But in the meantime
He still has work for him to do. There is nothing more amazing
than the patience of God.

**REFLECTION: Because God is patient He never acts out of
frustration when He sees our repeated failings.**

A sense of 'sentness'

'As the Father has sent me, so I send you.' John 20:21, NLT

The starting point for all of us is to know who we are, and what we are doing here. Our identity is that we are beloved of God, chosen to play a specific part in His programme. We need to be comfortable with that. Jesus knew that He had come from God and that He was going to God. You and I too come from God. There needs to be a sense of 'sentness' in us all, an understanding of why we came into the world. In being sent we are given opportunities to express different gifts and everyone is gifted to do certain things well. This sense of 'sentness' arises out of three convictions: knowing who we are, knowing that we are loved and knowing where we are going. It requires us to be wholly available for God, willing for Him to send us wherever He wants us to go. Our response must be that of the prophet Isaiah: 'Here am I. Send me!' (Isa. 6:8).

Some are sent and remain in the same place for years, others are continually sent to different places. The sense of being sent can hold us whenever we feel discouraged in our task as we remind ourselves that we were chosen and sent to do it. I have come to know that a telegram boy is all I am (bringing messages from God). Let me warn you that if you think too much of your importance then God will burst the bubble of applause!

REFLECTION: Have you considered creating a Mission Statement for yourself? It can be a very helpful exercise.

Equipping for the task

'I pray that out of his glorious riches he may strengthen you with power through his Spirit in your inner being ...'
Ephesians 3:16

The empowerment of the Spirit is the wonderful gift of God which is given along with the responsibility of the task. Did the Father leave Jesus to execute the task for which He was sent in His own strength? No. Heaven opened after His baptism in the Jordan and the Spirit descended upon Him. This was a special and particular anointing of the Spirit, a supernatural clothing for a special task. But before beginning His ministry Jesus was sent into the wilderness and was there tempted by the devil. It was a further empowerment because it is under test that the Holy Spirit makes us powerful. What we need most of all is a mighty empowerment of the Holy Spirit. Predicting His death, Jesus uttered these words: 'Now my heart is troubled, and what shall I say? "Father, save me from this hour,"? No, it was for this very reason I came to this hour' (John 12:27). It was by the Spirit's power He was able to accomplish His mission. In order to accomplish their mission, the Spirit's power was given to the disciples of Jesus. After His death and resurrection, Jesus came to His disciples, cowering behind locked doors, and breathed on them, saying 'Receive the Holy Spirit' (John 20:22). Fifty days later they received the full empowerment of the Holy Spirit as He descended on each of them in tongues of flame (Acts 2) and everything was different after that. The Spirit makes the difference.

REFLECTION: The apostle Paul understood he had been equipped for all God sent him to do through the empowerment of the Holy Spirit.

Fullness – only in God

'... to the only wise God be glory for ever through Jesus Christ!' Romans 16:27

God's boundless knowledge and wisdom are perfect in every way, and it is this that makes Him utterly worthy of our trust. But it must be said that one of the great difficulties we have in the Christian life is in trusting the divine wisdom. We can recognise wisdom only when we see the end to which it is moving. Yet God often calls us to trust Him when we can't see the end that He is pursuing, and at such times we have to ask ourselves: How much do I trust Him?

God's wisdom is not, and never was, intended to get us through life without being hurt. The goal of divine wisdom is to bring about the best possible results, which for us means making us holy. And sometimes pursuing that goal may involve us in considerable pain. 'And we know that all that happens to us is working for our good' (Rom. 8:28, TLB) must be read in connection with Romans 8:29. Because God is committed to making us like His Son, His wisdom will bring from every trial that comes our way something that will enrich our character and make us more like Jesus Christ. Infinite power is ruled by infinite wisdom. God could deliver us from difficult situations and make our lives comfortable, but in a fallen world that is not the *best* purpose. Understanding this is crucial if we are to live our lives in the way God desires

REFLECTION: No matter how hard the experience, God's power will be there to get us through, and God's wisdom will ensure that the benefit outweighs the cost.

The power of fasting

'So I turned to the Lord God and pleaded with him in prayer and petition, in fasting ...' Daniel 9:3

The New Testament makes clear that some spiritual victories can only be experienced when we know how to *fast* as well as pray. On one occasion Jesus said to His disciples, who were having some difficulty in casting out a demon, 'But this kind of demon won't leave unless you have prayed and gone without food' (Matt. 17:21, TLB). Fasting is the practice of deliberately abstaining from food in order to add greater power to one's prayers.

Let's consider a few points about this important spiritual exercise. (a) *Fasting puts the body in its place.* When a Christian practises the art of fasting his spirit says to his body: 'You will not dictate the terms of my life; I'm the boss – and don't forget it.' We can only conquer the enemy (Satan) after we have conquered ourselves. (b) *Fasting gives victory over temptation.* There can be no doubt that Christ's victory over Satan in the wilderness (Matt. 4:1) was due, in no small measure, to His forty days' fast. (c) *Fasting sharpens our spiritual understanding enabling us to make right decisions.* Is it not significant that Jesus spent a night in prayer before choosing His disciples? I have found in my own life that to precede the making of an important decision with a 24-hour fast enables me to come to the moment of decision with clarity and conviction.

REFLECTION: Fasting reinforces the human spirit, enabling it to deal more efficiently and effectively with the devil's strategies.

Fasting and prayer

'Jesus ... ate nothing during those days, and at the end of them he was hungry.' Luke 4:1–2

In Leviticus 16:29 God instructed the children of Israel to set aside a special day annually for the purpose of 'afflicting their souls' (AV). Jesus and the apostles fasted. Church history shows that many of the men who figured greatly in the growth and development of the Christian Church often fasted. John Wesley so believed in the importance of fasting that he refused to ordain young men who would not fast two days each week. Martin Luther fasted regularly, and so did John Knox. The great evangelist Charles Finney said, 'When empty of power I would set apart a day for private fasting and prayer ... after this, the power would return in all its freshness.'

I am convinced myself that if Christians were to fast as well as pray we would see a move of the Holy Spirit throughout the world such as we have not seen since the days of the Early Church. If you have never fasted before and you want to learn the art, then begin in a small way by entering into a 12- or 24-hour fast. Believe me, fasting is not easy. The first time I tried to fast I could go no longer than six hours! But I persisted and within a year I was able to fast for a week without any difficulty at all. No one should enter on a long fast before checking with a doctor. And if you have serious medical problems (such as diabetes) then fasting is not for you.

REFLECTION: Fasting together with prayer is often seen as a hallmark of great revivals.

What is heaven like?

'... glory, honour and thanks to him who sits on the throne ...' Revelation 4:9

Though it is not possible to buy a guide book or a map of the celestial city, the book of Revelation gives us some idea of what heaven is like. I am reminded of the story of a little girl who was born blind. Her mother used to describe the beauty of the world to her but the little girl did not have any real idea of what was being described. When she was twelve years old an operation was performed on her eyes which resulted in her gaining sight. When, for the first time, she saw the beauty of creation she turned to her mother and exclaimed, 'Oh Mother, why didn't you tell me it was so beautiful?' Her mother responded, 'I tried, my darling ... I tried. But I just couldn't find the words.'

That is how I feel as I read John's description of heaven. He tries to tell us what it is like, but eloquent and descriptive as he is, one has the feeling that language is being stretched to the utmost. In Revelation chapter 4 John shows us that heaven is a place of perpetual praise. All eyes in heaven seem to be directed towards the throne and every creature is vocal in the worship of God and of the Lamb. One of the great delights of earth is when the soul is caught up in praise of God. But in heaven we shall not just be caught up in it; we shall be lost in it.

REFLECTION: Here our praise is just a rehearsal; there it will be a realisation.

Indescribable joy

'... you will fill me with joy in your presence, with eternal pleasures at your right hand.' Psalm 16:11

A s well as being a place of praise and service heaven is a place of indescribable joy. Heaven and joy are often linked together. Jesus said on one occasion, '... there is joy before the angels of God over one sinner who repents' (Luke 15:10, RSV). And when telling the parable of the Talents He promised that those who use their talents and multiply them will hear the Master say, '... enter into the joy of your master' (Matt. 25:21, RSV). Frequently I have been asked: Will there be laughter in heaven? Personally, I have no doubt about it. The God who made Sarah to laugh, does He not laugh Himself? I believe that gales of laughter will echo from the redeemed, and we shall discover, I think, that however much we have laughed down here on earth it will be as nothing compared to the laughter of heaven.

Another characteristic of heaven is that it is a place of absolute perfection. In the last two chapters of the book of Revelation the apostle John uses a succession of negatives to help us develop a picture of heaven. There will be no more death, he says, no more crying, no more sorrow, no more pain, no longer any curse, no more night, and so on. The reason for heaven's perfection is that sin, which is the cause of all imperfection, has no place or part in that eternal realm.

REFLECTION: Heaven is a place of perpetual praise, a place of endless service, a place of ineffable joy and a place of absolute perfection.

God's indescribable gift

'For God so loved the world that he gave his one and only Son ...' John 3:16

When John Newton wrote his hymn about grace he used the word 'amazing' to describe it. As someone who constantly uses words, I have tried to think of a better word to describe it, but there just isn't one. It really is amazing. When Jessye Norman sang 'Amazing Grace' during a rock concert at Wembley, a strange power descended on the stadium. Without any accompaniment she began to sing slowly: 'Amazing grace! how sweet the sound, That saved a wretch like me! I once was lost, but now I'm found; Was blind, but now I see.' By the time she reached the last verse all was quiet. Non-Christians as well as Christians are amazed by grace. Though they may not realise it, that is what they thirst for.

A friend once sent me a Christmas card with these words which impressed me deeply: 'If our greatest need had been information, God would have sent us an educator. If our greatest need had been technology, God would have sent us a scientist. If our greatest need had been money, God would have sent us an economist. If our greatest need had been pleasure, God would have sent us an entertainer. But our greatest need was forgiveness, so God sent us a Saviour!' When, on that first Christmas morning, Mary looked at the face of her newborn son, I wonder, did she realise that she was unwrapping for humanity what Paul calls God's indescribable gift? That indescribable gift of grace was the gift we needed most.

REFLECTION: Thank God for His indescribable gift of grace of Jesus Christ our Saviour.

Empty promises

'You open your hand and satisfy the desires of every living thing.' Psalm 145:16

I f contemplation of the goodness of God does not drive us to Him, perhaps weariness with the pleasures of the world will have the desired effect. Pleasures, beauty and personal relationships all seem to promise so much, and yet when we grasp them, we find that what we were seeking was not located in them, but lies beyond them. There is a divine dissatisfaction within human experience which prompts us to ask whether there is anything which may satisfy the human quest or fulfil the desires of the human heart.

Clearly in every one of us there is something that earth cannot satisfy – not even the best things of earth. There still remains a hunger and a longing that nothing on earth can meet.

Human love is probably one of the most powerful and satisfying things one can experience on this planet. To love someone deeply and to have that love reciprocated is one of earth's greatest joys. Yet deep within our souls is something that not even the most loving wife, husband or dearest friend can meet. What we long for at the core of our being simply isn't there in any earthly relationship. The sooner we realise this the better. Not to realise it means we might demand from those who are closest to us something they are not really able to provide. This is what kills relationships.

REFLECTION: Are you demanding that others provide for you fulfilment and happiness or are you growing closer to the One who meets these needs in you?

Caring for others

'Share each other's troubles and problems, and so obey our Lord's command.' Galatians 6:2, TLB

Almost every day of our lives we find ourselves confronted by someone who has a problem, a marriage difficulty, the loss of a loved one, a desperate prayer that seems to go unanswered, a financial difficulty, ... a serious sickness, lack of spiritual growth ... and what can we say? Every Christian is encouraged in Scripture to have a practical and sacrificial concern for others. James tells us, 'Now what use is it, my brothers, for a man to say he "has faith" if his actions do not correspond with it?' (James 2:14, Phillips). A similar thought is expressed in Philippians 2:4, 'Don't just think about your own affairs, but be interested in others, too, and in what they are doing' (TLB). In 1 Thessalonians 5:11 we are told to 'encourage each other to build each other up' (TLB), and in Galatians 6:2 we are commanded to 'Share each other's troubles and problems, and so obey our Lord's command' (TLB).

Answering questions and helping people from a Christian perspective is ultimately guiding people to what God has to say about the situation in His Word, the Bible. The same breath that went into the making of man has gone into the making of the Bible (2 Tim. 3:16), for it was God's intention that the Scriptures should become the reference book for mankind's continued spiritual and psychological development on this earth.

REFLECTION: It was God's intention that the Scriptures should become the reference book for mankind's continued spiritual and psychological development on this earth.

Do you feel like praying?

'Devote yourselves to prayer ...' Colossians 4:2

Some Christians think that it is no good praying unless you 'feel like it'. The precise opposite is nearer the truth. Our prayers are often more effective when we pray even though we don't feel like praying. And it is not difficult to understand why. When we pray because we feel like it there is often a degree of pleasure that we give ourselves. It feels good to hear our own voice putting together words that address the Almighty God, to sense a flexibility of language as our tongue becomes like 'the pen of a ready writer'. We can feel good about ourselves when we pray like that.

When, however, we pray though we do not feel like it, we bring to God not only the content of our prayer but the evidence of a disciplined spirit. We have gone to Him against our natural inclination. We have displeased ourselves in order to please Him. Prayer is too important to depend on the vagary of feelings. Feelings fluctuate with our health, the weather, the news, circumstances, what we eat and whom we met last. Our prayer lives cannot be conducted on things so fortuitous. Forbes Robinson, himself a man of prayer, said: 'Do not mind about feelings. You may have beautiful feelings. Thank God if you have. He sends them. You may have none. Thank God if you have not, for He has kept them back. We do not want to *feel* better and stronger; we want to *be* better and stronger.'

REFLECTION: If in times past you have prayed only when you felt like it, then in future, determine to go to God whether you feel like it or not.

Waking with God

'When I awake, I am still with you.' Psalm 139:18

Our first thought upon waking ought to be of the Lord. A friend of mine says that this suggestion, given to him in the early days of his Christian experience, has been the means of sharpening the sense of God's presence in his life more than almost any other single thing. Listen to how a poet put it: 'Every morning lean thine arm awhile Upon the window sill of heaven And gaze upon thy God; Then with the vision in thy heart Turn strong to meet the day.' 'Turn strong to meet the day.' What an optimistic thought! And why not? Anyone who looks into the face of God during the waking moments is fortified to look into the face of anything the day may bring. Someone has said there are two kinds of Christians; those who wake up in the morning, look around the room and say rather gloomily: 'Oh, Lord, another day,' and those who wake up, look into their heavenly Father's face and say brightly: 'Oh, Lord, another day!' Which kind, I wonder, are you?

Those who study the effect of thought upon the personality tell us that our last thought at night and our first thought in the morning are greatly influential in determining the quality of our sleep and our attitudes towards life. Waking with God gives a divine perspective to the day because if your day begins with God, it is more likely to continue and end with Him.

REFLECTION: Learn to push expectantly on the gates of abundant living as you awake each morning and as surely as day follows night, those gates will open wide.

A praising heart

'But you are holy, Who inhabit the praises of Israel.'
Psalm 22:3, NKJV

Reading the Bible, we are constantly reminded that God delights to dwell in the midst of His people's praise. On the basis of Psalm 22:3, I can promise you that the more you cultivate a praising heart, the more deeply you will feel the Lord's presence in your life. We might not always be able to find a reason to be thankful but we can always find a reason to praise. The prime purpose of praise is to honour and glorify God and because He never changes, then it follows that praise of Him is always appropriate. Some may feel they have little for which they can give thanks, but no one, no matter how poor, deprived or downcast has any excuse not to praise.

Whenever you feel sad or depressed, here's a secret that has taken me a lifetime to learn: acknowledge your feelings and then decide by an action of your will to focus your thoughts upon the goodness of God and praise will flow. Praise, unlike thanksgiving, begins not so much in the feelings as in the will. We can choose to praise the Almighty whether we feel like it or not. Can I ask you to determine right now that you will make it a daily habit to spend some time in praise of God? We pick up bad habits all too quickly. What is wrong with setting up a habit that enables us to turn our minds towards the Lord and give Him the praise which He so wondrously deserves?

REFLECTION: We are made in our innermost beings for praise. We naturally praise actors, sports stars, musicians and heroic actions. We naturally praise our Creator and Saviour.

God's kindness

'... God's kindness is intended to lead you to repent ...'
Romans 2:4, Amp.

A lthough God commands us to be kind, He goes further than that: He exemplifies it in the Person of His Son. Our text is a favourite verse of mine. Imagine if God had never come to the world in the Person of His Son, Jesus Christ, but had simply shouted down to us from heaven through a megaphone, 'Repent!' But, no, He came into the world, wore our flesh, measured its frailty and earned the right to call us to repentance by His involvement in the messy business of living. He knows our condition because He has been in our condition. How does the kindness of God lead us to repentance?

Somebody has said that, if you wanted to represent Christianity in one English word and you were not able to use the word 'love', then the word 'kindness' would be the next best word. How kind God has been to us in giving His Son to die for us on the cross! Heaven's highest strategy for begetting a response in our hearts is to bring us to the cross and hold us there and, seeing God's kindness to us, our own hearts flame in response.

I have found, as an evangelist, that the most powerful motivator in bringing people to Christ is to show them what God has done for them. That's why the greatest evangelistic text in the Bible is John 3:16: 'For God so loved the world that he gave his one and only Son, that whoever believes in him should not perish but have eternal life.'

REFLECTION: Seeing how much we are loved we cry: 'Amazing love! How can it be That Thou, my God, shouldst die for me?'
(Charles Wesley)

Counting the cost

'Will he not first sit down and estimate the cost ... Will he not first sit down and consider whether he is able ...?'
Luke 14:28,31

Jesus here is illustrating that someone, before beginning to build a tower or going to war, sits down to count the cost, and that this is exactly what He Himself is doing. He is saying, 'I am in the world to build, I am in the world to overturn its systems ... and, in order to do it, I want to be absolutely certain that the people who come to me are totally committed.' He is counting the cost and He is making it absolutely clear that, if He is to change the world, then He is thinking very carefully about the breed and the brand of people that He wants to follow Him.

He is saying, 'Now here are my commands. Here is my standard. This is what I am asking for.' So, there are three tests of discipleship: Are you willing to put Christ first and foremost before every other person in your life, every other pleasure, every other possession? Somebody said that the stages of the Christian life could be described in four words: easy, hard, difficult, impossible. Some people think that it is easy to be a Christian: all you have to do is sign on the dotted line, say a prayer and you are in. When they get in, they find that it is a little harder than they thought. And then they go through a phase where it is extremely difficult and, finally, they come to a stage where it is impossible. When they come to this final stage they are at the point of their greatest breakthrough, because, actually, you cannot live this life in your own strength.

REFLECTION: You become a disciple by committing yourself to Him.

Keeping on keeping on

*'... I'm running hard for the finish line. I'm giving it
everything I've got. No sloppy living for me! I'm staying
alert and in top condition.*
1 Corinthians 9:26–27, The Message

There are some Christians who appear in church on Sundays,
but they do not persevere and engage in a personal life
with the Lord through the days of the week. They don't go
through the tough times, praying through the loneliness and keeping
on and staying true during the lonely, anxious hours.

Two frogs fell into a vat of cream. They tried very hard to get out
by climbing up the side of the vat but it was too slippery and steep.
They could not get a purchase to hop out. Each time they slipped
back again. Finally one frog said to the other, 'We'll never get out of
here. I give up.' So down he went and eventually drowned. The other
frog decided to keep trying and kept kicking and kicking hoping he
would get some purchase and be able to hop out. Eventually the
constant kicking turned the cream into butter, and so with one final
effort the frog leapt out.

Whenever I think of the word perseverance I think of Jeremiah.
He had some pretty hard times to put up with but he never allowed
himself to get into a rut. How did he manage it? He got up every
morning with the sun. The day was God's day, not the people's.
He didn't get up to face rejection; he got up to meet with God.
He didn't rise to put up with another round of mockery; he rose to
be with his Lord.

**REFLECTION: Don't think about the long road ahead but greet
the present moment with obedient delight and expectant hope.**

Loving and giving

'Each of you should look not only to your own interests,
but also to the interests of others.' Philippians 2:4

B egin to think of ways in which you can minister to others in
love. Tilt your soul in the direction of serving rather than
being served, of giving rather than receiving. Develop an
attitude of giving. All actions begin with the right attitude.

Early one chilly winter morning in London during the Second
World War a soldier was making his way to the barracks and spotted
a lad with his nose pressed against the window of a baker's shop.
Inside the baker was kneading dough for a fresh supply of doughnuts.
The hungry boy stared in silence watching every move. The soldier
walked over to the shop and stood at the side of the little boy.
Through the steamed-up window he could see the mouth-watering
items that were being pulled from the oven. They watched as the
baker put them in a glass enclosed counter. The soldier's heart went
out to the little boy. He said, 'Son, would you like some of those
doughnuts?' The boy was startled. 'Yes, I would,' he said. The soldier
stepped inside the shop, bought a few of the doughnuts and walked
back to where the lad was. He smiled as he held out the bag and said
simply, 'They're yours.' He walked away but he hadn't got far when
he felt a tug at his coat. He looked down and heard the child ask
quietly, 'Mister, are you Jesus?'

We are never more like Jesus than when we give ourselves to
others. It's the law by which every one of us should live.

**REFLECTION: Life is more about giving than getting – see who
you can bless today.**

The Servant King

'May they be brought to complete unity to let the world know that you sent me and have loved them even as you have loved me.' John 17:23

W e need to focus on the fact that what our Saviour longs for every one of His children is that we might give ourselves to others in the same way that He gives Himself to us. You are to love one another, He said, in the same way that I love you. Jesus Christ was the only one who has ever lived on this earth completely free from self-centredness. Listen as He declares one of His primary reasons for coming to this world: 'For even the Son of Man did not come to be served, but to serve, and to give his life as a ransom for many' (Mark 10:45). No prevaricating. No fudging of the issue. He gives us in those words a crystal clear statement of why He is here. He came to serve and to give. John Wesley said of our Lord, 'All his life was prayer and love.' We have only to study the Gospels to find Wesley's words confirmed. Jesus' first thought was not of Himself but to do His Father's will and His Father's will was one of costly serving of others.

The apostle Peter summarised our Saviour's life by saying, 'he went around doing good' (Acts 10:38). He fed the hungry, cheered the sad, preached good tidings to the poor. One preacher said of Him, 'In Jesus Christ there moved on the surface of this planet for the only time in history a completely *un*self-centred person.' It makes sense then that the one who so brilliantly modelled the other-centredness of the Trinity desires that our lives should be run in the same way.

REFLECTION: He longs that we might run our lives in the same way He did.

Clarifying the emotions

'There is a time for everything ... a time to weep and a time to laugh ...' Ecclesiastes 3:1,4

One of the great mistakes many of us make with regard to our feelings is to conclude that all unpleasant emotions are bad and all pleasant emotions are good. The death of a loved one, for example, will almost certainly produce unpleasant feelings, but the grief that is in the heart should not be thought of as a negative emotion. You are supposed to feel grief when a loved one dies. Similarly, not all pleasant feelings are to be viewed as positive. A man may have pleasant feelings when he has succeeded in seducing a woman, but in a moral context those feelings cannot be described as good.

Psychologist Larry Crabb prefers to categorise emotions as constructive or destructive. Constructive emotions, he says, are emotions that lead us towards God, and destructive emotions are those that lead us away from Him. If whatever we feel is hindering our loving involvement with God or with others then the emotion is destructive and needs to be traced to its root, for something is going on inside that needs correction. When our feelings turn us towards the Lord in deeper dependence on Him and more loving attitudes towards others then the emotion is praiseworthy.

Somehow we have developed the idea that mature Christians should always feel good. Our Lord was a Man of sorrows even though He delighted in pursuing His Father's will.

REFLECTION: Joy is given to us now not to replace suffering and pain but to support us as we go through it.

Seeing God in Jesus

'Anyone who has seen me has seen the Father.' John 14:9

E. Stanley Jones tells the story of a little boy who one Christmas Day stood for several minutes before a picture of his absent father and then turned to his mother and said wistfully: 'How I wish Father would step out of the picture.' A similar cry must have arisen in the heart of all those who lived in Old Testament times, who believed in God and longed for His appearing.

One day the Father stepped out of the picture. He stepped out at Bethlehem. John's Gospel says simply but sublimely: 'The Word became flesh and dwelt among us ...' (John 1:14, NKJV) He also said: 'No-one has ever seen God, but God the One and Only, who is at the Father's side, has made him known.' (John 1:18). Our Lord's coming into this world gave us a true picture of what God is like and reflected His image to us. What I am now about to say may seem strange, but the truth is in the perfect life of Jesus of Nazareth we see a lot of God, but we do not see all we need to see. It took something more than a perfect life to reveal God fully. That unfolding comes only at the cross. It was as Jesus hung upon a Roman cross, that He lay completely bare the heart of the Eternal and revealed the beauty and perfection of His being in sacrificial love. Solemnly I say, it took a cross to reveal God fully.

REFLECTION: The cross is God's magnet to draw men and women to Himself and the power by which God's image can be restored in us.

Be wise

'Be wise in the way you act towards outsiders; make the most of every opportunity.' Colossians 4:5

Many Christians are not very wise in the way they relate to others. Once, I stayed with a very friendly couple and on the Sunday morning the man said, 'It's such a nice day, let's not bother with the car, we'll walk to church.' As we set out, he said, 'You might be interested to see what will happen as we walk to church this morning. Because I am a Christian many of my neighbours go out of their way to avoid me.' He pointed to one up ahead who had just come out of a newsagent's shop obviously buying his Sunday paper and said, 'Now watch what he will do as soon as he catches sight of me.' Sure enough, as soon as the neighbour spotted my friend, he went back inside the shop. A few minutes later we came across another neighbour who when he caught sight of us crossed to the other side of the road. At this point my curiosity got the better of me and I said, 'How has all this come about?' 'It's simply because when I first moved here I witnessed to my neighbours that I was a Christian.' 'And how did you do that?' I asked. He replied, 'I began my witness by saying to them: Good morning, do you know you are going to hell?'

It is one thing when we are ostracised because of Christ; it is another thing when Christ is ostracised because of us.

REFLECTION: It is a tremendous privilege and a tremendous responsibility to belong to the people of God.

God does listen

'Before they call I will answer; while they are still speaking I will hear.' Isaiah 65:24

B etween people there is frequently a communication breakdown. Many people do not actually listen but simply wait to have their turn at talking. But perhaps some don't listen because they have never been listened to. Listening is the most powerful way of showing someone you care. When it comes to talking to God, I am totally confident, on the basis of numerous scriptures, that He always listens. We have His full attention and He both hears and answers our prayers.

Prayer is powerful and we should be praying frequently. But people often tell me that they have given up on praying 'because God doesn't listen'. That does not accord with God's Word, but undoubtedly the matter of God's response can be problematic for people. God gives us this assurance: '... if my people, who are called by my name, will humble themselves and pray and seek my face and turn from their wicked ways, then will I hear from heaven and will forgive their sin and will heal their land' (2 Chron. 7:14). But we are not to expect that He will always answers our prayers in the way we want them answered. His answer may be 'Yes', 'No', 'Not yet' or, as I have personally experienced, 'I will give you something better'.

I know that God listens to me when I talk to Him, and I know this doesn't mean He is going to do everything I ask. I leave the judgment to Him and thank Him for all my answered prayers, no matter what His responses have been.

REFLECTION: God hears and answers: 'Call to me and I will answer ...' (Jer. 33:3).

The time had come

'But when the time had fully come, God sent his Son,
born of a woman, born under law, to redeem those
under law, that we might receive the full rights of sons.'
Galatians 4:4–5

The coming of Christ to Bethlehem was neither late nor early, neither behind nor beforehand, neither tardy nor premature. Charles Wesley's carol, 'Hark the Herald Angels Sing', says: 'Late in time, behold Him come ...' As a boy, whenever I sang that carol, I used to ponder how it was possible to be both things at once, late and in time, wondering if I could achieve the same feat in relation to my school attendance. But Jesus was not late. Although it might have appeared that He was late, He came at the divinely appointed hour. His advent chimed exactly with the striking of the great clock of God.

Make no mistake about it, His birth was not a last minute brainstorm by the Creator, some hectic attempt to rescue mankind. God had prepared this even before the foundation of the world. He announced His coming way back in time. He predicted it through prophecy. People get some predictions wrong. We can't predict the weather exactly, for example. But there are hundreds of prophecies about Jesus' coming: Genesis 3:15 was the first prophecy of Scripture, Micah 5:2 speaks prophetically of Bethlehem as His birthplace, Isaiah 7:14 says He will be born of a virgin and Hosea 11:1 refers to the time when the family of Jesus would take refuge in Egypt. It was no fluke that Jesus arrived when He did.

REFLECTION: God sent His Son into the world to save us – at exactly the right time – foretold years before. How amazing!

'For to me, to live is ...'

'For to me, to live is Christ and to die is gain.'
Philippians 1:21

Before we can thrive spiritually we must replace our foolish thinking with right thinking. There are many thoughts in our minds that need to be changed, but we must be careful that we understand what is the mind's *core* wrong belief. Many Christians have spent years countering wrong ideas in their minds but have made little progress in their spiritual development because they did not challenge the wrong core belief.

So what is this wrong core belief? Well, embedded like splintered glass in our minds is the belief, laid there by Satan, that we can make our lives work independently of God. Often I have said to Christians in counselling, 'Finish this sentence for me: "For to me, to live is ..." But before you say "Christ" ask yourself if that is really true. Is Christ really your life or are you finding it in other things?' Honest people who have risen to that challenge have responded with a variety of different answers: 'For to me, to live is ... success, happiness, getting my husband's attention, a big house, a new car, the acceptance of others.'

It is not enough, however, to confront our wrong beliefs; we must replace them with the truths found in the Word of God. You will never be a spiritually thriving Christian unless you expose your soul to the nourishment and energy that comes from the Scriptures.

REFLECTION: The more you bring your thinking in line with God's thinking the easier it will be to say and mean, 'For to me, to live is Christ.'

God came to earth!

'While they were there, the time came for the child to be born, and she gave birth to her firstborn, a son.'
Luke 2:6–7

Why did God come in the form of a baby? Because He did not come to scare us, but to save us. Many people are afraid of God. If I were God I would have lit up the heavens and shaken the earth to get people's attention. But it would have been frightening if God had come in thunder and put on a giant light show. Who is afraid of a baby? The Word became flesh and a little bundle of life moved in a crib at Bethlehem – the greatest mystery. God came to earth in the form of a baby. Wow! What a baby! He is the only baby who ever lived before He was conceived! Jesus' birth is the most significant event in history. That's why we celebrate it.

In fact, all of history is split in half by this one event. He is the reference point for every date in history because He was that important. Every time we write the date, who are we using as a reference point? Christ and His birth. Caesar Augustus was in power at the time Jesus was born, and little did he know when he called for a census that he was, in fact, doing God's will. The edict that all people return to their place of origin to be counted, meant a pregnant Mary with Joseph made the historic journey to Bethlehem. She was guided by the sovereignty of God to the place where Jesus was to be born, as prophesied in the Old Testament.

REFLECTION: Reflect on what it means that God – the Word – became flesh and came to earth – for us!

The final transformation

'For those God foreknew he also predestined to be conformed to the likeness of his Son ...' Romans 8:29

A major emphasis of my writings has been the fact that all of life is based on transformation. We are transformed either upwards or downwards depending on which side of life we stand – God's or the devil's. For those of us who have received Jesus Christ into our lives, we are able, in His name, to transform everything we touch. And why is this? Because God transformed Himself into man, became like us, so that we might become like Him. 1 John 3:2b introduces us to the breathtaking fact that the final goal of transformation is to make us like Christ: '... what we are to be is not apparent yet, but we do know that when he appears we are to be like him' (Moffatt).

Just think of it! We, who are born of the dust, are being gradually transformed into the most beautiful image this planet has ever seen – the image of Christ. This road, which takes us from 'glory to glory' will lead us eventually to the final goal of being transformed into the perfect image of Christ. We are to be with Him and like Him for ever and ever. We, who love the Lord Jesus Christ, who daily walk in His light and delight in His truth, will one day *see* Him, and the sight of Him will be so breathtaking, so positively absorbing, that we shall suddenly become like Him, not only in thought, *but in appearance*. This is the final consummation. This is the final transformation.

REFLECTION: We can, like Israel's kings, become worse and worse, or we can be transformed from glory to glory into the image of Jesus.

King Jesus

'On his robe and on his thigh he has this name written:
KING OF KINGS AND LORD OF LORDS.*' **Revelation 19:16**

Billy Graham has often pointed out that it is not as a president but as a king that Christ wants to rule our lives. A president serves for a period of time and then goes out of office. A king rules for life. It is one thing to have Christ in our lives; it is another thing to let Him reside permanently at the centre. Throughout time many people have professed to welcome Christ as King but then have sought to retain their own authority in certain areas of their lives. Then He is not *King*. 'A truly kingly rule', one preacher said, 'is without limit, and it is that kind of rule He [Christ] asks us willingly to accept.'

Jesus Christ wants to rule in us over the whole of our lives – home life, business life, social life, public life and, of course, the inner life. He is not willing to be shut out from even one part of our personalities. Only as Christ and His principles are allowed in every part of our lives can He empower us to live the life He designed for us. Surely this makes sense. If Jesus Christ is to empower us to live life the way it should be lived, then He cannot consent to be excluded from any territory that Satan could use. If Christ is to come and live in you, then He can only do so if He is given access to your personality in as full a way as possible.

REFLECTION: Jesus is a loving King who cares for His people, not an ogre who uses and subjugates them.

A second chance

'Go to the great city of Nineveh and proclaim to it the message I give you.' Jonah 3:2

What God longs for is enthusiastic obedience, but He remains patient even when our obedience is shot through with imperfection. What a thrill it is to realise that the grace of God which accepts a repentant heart, seals the act of acceptance with the gift of a new opportunity. The runaway prophet is given a second chance. How many of us would be where we are today if God had not given us a second chance to participate in His work? Who reading these lines has not been guilty of desertion or defiance of the Lord's commands?

Perhaps you are in the situation right now of having wandered off the course set by the divine will and are wondering if God will ever accept you or use you again. You feel disqualified from future service because of past mistakes. Take heart my friend, serving God is not an honour that is earned. None of us qualifies for God's service by merit. It is His mercy, not our merit, that enables us to do anything at all for Him. If you feel I am describing you at this moment then this message from the Lord is for you: God is giving you another chance. Many of the people we read about in Scripture were given a second chance: David, Elijah, Simon Peter, John Mark, to name just a few. So open your heart now and have done with all self-pity and self-derogation. Tell God you are sorry and be restored to the God-of-the-second-chance.

REFLECTION: You may be a million miles from God, but if you turn around He is right beside you.

A big task

'Jonah obeyed the word of the LORD and went to Ninevah. Now Ninevah was a very important city – a visit required three days.' Jonah 3:3

I imagine Jonah experienced a culture shock as he first set foot in Nineveh. One commentator, H.L. Ellison, says, 'To the provincial Galilean familiar with the small, tightly packed Israeli towns on their tells, the wide expanse of Nineveh, including even open land within its walls, must have seemed enormous.' Jonah had a big task ahead of him. But it had to be done. However, God's enabling is always equal to the task. I saw this once on a poster outside a church: 'The task ahead of you is never as great as the power behind you.'

Once when I was in London I saw a man with a placard on which was written: 'This city is doomed. Get out of it as fast as you can.' People smiled as he passed and totally ignored him. They are used to seeing this kind of thing. But the people did not smile when Jonah proclaimed his message. And why? Because it was a message that carried with it the convicting power of God's Holy Spirit. All that Jonah was required to do was to speak the words; God's Spirit then took over and applied the message to the hearts of the people. Nowadays we would describe these circumstances as a 'revival', or an 'evangelical awakening'. Indeed, what we are about to see in Nineveh is one of the greatest evangelical awakenings recorded in the Old Testament. One of the shortest sermons ever preached – just eight words – brought the biggest response.

REFLECTION: The task ahead of you is never as great as the power behind you.

Not much time left

'Forty more days and Nineveh will be destroyed.'
Jonah 3:4

I n Nineveh the forty-day period of grace had a salutary and
sobering effect. It concentrated people's minds on the fact that
time was running out. It spelt out doom, but it also spelt out
hope. The old Nineveh was to go, but a new Nineveh was possible
– a Nineveh whose citizens put their trust in the living God. Hope
was at hand if they turned their eyes to the living God. Perhaps we
need to bring back into modern evangelism the emphasis that time
is running out. Billy Graham said at a conference at which I was
present, 'Evangelism devoid of eschatology [the doctrine of judgment
and the last things] will get us nowhere fast.'

In Nineveh the announcement that the citizens had forty days to
decide whether or not they would turn to God achieved its aim: 'The
Ninevites believed God' (Jonah 3:5). The Ninevites were obsessed
with the present, taken up with the way things were, but Jonah
pointed them to what was to be. The thing that concentrates people's
minds is the announcement that the future is bleak without God and
they should relate to Him now before it is too late. I believe we are
living in the last days and that there is not much time left. The day is
coming when the whole world will be judged by Jesus Christ. This is
the message we should be preaching from our pulpits.

**REFLECTION: The men and women of this world think the
future is in some way magical; they cling to the illusive hope
that things will get better. They won't.**

Turning to God

'By the decree of the king ... Let everyone call urgently on God.' Jonah 3:7–8

T he people of Nineveh did not need a royal decree to repent; the Spirit of God had already been at work in their hearts and brought them to the point of repentance. A similar revival occurred in my own nation of Wales in 1904. Oh that God would bring revival again – not only in my country but also in yours. The inclusion of animals in the fast underlined the depth of repentance that was needed in the city, and thus reinforced the seriousness and solemnity of the moment. Would to God present-day kings, presidents and political leaders had as much concern for the spiritual wellbeing of their people, and would likewise encourage them to turn to Him. But if it is too much to expect political leaders to take a lead in turning to God, it is not too much to expect it of the Church.

When we Christians demonstrate to the world our sincere repentance for sin, when we adopt measures that are uncompromising, when we decide that we will take a lead in this matter and put righteousness first, then, though we cannot legislate for righteousness we will, I believe, see a tremendous move of the Spirit of God across many lands. We cannot force salvation on people but we can make it possible for God to act. God will come through a breach. All He asks is for His people to provide Him with an opportunity – then He will make His move.

REFLECTION: Can you imagine what would happen if a city today were to proclaim a fast and announce that the entire population was turning to God? What a glorious day!

Extracts in this book are taken from the following publications

Published by CWR:

7 Laws of Spiritual Success (2008, last reprinted 2010)

9 Steps to a Renewed Life (2001, out of print)

10 Principles for a Happy Marriage (2001, last reprinted 2003, out of print)

15 Keys to Experiencing the Presence of God (2002, out of print)

15 Ways to a More Effective Prayer Life (2001, last reprinted 2003, out of print)

Christ Empowered Living (2002, 2008, last reprinted 2011)

Christ Empowered Living Devotional (2006)

Every Day with Jesus Jan/Feb 2007 (first published 1994, out of print)

Getting the Best from the Bible (1989, latest reformatted edition 2011)

Grace – The marvellous gift of God (2005, out of print)

Heaven Bound (2003, last reprinted 2004, out of print)

Jonah – God of the Second Chance (2003, out of print)

Spoken from the Heart (2005, out of print)

Spoken from the Heart Volume 2 (2006)

The 23rd Psalm (2001, out of print)

The Divine Eagle (1988, revised edition 2001, out of print)

The Divine Gardener (1989, revised edition 2001, out of print)

The Holy Spirit, Our Counsellor (2004, out of print)

What to say when people need help (material first published 1977,
this title last reprinted 2011)

Why Revival Waits (2003)

Published by Kingsway – copyright CWR:

A Friend in Need (1981)

God Wants you Whole (1984, last reprinted 2001)

When nothing you ever do seems to satisfy (1994)

Published by Marshall Pickering – copyright CWR:

Sharing your Faith (1983, last reprinted 1990

NOTES

1. *The Silver Chair* by C.S. Lewis copyright © C.S. Lewis Pte. Ltd. 1953. Extract used by permission.
2. *The Problem of Pain* by C.S. Lewis © C.S. Lewis Pte. Ltd. 1940. Extract used by permission.
3. *Mere Christianity* by C.S. Lewis © C.S. Lewis Pte. Ltd. 1942, 1943, 1944, 1952. Extract used by permission.
4. *The Problem of Pain* op. cit. Extract used by permission.

National Distributors

UK: (and countries not listed below)
CWR, Waverley Abbey House, Waverley Lane, Farnham, Surrey GU9 8EP.
Tel: (01252) 784700 Outside UK (44) 1252 784700 Email: mail@cwr.org.uk

AUSTRALIA: KI Entertainment, Unit 21 317-321 Woodpark Road, Smithfield,
New South Wales 2164. Tel: 1 800 850 777 Fax: 02 9604 3699
Email: sales@kientertainment.com.au

CANADA: David C Cook Distribution Canada, PO Box 98, 55 Woodslee Avenue,
Paris, Ontario N3L 3E5. Tel: 1800 263 2664 Email: sandi.swanson@davidccook.ca

GHANA: Challenge Enterprises of Ghana, PO Box 5723, Accra.
Tel: (021) 222437/223249 Fax: (021) 226227 Email: ceg@africaonline.com.gh

HONG KONG: Cross Communications Ltd, 1/F, 562A Nathan Road, Kowloon.
Tel: 2780 1188 Fax: 2770 6229 Email: cross@crosshk.com

INDIA: Crystal Communications, 10-3-18/4/1, East Marredpalli,
Secunderabad – 500026, Andhra Pradesh. Tel/Fax: (040) 27737145
Email: crystal_edwj@rediffmail.com

KENYA: Keswick Books and Gifts Ltd, PO Box 10242-00400, Nairobi.
Tel: (254) 20 312639/3870125 Email: keswick@swiftkenya.com

MALAYSIA: Canaanland, No. 25 Jalan PJU 1A/41B, NZX Commercial Centre,
Ara Jaya, 47301 Petaling Jaya, Selangor. Tel: (03) 7885 0540/1/2 Fax: (03) 7885 0545
Email: info@canaanland.com.my

Salvation Book Centre (M) Sdn Bhd, 23 Jalan SS 2/64, 47300 Petaling Jaya,
Selangor. Tel: (03) 78766411/78766797 Fax: (03) 78757066/78756360
Email: info@salvationbookcentre.com

NEW ZEALAND: KI Entertainment, Unit 21 317-321 Woodpark Road, Smithfield,
New South Wales 2164, Australia.
Tel: 0 800 850 777 Fax: +612 9604 3699 Email: sales@kientertainment.com.au

NIGERIA: FBFM, Helen Baugh House, 96 St Finbarr's College Road, Akoka, Lagos.
Tel: (01) 7747429/4700218/825775/827264 Email: fbfm_1@yahoo.com

PHILIPPINES: OMF Literature Inc, 776 Boni Avenue, Mandaluyong City.
Tel: (02) 531 2183 Fax: (02) 531 1960 Email: gloadlaon@omflit.com

SINGAPORE: Alby Commercial Enterprises Pte Ltd, 95 Kallang Avenue #04-00,
AIS Industrial Building, 339420. Tel: (65) 629 27238 Fax: (65) 629 27235
Email: marketing@alby.com.sg

SOUTH AFRICA: Struik Christian Books, 80 MacKenzie Street, PO Box 1144,
Cape Town 8000. Tel: (021) 462 4360 Fax: (021) 461 3612
Email: info@struikchristianmedia.co.za

SRI LANKA: Christombu Publications (Pvt) Ltd, Bartleet House,
65 Braybrooke Place, Colombo 2. Tel: (9411) 2421073/2447665
Email: dhanad@bartleet.com

USA: David C Cook Distribution Canada, PO Box 98, 55 Woodslee Avenue, Paris,
Ontario N3L 3E5, Canada. Tel: 1800 263 2664 Email: sandi.swanson@davidccook.ca

CWR is a Registered Charity - Number 294387
CWR is a Limited Company registered in England - Registration Number 1990308

Courses and seminars

Publishing and new media

Conference facilities

Transforming lives

CWR's vision is to enable people to experience personal transformation through applying God's Word to their lives and relationships.

Our Bible-based training and resources help people around the world to:
• Grow in their walk with God
• Understand and apply Scripture to their lives
• Resource themselves and their church
• Develop pastoral care and counselling skills
• Train for leadership
• Strengthen relationships, marriage and family life and much more.

Our insightful writers provide daily Bible-reading notes and other resources for all ages, and our experienced course designers and presenters have gained an international reputation for excellence and effectiveness.

CWR's Training and Conference Centre in Surrey, England, provides excellent facilities in an idyllic setting – ideal for both learning and spiritual refreshment.

CWR Applying God's Word
to everyday life and relationships

CWR, Waverley Abbey House,
Waverley Lane, Farnham,
Surrey GU9 8EP, UK

Telephone: **+44 (0)1252 784700**
Email: **info@cwr.org.uk**
Website: **www.cwr.org.uk**

Registered Charity No 294387
Company Registration No 1990308

Meet with Jesus through His Word each day

Drawing on his fifty years of pastoral and counselling experience, Selwyn Hughes has authored one of the most popular daily Bible study tools in the world with around a million readers.

• Get practical help with life's challenges
• Gain insight into the deeper truths of Scripture
• Be challenged, comforted and encouraged
• Study six topics in depth each year.

Written by Selwyn Hughes; edited and updated by Mick Brooks
170x120mm booklet
Large-print edition also available: 297x210mm